DINING with STARS

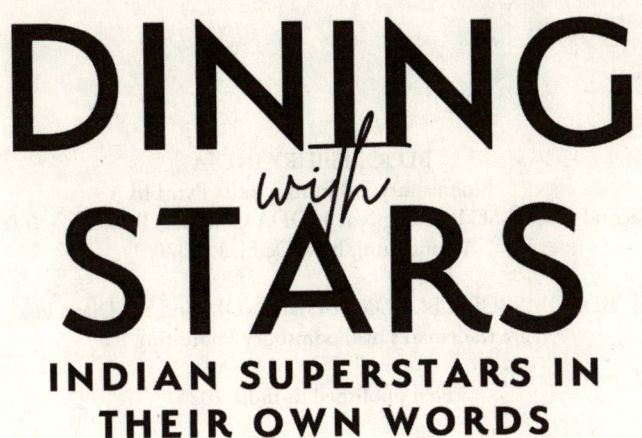

DINING with STARS

INDIAN SUPERSTARS IN THEIR OWN WORDS

ANUPAMA CHOPRA

BLOOMSBURY
NEW DELHI · LONDON · OXFORD · NEW YORK · SYDNEY

BLOOMSBURY INDIA
Bloomsbury Publishing India Pvt. Ltd
Second Floor, LSC Building No. 4, DDA Complex, Pocket C – 6 & 7,
Vasant Kunj, New Delhi, 110070

BLOOMSBURY, BLOOMSBURY INDIA and the Diana logo
are trademarks of Bloomsbury Publishing Plc

First published in India 2025

Copyright © Anupama Chopra, 2025

Anupama Chopra has asserted her moral rights to be identified as the author of this work in accordance with the Indian Copyright Act, 1957

All rights reserved. No part of this publication may be: i) reproduced or transmitted in any form, electronic or mechanical, including photocopying, recording or by means of any information storage or retrieval system without prior permission in writing from the publishers; or ii) used or reproduced in any way for the training, development or operation of artificial intelligence (AI) technologies, including generative AI technologies. The rights holders expressly reserve this publication from the text and data mining exception as per Article 4(3) of the Digital Single Market Directive (EU) 2019/790

ISBN: PB: 978-93-61317-17-0; eBook: 978-93-61317-58-3

2 4 6 8 10 9 7 5 3 1

Typeset in Adobe Garamond Pro by Manipal Technologies Limited

Printed and bound in India by Gopsons Papers Pvt. Ltd., Noida

To find out more about our authors and books visit www.bloomsbury.com and sign up for our newsletters

Contents

Preface — vii

1. 'Life Will Surprise You': Sushant Singh Rajput — 1
2. Shah Rukh Khan Beneath the Surface — 8
3. Everyone Needs S.S. Rajamouli's Approval — 12
   With Nandamuri Taraka Rama Rao Jr. & Ram Charan
4. 'My Time Has Come': Pankaj Tripathi — 19
5. Sandeep Reddy Vanga on Films, Processes, Beliefs — 28
6. Deepika Padukone: The Best That Earth Has to Offer — 38
7. Ranveer Singh: The Human Chameleon — 51
8. Stage Queens: Zeenat Aman & Shabana Azmi — 63
9. 'We're Not Damsels': Ratna Pathak Shah & Ayesha Jhulka — 70
10. Hrithik Roshan: In Search of New Experiences — 80
11. 'I Marry the Director's Mind': Ranbir Kapoor — 92
12. Celebrating *All We Imagine as Light*: Payal Kapadia & Ranabir Das — 101
13. The Versatile Fahadh Faasil — 105
14. Priyanka Chopra Jonas: Redefining 'Bold' — 114
15. Imran Khan: Planning the Comeback — 126
16. In Their Own Voice: Vicky Kaushal & Katrina Kaif — 140
17. Becoming, Not Performing: Vidya Balan & Shefali Shah — 145
18. 'A Love Affair with the Camera': Madhuri Dixit — 153
19. Sanjay Leela Bhansali on Silence, Scars, Cinema — 159
20. Shabana Azmi on the Golden Era — 171
21. Alia Bhatt: The Bhansali Heroine — 177
22. Karan Johar Unfiltered: Love, Legacy, Rocky Randhawa — 183
23. 'I'm Sexy and I Know It': Diljit Dosanjh — 192
24. In Conversation with Decade-Defining Actors — 202
    Ranveer Singh, Ayushmann Khurrana, Deepika Padukone, Alia Bhatt, Vijay Devarakonda, Vijay Sethupathi, Manoj & Parvathy Thiruvothu

25.	Of Masks and Monsters: Nawazuddin Siddiqui	218
26.	Saif Ali Khan on Privilege, Parenting, Passion	227
27.	'Enrich Your Soul Through Your Job': Irrfan Khan	235
28.	Twenty Years of Kareena Kapoor Khan	243
29.	The Inner World of Konkona Sen Sharma	251
30.	'Every Day Is a New Costume': Mohanlal	262
31.	Vikrant Massey Spills the Tea	266
32.	'I'll Graduate Life with Honours': Sushmita Sen With Ram Madhvani	275

Acknowledgements   291

Preface

In July 2024, I shut down *Film Companion*. It was a little like cutting out a piece of my heart. For ten years, the platform had been an all-consuming passion and a sanctuary. When you function as everything – PR to peon to salesperson to boss – there is a singular excitement, freedom and panic. It was a blazing, exhilarating ride. But I instinctively understood at some point that we had peaked, that the learning curve had flattened and that if we were to continue, it would be a familiar retread. We had become comfortable in our routine, and comfort is as stunting for journalists as it is for artists.

The announcement that we were shutting down brought forth an outpouring of love and gratitude. Karan Johar posted on Instagram that *Film Companion* was always 'looked at like the enemy with no boundaries and barriers … that they were certainly no companion to the fraternity'. He also said that he 'was sad that a media hub of opinion and analysis won't exist anymore'. He wrote, 'I won't say that I agreed with everything that was said and written but the democracy and transparency of it all has my vote.' National Award-winning cinematographer Sudeep Chatterjee posted, 'We cinephiles owe it big time to you for giving us *Film Companion*. It enriched us and bonded us.'

My farewell video on our YouTube channel got over 300 comments. These ranged from 'As a loyal FC follower of nearly eight years, I feel betrayed and terribly sad by this sudden decision to shut things down without any warning or explanation! First, I thought only Anupama ji is leaving but now it seems that FC itself is closing? I have no clue what is happening and why. This feels like a break-up over a text message' to 'What am I gonna do with my life now?' At the office we joked that if we had known that people cared so much, perhaps we would have stuck around. The last month was gutting. At the farewell lunch, we ate pizza and exchanged memories and somehow avoided tears.

That name – *Film Companion* – came from a line by the American philosopher and film critic Stanley Cavell. He said, 'The writing about film that has meant most to me has the power of a missing companion.' Our ambition was to be that missing companion, that friend you discuss movies, shows, trends and pet peeves with. You don't have to agree but the conversation is robust and invigorating.

I believe that *Film Companion* altered the landscape of entertainment journalism. I'm proud to say that we were pan-India before the *Baahubali* franchise. Film Companion South covered the major cinemas of the South with rigour and verve. We also had contributors reporting on the Bengali, Marathi and Punjabi film industries. When streaming arrived in India, we made it a focus with reviews, interviews and roundtables devoted to OTT. Along the way, we also launched e-learning modules on film criticism and writing for the screen.

One of our overarching ambitions was to move the needle for the film industry. With this aim, we created *O Womaniya*, in partnership with research firm Ormax Media and Amazon Prime Video – a first-of-its-kind report on women in the entertainment business. The idea was to put out concrete numbers, year after year, that recorded the skewed gender equation and prompted conversation. Our hope was that this conversation would bring change.

Another flagship initiative was Take Ten, in collaboration with Netflix's Fund for Creative Equity – a programme that found and funded new filmmakers to make short films in the first year and series pilots in the second. At the 2024 Cannes Film Festival, I found myself getting teary because the crew of Payal Kapadia's Grand Prix-winning film *All We Imagine as Light* included Suyash Kamat as an assistant director – he was a finalist of our Take Ten series. In 2023, we also curated and ran the Himalayan Film Festival in Ladakh – the ambition was to celebrate and showcase filmmakers from across the Himalayan states, filmmakers who often struggle to find their place in the business.

The industry, meanwhile, changed rapidly through the decade. According to Ormax Media, the Indian box office grew by 59 per cent over the decade – from ₹7,400 crore in 2014 to ₹11,800 crore in 2024 (though the increase was largely due to ticket rates going up while footfalls remained static). The two most seismic events were the arrival of streaming and the emergence of the pan-India movie. I would argue that the OG pan-India makers were actually Mani Ratnam and S. Shankar – audiences in the North watched *Roja* (1992), *Bombay* (1995), *Indian* (1996). But S.S. Rajamouli's flamboyant, riveting storytelling in *Baahubali: The Beginning* (2015) roused and united contemporary audiences across the country.

Until *Baahubali 2: The Conclusion* arrived in 2017, the biggest mystery in the country was: kattappa ne Baahubali ko kyun mara (why did Kattappa kill Baahubali)?

Streaming did the opposite – by facilitating individual viewing on phones and laptops, it splintered the audience. Dozens of OTT platforms delivered thousands of hours of content, and algorithms became tastemakers. I'm a die-hard theatre lover, but through the devastating years of the Covid-19 pandemic, stories on streaming sustained us (at least those of us who were privileged enough to have food and shelter). Even as streaming divided the viewing experience, it played a key role in uniting the Indian film industry. Thanks to access and subtitles, we started to discover Indian films that were not in our first language. My gateway drug to Malayalam cinema was director Madhu C. Narayanan's *Kumbalangi Nights* (2019). Like me, viewers across the North discovered the brilliance of artistry beyond Bollywood. Despite not doing a single Hindi film, Fahadh Faasil became a national superstar. As did Allu Arjun who took Telugu cinema to the Hindi heartland as the sandalwood smuggler Pushpa. The dubbed version of *Pushpa 2* (2024) is the highest-grossing Hindi film in India.

Streaming also vastly strengthened writers and women. The lack of a box office brought freedom (at least in the early years). Writers' rooms took shape and for a brief, blazing moment, the stories became bigger than the stars. In fact, OTT gave rise to a new breed of stars such as Jaideep Ahlawat and Prateek Gandhi, and it galvanized the careers of talented actresses – Sushmita Sen (*Aarya*), Madhuri Dixit (*The Fame Game*), Raveena Tandon (*Aranyak*; *Karmma Calling*), Kajol (*The Trial*; *Lust Stories 2*; *Do Patti*), etc.

Meanwhile, theatrical films did the opposite. The mantra became 'go big or go home'. Conventional wisdom stated that audiences now had so much entertainment at home that they would only come to theatres for a larger-than-life event of a film, which inevitably translated into heroes saving the world in action movies – such as *Pathaan, Jawan, RRR*, the *Pushpa* franchise, and *Vikram*. Heroines were largely relegated to the sidelines. Franchises and universes built around men (the *Stree* franchise directed by Amar Kaushik being an exception) became a way to battle the threat of streaming, YouTube and the relentless seduction of social media.

X (formerly Twitter) was the first social media platform I went on. I joined in February 2010. Back then, it was a more convivial space – a community of film critics and film lovers were able to exchange takes on movies and artists without jostling for space and without hate. Twitter's biggest gift to me was that I was able to connect with the great Pulitzer

Prize-winning American critic Roger Ebert. We met online and then at the Cannes Film Festival. By then, cancer had taken his ability to speak, so he communicated via written notes. My meeting with him remains a treasured memory.

But social media and especially Instagram would change the nature of the celebrity. Stars, especially younger, upcoming names, became increasingly accessible, content creators became stars and fame became even more fleeting. Our current moment of everyone having fifteen minutes of fame (as was supposedly predicted by Andy Warhol) was further fuelled by Mumbai's paparazzi culture. And the lines between who qualifies to be an entertainment journalist and who doesn't blurred dangerously. By year ten of *Film Companion*, paps were also reporters and podcasters were conducting two-hour-long interviews with movie stars. The churn was constant and breathless and somehow both deflating and exhilarating! We covered it all.

The pillars of *Film Companion* were reviews and interviews. Over 3,500 videos on YouTube attest to the breadth and depth of our work. I have fond memories of our shoots – walking and talking with Shah Rukh Khan in Lisbon in 2016 for *Beneath the Surface*, which was the first branded show we did; our first actors' roundtable in 2019, in which eight actors from across the country, including Ranveer Singh, Deepika Padukone, Alia Bhatt, Vijay Sethupathi, Vijay Deverakonda and Manoj Bajpayee, participated; and the *Front Row* series, a conversation in front of a live audience (I was teary when I walked on stage for the first one with Deepika). The world was just emerging from the shadow of Covid-19 and to be in a room with people wearing masks and sitting one seat apart made me emotional.

There was also *TapeCast*, a show in which artists spoke to other artists, prompted by questions we put on a tape that played through the interaction. The first public interaction between Vicky Kaushal and Katrina Kaif took place on *TapeCast* in March 2019. When they got married, I was labelled Sima Aunty from *Indian Matchmaking*! And then there was Diljit Dosanjh – I first interviewed him in April 2016, months before the release of *Udta Punjab*. He was a bona fide star of the Punjabi music and movie industry, but international superstardom was still a few years away. He came in a simple white shirt and spoke with candour about his humble beginnings. When I interviewed him again in 2018, he was attired from head to toe in Gucci. When I asked where the fashion sense came from, he laughed and replied, 'Thi, par paise nahin the (Always had it, but didn't have the money)!'

There was also *Cheat Sheet*, hosted by Sneha Menon Desai – a show that broke down the mechanics of making movies. Sneha took viewers behind the scenes of how artists lived and functioned – her conversation with intimacy coordinator Aastha Khanna and another discussion with bodyguards in Bollywood have over a million views. It's a matter of great pride that *Cheat Sheet* was used as teaching material in film schools.

This book is a compilation of some of the best interviews that Sneha and I did – from Diljit Dosanjh to Alia Bhatt to Ranbir Kapoor to Hrithik Roshan to Deepika Padukone to Zeenat Aman to the maestro Mohanlal to the late Irrfan Khan and Sushant Singh Rajput, they are all here. These conversations capture a certain moment in Indian cinema. They speak to a mood. I've been a film journalist for over thirty years, but I don't take these interactions for granted. It's a privilege to spend time with artists who are shaping film, popular culture and society.

One of my favourite quotes comes from American president Theodore Roosevelt. He said, 'It is not the critic who counts; not the man who points out how the strong man stumbles, or where the doer of deeds could have done them better. The credit belongs to the man who is actually in the arena, whose face is marred by dust and sweat and blood, who strives valiantly, who errs, who comes short again and again, because there is no effort without error and shortcoming, but who does actually strive to do the deeds; who knows great enthusiasms, the great devotions, who spends himself in a worthy cause, who, at the best, knows, in the end the triumph of high achievement, and who, at the worst, if he fails, at least fails while daring greatly.'

I wasn't a very good entrepreneur, but *Film Companion* did require some daring. And the decade-long hustle has only fuelled my desire to do more. I hope you enjoy these conversations. Do note that the interviews you are about to read are edited and excerpted from the longer versions for the sake of clarity, readability and smooth reader experience.

Onwards and upwards.

Anupama Chopra
October 2025

1

'Life Will Surprise You': Sushant Singh Rajput

Anupama Chopra: I want to go back a little bit to the beginning. You grew up in a middle-class house with four older sisters. You've talked about being a very shy child who couldn't express himself but then discovered that he wanted to be an actor. Do you have a memory of the first time you acted?

Sushant Singh Rajput: Very vividly – that was the first time I was saying something confidently in front of strangers. Back in 2003 or 2004, there was this play I was doing with Barry John and that was the first time I realised I could influence people. That was such a fascinating feeling. I told myself, 'Wow, I can hide behind all these interesting characters and tell everybody not to judge because it's not me.' When I play a character, I find a way to fool myself, convince myself that I'm not me but somebody else, and that's such a relief.

AC: To not be you?
SSR: Every day we try and project a personality we think we are and it's too much effort. So, when you play a character, it's so much of a relief to play somebody else and you get paid for it.

AC: You were pretty good academically but you dropped out of engineering college because you wanted to be an actor. Tell me, where did you find the clarity to do that and what did your parents say?
SSR: So, for sixteen to seventeen years of my life, I somehow convinced myself that I didn't need to speak. I had two or three friends and I was very open with them. I had four sisters and was so pampered and protected in my family that when I used to step out as a kid, I didn't know how to deal with people. And then Shiamak (Davar) got me into dancing on stage. And he asked me to join theatre and the first play that I did … I think the most important thing that we miss or want in our lives is to be understood by somebody else. And when you act, that is what happens. When that resonance happens, when you feel something, you feel so good about it. So, I took three years wondering, 'Do I want to be the next Shah Rukh

Khan? Or is it the thing that I'm doing right now that excites me so much?' And I was sure 'I'd be wasting another year in engineering'.

AC: So, three years of engineering.
SSR: Two more semesters and I would have been an engineer.

AC: And we would have been a lot sadder, right?
SSR: My dad would be very happy. He still tells me all the time, 'I know that you're doing well and everything and I like you when you act. But that degree you could have.'

AC: An engineering degree is such a big thing in India. How do you take that call when you're that young?
SSR: We are so conditioned into thinking that there will be a day when we'll do something and people will recognise who we are. There is a thing in psychology which we call impact bias: this tendency of overestimating the hedonic impact of anything that has to do with the future. So, we think if I get there, everything will change. Or if I fail, that's the end. But it doesn't happen like that. When I started making a lot of money in TV – money was a big differentiator in my life, by the way – and people started recognising me for the first time, it was a very strange feeling. But I was very excited. I used to go to malls so that people would talk to me. But after a point of time, say, three months, four months – you get used to it. And you come back to the same mental state. So, it is not what would drive you for the rest of your life. No matter how successful you are, no matter how rich or recognised you are. I think it's not the pursuit of happiness; it's the habit of happiness. So, when you do what you want to do, you don't care what people say.

AC: You were a big television star. You had money. You had fame. And then, at the peak of television success, you quit, again, because now you want to do something else. How do you walk away from success to pursue something that you think will satisfy you?
SSR: It's a very simple thing. You just need to stop and reflect on what you're doing. That's it. Normally what happens is, after such strong momentum and conditioning, when we get what we want, we somehow fool ourselves that this is what we want for the rest of our lives. So, what I want to say at this point of time is – it's not that I'm doing it to prove a point to somebody that I'm different; it is just that something that gets

me up ten minutes early in the morning. So, it's the same thing that I have followed for the last twelve years. I was making money; everybody was very happy with me. But I knew every morning what I was supposed to do. No excitement. So, I didn't quit [TV] to get into films because I very genuinely believe that it's not an organic progression from theatre to TV to film. It was because I wanted to go to UCLA to know how to read the film so that I can do it better as an actor. And fortunately, I got the role in *Kai Po Che!* and I stayed back.

AC: But between the time when you stopped doing *Pavitra Rishta* and you landed *Kai Po Che!*, did you have like a dark night of the soul, some moment of confusion, anxiety, insecurity?
SSR: No, nothing. Absolutely nothing. When you're continuously thinking about what people think of you, failure is defined, success is defined, your excitement is defined. I think nothing, absolutely nothing, should come between you and your work. I always used to think that there is one right way of doing it and that there are several wrong ways. I realised there are several right ways of doing it.

AC: So, for six months, you didn't know that you would land a film, but you were fine?
SSR: Completely fine. I would just sit and think about the different ways that I could do the same thing in a slightly better way so that I felt better about it.

AC: Dibakar Banerjee, who directed you as Byomkesh Bakshy, said that you have a quiet arrogance that all actors should hold on to. Is that what gives you clarity? The clarity to stay at home for six months and not be insecure?
SSR: Probably. Yes. If you ask me right now what I am doing right, I wouldn't know. I just do what I want to in a way that I think that I should go about. If I don't get films next year, I would do a play, or I would probably work in TV, but in a nice project. I would buy a 5D camera . . . make a short film. I'll be the solo hero in that short film. I just want to act so that there's some relief in between, so that I don't take myself so seriously all the time.

AC: The film industry has now become far more professional. Still, no matter what we think and say, it is a very nepotistic place. As an outsider, how difficult was it for you to negotiate this?

SSR: It would not be very right for me to say anything about this because I landed all the films that I wanted to work on. So, I can't complain, but it is there. When you are successful as an outsider, you'll be discussed but in a very hushed tone and that's about it.

AC: You're not invested in box office success or failure?
SSR: Nobody can guess. I have still not found any book that claims that this is how you'll get ₹100 crore in your next film. I've read it all, trust me. It's only after a film does something that we sit down and we try to logically explain. So, it's always the effect and then we manufacture the cause after that. Nobody knows what's going to happen. So, if *this* is the chaos, let me find a pattern in that. Let me just not care about it. And let me be very selfish. This is the film. I like the script. I'll do it.

AC: Do you have any rituals that you follow to hone your craft? I read somewhere that you always find a song for each character.
SSR: Yes. They tell you how to do the research but when you're in front of the camera, it doesn't translate into what you do. So, the best way to do it, I think, is the rhythm. Also, because I started as a dancer, I get the rhythm correct. So, I somehow find a song for each character. I was going through the YouTube songs, the VMs on Dhoni, and there was this South Indian song which I don't understand, but it was so right with the visuals.

AC: And that was the Dhoni character rhythm? Dhoni is the fifty-third character you played across television, screen, theatre. And I read about the amazing prep that you did. Watching over a 1,000 hours of footage of Dhoni, training with Kiran More and practising one shot 300 times, just keep going so your body language is exactly right. Talk a little bit about the importance of that work ethic.
SSR: I think [it's] the way we look at it. But it was not hard work for me. I started with signing a contract. This film is [Mahendra Singh] Dhoni's biopic. So, what are the things I want to do? I have to be very good at cricket; I have to get his body language, intonation, diction, everything correct. And I need to somehow – the most difficult part – understand the guy so that even in the scenes in which I improvise, I should be confident that it's not me improvising but him. I was the one playing all the shots. These are relatively easier things to do. I like to play cricket. I was never very good at it . . . . Here I am getting the M.S. Dhoni kit. Kiran More

is training me. And this is what I wanted to do. I wanted to play more. I was like, can we play for another two hours? So, it was not hard work. It commands your attention so much that you're just there. And you just don't care. Time is so subjective: when you enjoy doing something, you don't feel like you're working so hard.

AC: Somebody asked you in an interview about becoming a star. And you said, 'I don't know what that is and I don't intend to become one.' Are you not at all seduced by the notion of stardom?

SSR: No. If you give it to me, I'll keep it. Because I don't know what I would do without it. But if you don't give it to me, I don't miss it. Because that's not something that I'm looking forward to. I'll be very honest. When I started, that was the incentive that I was trying to give myself [while] dropping out of college. *I'll be a star. I'll be the next big thing.* So, I convinced myself, and I wanted that to some extent, just because I didn't have those things. All my eighteen, nineteen years of life, nobody had actually looked at me and said, 'Oh, you exist.' I was such an introvert. And we were not that poor, but money was a differentiator in each and every decision that my family used to take. When you don't have it, a small amount of money can buy you a lot of things. But after that point of inflexion, a lot will buy you just a small thing. So that is the irony of it. But thankfully, I was doing something that kept me going, something that I really wanted to do and that I had been doing all the while.

AC: You also said you don't know how much money you have in your bank account.

SSR: Yes, I know that I have enough to go about everything that I want to do in my life. For instance, there was this bike – BMW K1300R. It cost between thirty and forty lakh rupees. This would have been a dream for me five years back. And so I bought it. So, there are times when I tell myself, 'Sushant, you have done well.'

AC: But what we see so much is the glamour, the red carpet, all of that. What we don't see, really, is the failure, which is also very public. You've had films that didn't do well that you put your heart and soul into.
SSR: *Byomkesh Bakshy!*

AC: Yeah, *Byomkesh*, which I love, but not many other people did. You were doing *Paani* with Shekhar Kapur. After months of conversation, that project didn't take off. How do you move forward? How do you get up and say, I'm going to do it all over again?

SSR: I do it all the time. And you all do it all the time. No matter what your Friday is like when your film releases, the next Friday, you'll come back to the same mental state. This is what we do. We overestimate the impact of [what's] going to happen if we are successful or if we fail.

AC: And do you get sad?
SSR: Of course, I do get sad all the time. I look at the work I do. *Dhoni* is the only film in which I was not watching the monitor when I was shooting. Before that, when I used to dub, I used to say, 'I know that you're pretending. You're not that honest. I could have done that.'

AC: So, *Dhoni* is the first time you felt like you were acting?
SSR: Yes. I was smiling all the time. It was a very tricky thing. Now, when you, the audience, don't know anything about a character – and I'm a very confident actor – I can convince you that this is what I'm feeling. But when you have a very strong visual reference of a guy who's immensely popular and then somehow find a way to not imitate, you're not conscious about, 'Okay, let me do this so that people think that I'm Dhoni.' And it happened. And I felt like, 'You're a star, man.'

AC: Which you are. Yeah, let's agree on that.
SSR: Thank you.

From the Floor: Q&A

Nidhi (BMM student, II year): Which do you think is more challenging: films or television?
SSR: Equally challenging, and no challenge at all at the same time. If you really like doing what you want to do, [it doesn't matter if] you are performing in front of a live audience or a TV camera. I would do the same. Just the paychecks are different.

Sonali (BMM student, II year): I would love to know how you personally deal with criticism, rumours, failures, etc.
SSR: Failures and successes are very subjective. But I realise that even when I insulate myself, criticism is something that can actually bother you all the time. If you don't get to know what they're saying, you can imagine whatever you want it to be. And that's how I do it. I call it

a Teflon coating. I don't read newspapers. I don't watch TV. Netflix? Good. Unless you walk up to me and say that you were bad or good or whatever – and even then – I'll forget in the next ten minutes.

Nishtha: Anupama ma'am, I'm really curious to know what you feel are the few qualities that a film critic should possess, and what you should look at.
AC: The first thing that a film critic needs to have is a great love for cinema. And not selective cinema, but all cinema – so that every Friday you go into the theatre feeling optimistic. I mean, you've got to walk in thinking this one's going to be *Sholay*. You can't go in with cynicism. I know what it takes to make a movie. And nobody sets out to make a bad film. So, you've got to have that respect and love for what you're seeing up on the screen. Of course, you'll have things that you like more than other things. I mean, I can't watch gore. It just freaks me out. So, you'll have biases, but overall, you've got to be expansive in your love for movies. And then you have to have integrity. You must be able to say what you actually feel. I mean, I'm making people mad all the time. That's what I do for a living. But I have to be honest to my response to a film. I can't lie. I can't soften it because I know someone or because they're my husband's friends or something. Everybody has a platform to express an opinion about cinema. What makes mine more special than anybody else's? And then you just keep watching and learning and writing.

SSR: I'm very intrigued. Please tell me about all the fundamentals that you use to read the film.
AC: For me, the first thing is really just engagement. I'm not so invested in technique. I'm old school. It's story, character, narrative. If that connects and then the rest of it is amazing, then that's wonderful. I would never be seduced by film because the photography is amazing, but the character is not. You've got to move the heart. What is your mantra, Sushant? What's the one thing that you live by?
SSR: There's one thing that I really believe in: 'He who thinks he can and he who thinks he can't are both usually right.' So, at this point of time, no matter what you have, what your present circumstances are, I'm just not concerned about that. But if you somehow make yourself believe that it's going to happen, trust me, it will happen. It will surprise you.

5 December 2016

2

Shah Rukh Khan Beneath the Surface

Anupama Chopra: This is the twenty-first year of our conversations.
Shah Rukh Khan: Oh wow.

AC: I first came to see you in April 1995 on the sets of *Ram Jaane*. You were wearing a purple suit.
SRK: You know, my Kolkata Knight Riders uniform? That's why it's purple. I'm inspired by my purple suit.

AC: By *Ram Jaane*. This was, of course, pre-*DDLJ*'s release. But my sense is that inherently you're still that guy, you're still charming, a little cocky, very funny, relatable and somehow still larger than life. Is that a correct assessment?
SRK: You know, people don't really change. People talk about evolving and XYZ, but there are certain beliefs that we live by. When you're younger, maybe it seems stupid, even. I think what you say in your childhood is who you are. You may garb it in better speech patterns.

AC: You're just a more polite man now.
SRK: I'm just polite now. But I think whether that belief was misplaced, whether the belief was right, whether it was something that comes instinctively from inside, I think that's who you are.

AC: That's your essence.
SRK: I think the essence comes out in that period of life, which kind of defines us finally.

AC: You know, you've spent half your life playing a man in love.
SRK: (Laughs) With women who belong to other men, to begin with. I've made an art and profession out of loving women who are going to get married to someone else, are already married or are engaged. And then I run after them. And then I get them, sometimes with charm,

sometimes with goodness. Sometimes I throw them off the building. I have a problem.

AC: Has your understanding of love and its portrayal in Hindi cinema altered a lot? Or do you find yourself going through the same beat?
SRK: It will sound a little pompous, but I know all facets of love.

AC: What does that mean?
SRK: I am beautiful. Not physically only, [but] in a different way. I'm unpredictable. I'm charming. I make you glow. I make you sad. I destroy you. I distress you. I create longing for you. I create belonging in you. I can be the worst thing that happened to you. I could be the best thing that could happen to you. So, I am genuinely love. And I believe in love like that. And not just man–woman love or man–man love or woman–woman love of sensuality.

AC: All kinds of love?
SRK: All kinds of love. I know love very well. So, I understand Aditya Chopra's love when he tells me to do *Dilwale*. I understand Imtiaz's very well. All of us have a backstory, which we kind of expose in our cinema. Especially writers and directors. Actors still less. I'm not saying I'll be able to deliver just because I know love. Because obviously I'm bound by my five expressions. But I really, really need to say, 'Can I sense this? Can I feel it? Can I hold myself back? Okay, this scene is actually in a love story.' I keep doing it actually. As you see, Adi would do the scene like this. Karan would do it like this. Because he's that lover. Imtiaz is going to do it like this. I get really intrigued by it. If you try something completely in a dark space in a love story, I think people will get a little…

AC: It'll be too shocking. I mean, in *KANK*, when you went into that hotel room, people couldn't believe it was you with somebody else's wife.
SRK: Yeah. And just to tell you, it was a body double. It wasn't me. I don't do love scenes or kissing scenes, so I don't know. And I watch movies – everybody's doing it.

AC: That's right.
SRK: I was really taken aback when people reacted to that film. As an actor, it was a nice, cynical, angry riot. Somebody said, 'Woh toh uske face

pe dikhne lag gaya hai (It's showing on his face),' so I kept my face in angst all the time.

AC: Yeah, you were very curdled.
SRK: Suddenly, I got feedback. 'Ye sab harkatein kar raha hain na ye, filmon mai ab sab, uski shakal pe dikh raha hai aisa (He's doing all these actions in movies nowadays, it shows on his face).' I was like, 'Arre, It's just a movie.' That's one place you have to have extreme freedom of expression. But reactions curb you, you know, shock you.

AC: Does it bother you?
SRK: No. But it does make the filmmaker think.

AC: They become a little wary.
SRK: I didn't talk to Karan. Maybe he'd say, 'Bhai, ye nahi karte aapke saath, bada backlash hoga (Brother, let's not do this with you, there will be a lot of backlash).'

AC: I saw Suhana in a school play. I tweeted about how she was really good. You tweeted back to say she has so much more brevity and grace. Do you think you still haven't cultivated that?
SRK: No. I see Suhana or Alia – they haven't lived much but express so much. My assumption is there's still more to see. But even without the experience, they're still able to convey emotions. I would take much longer. So, is it that my experience has given me more expressions and my brevity is gone? Craft is tangible. Art is free-flowing.

AC: Instinctive.
SRK: Instinctive. It flies. But craft starts binding you. Stops the free flow. You start thinking of things to fix. 'Is it right?' you ask too often. So, when I see Suhana do what she does – she's not bound by craft. Hopefully, before she gets bound, her art would have taken place. I had that opportunity. But naturally, craft takes [you] away. And then, to deal with it, work with people who are not bound as yet. Imbibe what they're doing. I think Alia is very good. I think she's really new.

AC: But it genuinely makes you happy.
SRK: It makes me happy. I don't like many actors. I have malice towards one and all.

AC: Why?

SRK: All actors have that. Somebody told me politicians abuse in public and hug in private. Actors hug in public and abuse in private. It's good malice; it's not bad. But I have more ease now. I don't have to prove anything. I don't have to get it right. I just need to know my lines and focus points and understand what the scene is going to convey.

AC: I was reading David Fincher, and he said, 'I'm not interested in movies that entertain. I love movies that scar.' He said, 'What I love about *Jaws* is that I could never swim in the ocean again.' Do you want your cinema to scar? To educate?

SRK: You could put it like Fincher – *Jaws* was extremely entertaining. You can find a deeper meaning as time goes by. I can't make up my mind before (the release). I don't think so. I wanted *Fan* to shake you up a bit and entertain. You think, 'God, if this happens!' It is a scary thought and it can happen actually. I meet people who love me so much. People who look like me, want to look like me. I love you all. When I was young, I thought I looked like XYZ.

AC: Your mom thought you looked like Dilip Kumar.

SRK: I thought I looked like Amitabh Bachchan. Later on, girls said I was like Al Pacino, so I got the best of them all.

AC: But don't you decide, 'Primarily I want to entertain!'

SRK: I've never thought of a film as an entertaining medium. I'm like, 'Let me just do this. This is fun.' Like this film that Karan made – *Dear Zindagi* (2016). 'Shah Rukh ne ye role kyun kiya hai (Why has Shah Rukh done this role)? People have a lot of things to say but I think it's very interesting. I think it's a very nice film and [what] if I can add to it by just learning with this new experience. Perhaps, I don't have the age to do a full film like that anymore. Or stardom is too big, perhaps. It's very interesting to see what it does to the world. But then, I'd be lying if I said I would like my cinema to be like that and not commercially successful.

2 November 2016

3

Everyone Needs S.S. Rajamouli's Approval

With Nandamuri Taraka Rama Rao Jr. and Ram Charan

Anupama Chopra: I would love someday to be able to peek into your brain. I think your superpower is the ability to combine spectacle with emotion. Your movies are like modern-day mythologicals, but you never lose sight of the human relationships. How do you keep that balance?

S.S. Rajamouli: I don't try to balance it; I operate on the basis of emotion. I cannot function otherwise. Even for a song like *Nacho Nacho*, a mass dancing number, I need to have an emotional lead, emotional conclusion, underlying emotion.

AC: I interviewed Vijendra Prasad a couple of months ago and he said that in this film [*RRR*], there's going to be action and tears. How do you combine action and tears?

SS: I think if you close your eyes and think of an impactful action, there will be tears in it. It is only when the emotion is so nicely woven into the action that it will be so memorable.

AC: He [S.S.] said about the two of you [Jr NTR and RC] that you are both fantastic actors, but you don't know it. What did he mean?

Nandamuri Taraka Rama Rao Jr.: I think he knows us better than we ourselves do.

Ram Charan: His perspective was completely new to me. It was a good one, I think.

AC: But is that true? Do you feel that you're still unsure as an actor and are *you* very confident?

Jr. NTR: Well, he's been a lot of things to me, including a friend. There was this time in my career where I just didn't know what was happening. I was like, 'I don't know. My likes as an actor, what I want to do is completely different from what I'm doing now. Is it because of that that my films aren't working?' And very sweetly, he just pushed away that idea of mine. Today, I've turned out to be a better actor because of that. He makes you realise your potential. Probably I was prepped all these years to be Bheem in *RRR*. It was a very complicated character. Bheem has this brutal strength in him, but he's very innocent at heart. And that's what he made me search for. 'You don't know how you're going to perform for this character. Start being naive.' As Charan says, you have to unlearn a lot to be a Rajamouli hero.

AC: What did you have to unlearn?

RC: The assurance part, *that* I keep. Sometimes I'm not sure. And it's not always about what we think is right for the scene and the emotion. Of course, he explains everything to the T. But at end of the day, just before we move on to the next shot – that last yes from him is something that I look forward to. That assurance is always needed. Since we're kids now, we always need some kind of validation. Overconfidence doesn't work for me.

AC: Which is lovely, given that you're such a big star. Your father mentioned that you said, let's make a film with two big stars around two real-life freedom fighters. In the Hindi film industry, Rohit Shetty said that he could not make *Ram Lakhan* because no two male stars are willing to work together anymore. So, you have managed something quite exceptional here. How tough was this? Or are you now at this God-like stage where you say, 'Come' and everybody arrives?

SS: The moment I think I am in a God-like state, that is my first step to a downfall. I am not just talking about stardom. There is a friendship between Duryodhana and Karna, between Krishna and Arjuna. But what if there is a friendship between Krishna and Karna? That is how I think.

AC: It is exciting. I want to see that film.

SS: That kind of thing always excites me. Bringing two powerhouses together. When I thought of combining the lives of Aduri and Kumaram,

I needed fine actors and superstars. The moment I think of this idea, I know it is going to be two – two and a half years. But that excitement has to be there throughout. Not just at the onset. So, I have to keep them excited; write characters that will hook them. Not just for me, even for them. When all three of us are on the same page, the journey becomes easier.

AC: The other thing you said was, you said yes, but you didn't know the script. Is this something you do often?

RC: No.

Jr. NTR: No, it's just with him.

RC: And Sukumar.

AC: Your dad said you reject 90 per cent of the ideas he pitches to you. He said, he's very blunt. Is that how he is on the set?

Jr. NTR: Absolutely. He knows what he wants, but he's open to ideas. There was a key sequence he shot for sixty-five nights. So, I said, 'What if I emote like this?' He said no. But he came back to me and said, 'You know what? Actually, what you said was right. Can we do one more?' So, I just looked at him and smiled.

SS: It was a very emotional sequence. He said he will scream. I said no. But then, while shooting, I knew he had to scream. I said, 'No, I think you were right.' And he said, 'Okay, I'll do it.'

Jr. NTR: There are many incidents like that. I'm sure even Charan has experienced that. He's open, but if he knows it's not right, it's not right. He's blunt. And I think that's how you have to be as a filmmaker. You want people to carry your vision.

AC: What is he like on set? In interviews, he is a saint.

RC: It depends on the day. If stress levels are high and people are not performing, he blows the roof.

Jr. NTR: It's a process, becoming a saint — I think you have to be angry to become a saint. So, that's what he is. He's angry when he's making his movie.

RC: Otherwise, he's pretty much in zen mode.

Jr. NTR: He's a taskmaster.

AC: Perfectionist. You're chasing that one detail always.

SS: It's basically out of fear, not out of anything else — because you need to get it right. The images that we have in our mind — we have to get it right on the screen. If we don't get it right, then I'm afraid that it would not work out.

AC: Sanjay Leela Bhansali said to me, 'You want to perfect each frame. Because it's forever. You can't change it.'

SS: True.

Jr. NTR: The movie is there forever.

AC: Which is the great thing about this art form.

Jr. NTR: Absolutely.

AC: Patriotism is baked into this narrative. Two freedom fighters. But there's such a thin line now between patriotism and jingoism. How have you ensured that this film doesn't cross it?

SS: Even though it is set in the pre-Independence era and is the fictional tale of two real-life freedom fighters, the film itself is not about patriotism. It's about friendship. I love my country. I love my culture, but that doesn't mean I hate others. I respect other countries. But for me, my country is great. Respecting my country doesn't mean demeaning others. That's what I believe. But the film is about friendship.

AC: The conversation around this film is also, because it's so massive — the conversation is so much about the numbers. The budget is around

₹550 crore. I was like, 'Wow, how many zeros are there in that?' But do you all ever worry about whether, in this conversation, people will lose sight of the artistry, of your art and your craft and the amount of work you put into it.

SS: See, we make films for money, ultimately. If the film doesn't get that back in return, then it's a failure, for everyone. But as long as I'm making the film, those numbers won't affect me at all. Occasionally I look at them to have a perspective. But until my last CG shot is done, and everything is put together, I don't have space in my mind to do that. So once everything is out of my hand, then I become a spectator. Then it becomes that game.

AC: Then the artist is done and the businessman takes over.

SS: Yeah, then we'll start looking at the numbers. If the number is high, we celebrate. If the number is low, then we think about what can we do to push it up.

AC: Are the two of you thinking about numbers?

Jr. NTR: I personally feel that there needs to be one brain like Rajamouli's to think about numbers. But if I can speak on Charan's behalf also, right now for us, it's… We just want *RRR* to hit the theatres and we're waiting for the audience to give a verdict on what we've done as actors. But post that, yes. For me, *RRR* – or any film releasing post-pandemic – is about bringing back audiences to the theatre.

RC: Bring the old glory back to the theatres.

Jr. NTR: Watching a film in theatres . . . . When we came to Mumbai and when we were watching it on the PVR screen, I was like, 'Wow!' I don't know the last time I went to a theatre to watch a movie of mine. The whole feeling was so ecstatic. If *RRR* can bring back more audience, I'll be the happiest.

RC: The first few days – we speak about numbers more than the artistic form and appreciating our work. I mean when you spend ₹500 crore, I don't mind not being spoken about for two three days. Let's cross that number and hope our producers are fine, our distributors are fine. We can talk about our work, pause, replay.

AC: How much has he evolved as a director from *Magadheera* and *Student No. 1*?

RC: We all have evolved, but he evolved multi-fold. I would love to always be associated with somebody who is more evolved than me if it's the director.

Jr. NTR: From being a local Telugu director to being the first filmmaker to actually break the regional barriers. We are not regional anymore. We are one big Indian film industry.

RC: Indian cinema.

Jr. NTR: And it was him—

RC: —who did that.

Jr. NTR: Thanks to *Baahubali*. He's hungrier. He wants to tell stories to the world, share his ideas. And that perfectionist keeda – it's grown bigger.

AC: You talked about it being the Indian film industry. We've spent too long being Bollywood and Mollywood and Tollywood and pata nahi konse woods (and I don't know what -woods). I just think it's so amazing. You have Ajay Devgn. You've got Alia. And that's not just the one project. Fahadh Faasil can act with Allu Arjun. Cross-pollination across the country. Do you think it will grow?

RC: Absolutely.

Jr. NTR: You mentioned *Ram Lakhan* today. Certain filmmakers don't have that kind of confidence or infrastructure for that to happen. But now, here we are. Two actors coming from rivalry between the families.

AC: Of course.

SS: Everyone knows.

Jr. NTR: There was a thirty- to thirty-five-year-old rivalry. Today we are friends too. Positive rivalry. When was the last two big-star collaboration in Hindi? *Karan Arjun*. But we've seen this cross-pollination happen. And this is our patriotism towards our industry. We need to travel. We have actors all over our country in different languages. The language barrier, for me, is not a barrier at all. Filmmakers today believe in that idea of uniting. And it will just get bigger and better.

AC: And as a greedy viewer, I just want more. How does he come up with these images? That image of the woman carrying just the hand and the baby. From *Baahubali*. It was just unforgettable. What is the secret sauce?

RC: I don't think I want to get into his head.

AC: Might as well stay out of it.

RC: As a viewer, I enjoy it. I want to ask him one day. I hope he answers us.

Jr. NTR: He's a visual storyteller. *Baahubali 2* – watching the conclusion, you have a recap of what happened in *Baahubali 1*. How do you even think about something like that?

AC: Mystery, Sir?

SS: No mystery. I just like to wow my audience. But the imagery should have fantastic emotion underneath it. In the trailer, Charan appears from the fire. That's a strong visual. But what connects is the intensity in his eyes – he just needs to stand there and bring his bow down. But if your intention is being portrayed through your eyes – subconsciously you'll connect with it. People will only say, 'That's a great image.' I say the credit goes to the emotion.

25 December 2021

4

'My Time Has Come': Pankaj Tripathi

Anupama Chopra: Pankaj, welcome to *Film Companion*. First of all, many congratulations on *Stree*.
Pankaj Tripathi: Thank you, Ma'am.

AC: I read that the film *Stree* is the most profitable film of this year because the budget...
PT: Bohot chhota thha, kamayi zyaada hui hai. (It was very low, and the earnings were high.)

AC: It's at hundred crores now. You've made us laugh, cry, and scared us. So a big thank you, really. You know, you're such a fine actor.... Pankaj, you said in an interview of *Film Companion* that, 'The [right] time is for things like fruits, crops, and vegetables. How can there be a "right time" for an artist?' But don't you feel that now, after so many years and so many struggles, when you've become so successful, your time has really come?
PT: Haan, woh interview I think kuch ek ya do mahine pehle hua thha. (Yes, I think that interview was done one or two months ago.)

AC: Before *Stree*.
PT: But ab lag raha hai ki main itna pareshaan ho gaya hoon teen din ke liye Mumbai aake. Aur main aisi coma waali stithhi mein hoon kyunki mujhe bohot saare logon se milna hai, bohot saari jagah jaana hai. Itne saare offer hain, itna load hai kaam ka. Toh mujhe lag raha hai ki mera samay aa gaya hai shayad kyunki itni vyastata maine kabhi nahi dekhi. (But now I feel so overwhelmed on this three-day trip to Mumbai. I'm in a comatose state because I have a lot of people to meet and places to go. There are so many offers, so much work. So maybe my time has come, because I've never been busier.)

AC: But isn't that wonderful?

PT: Haan, achha bhi hai, but main thoda sukoon mein rehne wala aadmi hoon. Mujhe na itni bhaag-daud aur itna cut-to-cut ghanta ke hisaab se chalna pasand nahi hai. (Yes, indeed, it's good. But I'm a person who likes his peace. I don't like this mad rush or living hour to hour on the clock.)

AC: Pankaj, you call yourself an aware performer. What does that mean?
PT: Jo samaaj mein ho raha hai na iss waqt, social, political, economical level pe, toh bataur abhineta mujhe pata hona chahiye. Des aur kaal ka anumaan hona chahiye. Aur kya ghatit ho raha hai humare aas paas, middle class, upper class mai kya chal raha hai lower class mein kya chal raha hai. Toh woh aware rehne se na somehow hum apni performance ko zyada contemporary rakh paayenge. Main chahta hoon ki mere saare kirdaar na aware rahein. (As an actor, I should know what's happening in society right now, at the social, political and economic level. Be aware of the country and the times. And of things happening around us, what's happening in the middle-class, upper-class and lower-class strata. By being aware of that, somehow, we can keep our performance more contemporary. I want all my characters to be aware.)

AC: But Pankaj, isn't it difficult? The more successful you are, the more you are cut off from normal life. So how do you stay aware?
PT: Padhne se. Mere liye bada mushkil hai duniya se katna. Mujhe pata hai ki main abhineta banne aaya taaki log mujhe jaanein. Ya koi bhi jo abhineta banna chahta hai isliye banna chahta hai ki duniya usko jane. Aur jis din duniya jaanne lagti hai, uss din who apni gaadi mein kaale rang ki kaanch laga deta hai. Woh kala chashma pehen leta hai, aur khud ko sabse alag kar leta hai. (By reading. First of all, it's very difficult for me to cut myself off from the world. I know that I came here to become an actor, so that people know me. Anyone who wants to become an actor wants the world to know them. And the day the world gets to know them, they install tinted windows in their car, start to wear black shades, and isolate themselves.)

AC: You are the first actor who has come here with no entourage, no manager and no social media persons. There is no one. Why is that?
PT: Aisa yun hain kyunki akele hi aaye the, akele hi jaana hai. Aur iss baat ki anubhuti bohot achhe tarike se hai. Main apna saara kaam khud kar leta hoon. Main abhi aane se pehle ghar par khaana banake aaya hoon apni biwi aur beti ke liye. (This is so because alone we come, and

alone we go. And I have a very good experience of this. I do all my work on my own. Today, before coming, I cooked food for my wife and daughter at home.)

AC: Yes, I heard you are a very good cook!
PT: Bohot achha toh nahi hoon, simple banata hoon. Toh aaj patni boli ki, 'Tum banao mere liye', toh maine unke liye karela banaya aur phir tabhi idhar aaya. Cooking aur acting bada similar kaam lagta hai mujhe. (I wouldn't say I am very good; I cook simple food. So today, my wife asked me to cook for her, and I made some bitter gourd for her before getting here. I find cooking and acting very similar.)

AC: How so?
PT: Matraon ka gyaan hai na. Kitna daalna hai. Thoda sa amount badh gaya toh log bolte hain overacting hai. Waise hi thodi cooking zyada ho gaya toh bolte hain ki overcooked hai. Khaane mein jaisa amount haldi aur namak ka hona chahiye, waisa hi precision aur amount acting mein pata hona chahiye. Kayi baar flow mein hum thoda zyada kar jaate hain. Agar audience achhi mil gayi aur zyada hasne lag jaye, toh abhineta utsaah mein kuch zyada hi kar deta hai ki 'aur hasaunga'. (It's about the knowledge of measurements, and knowing how much to put in. If the amount increases even a little, people say it is overacting. Similarly, if something is cooked for slightly longer than required, they say the food is overcooked. The amount of turmeric and salt added to the food is also the precision you need when you're acting. Many times, one does more than necessary in the flow of things. If we get a good audience that's having a good laugh, then an actor can get carried away in that enthusiasm to make the audience laugh more.)

AC: Pankaj, we will show you three of your characters and you tell us how you created them.

(On playing Sadhya-ji in *Masaan*)

AC: This was such a small role in terms of footage, I mean, there were two scenes, maybe?
PT: Two and a half, yes.

AC: And such impact! I mean, I will never forget it. How did you do it?

PT: Iske writer Varun Grover, aur director Neeraj – dono mere dost hain. Jab *Masaan* ki script likhi gayi thhi, tab maine padhi thhi. Neeraj chahta thha main Sanjay bhaiyya waala role karoon, Devi yaani Richa ke papa ka. Main script padhne ke baad bola ki, 'Nahi main ye karunga, Sadhya-ji ka role.' Ye main hoon darasal. Isme abhinaya kam aur main zyada hoon. (The writer Varun Grover, and Neeraj, the director, both are my friends. When the script was written, I read it. Earlier, Neeraj wanted me to play Sanjay bhaiya's – Devi, that is, Richa's father's – role. After reading the script, I said, 'No, I will do Sadhya-ji's role.' Actually, this is me. There is less acting and more of me in this role.)

AC: Especially because it is about kheer?

PT: Kheer ki baat hai, ji. Aur itni sehejta main chahta hoon jeevan mein, itna thheraav. Toh maine socha karke aata hoon do scene, kyunki likhi acchi gayi thhi. Plus, main iss ilaake se bhi aata hoon. Woh Kashi ka railway station hai jahan hum shoot kar rahe the. Mere chacha ka naam Kashi hai, mere pita ka naam Banaras hai. Toh mere liye ye ilaaka ghar jaisa hai. Main aath filmein kar chuka hoon, aur ab toh wahan ka har driver mujhe jaanta hai ... bolte hain ki 'Pankaj bhaiyya aa gaye hain.' Toh bohot aasaan thha mere liye ye part karna. But around the same time *Wasseypur* aayi thhi, aur logon ne uss film mein Sultan dekha thha aur bole, 'Arre yaar ye itna seedha saada hai. Itna kaise transform ho sakta hai ek abhineta?' But ye main zyada hoon. (It is about kheer, yes. And I want this much ease in life, this much calmness. I went thinking I will do two scenes, and they were well written, too. Plus, I come from this area. We were shooting scenes at the Kashi railway station. My uncle's name is Kashi, my father's name is Banaras. So this area is like home for me. I have done eight films and now every driver there knows me. They say, 'Pankaj bhaiyya is here.' So it was very easy for me to do this part. But around the same time, *Gangs of Wasseypur* came out, and people had seen me play Sultan in it and said, 'Oh, he is so simple. How can an actor transform so much?' But this [Sadhya-ji's] role is closer to who I am.)

AC: But Pankaj, after reading a script, how does an actor choose a role with less footage?

PT: Mujhe na aksar lagta hai ki match mein tabhi mazza hai jab ek ball mein chheh run banane hon aur akhri ball ho. Toh mujhe humesha se chhote kirdar na bade attract karte hain kyunki isme possibility bohot kam hai, lekin mujhe pata hai main isme bhi kuch kar loonga. (I often feel that a match is fun only when six runs have to be scored through the very last ball. So I am always attracted to such small characters, which have very little possibility but I know I will manage to create impact through these, too.)

AC: Okay, let's see the second one.

(On playing Kehri Singh in *Gurgaon*)

AC: This is also a very good film. You were so scary, but it was controlled menace. How did you do this?
PT: Bahut complex, bahut layered kirdaar thha ye mere liye. Itni mehnat maine isme aur *Powder*, ek series thhi, inn dono mein ki hai. Isme maine attempt kiya ki jo aam taur par ek actor ke jo tools hote hain – aankhein, chehra, haubhau, kab sakhti se bolna hai, kab narmi se – main inka na minimum istemaal karoon, aur phir dekhoon ki baat communicate kar pa raha hoon ki nahin. Kyunki chhoti film thhi, yahan scope hai ki aap experiment kar sakte ho, director allow kar raha thha. Aur chhote-chhote details pe zyada dhyaan diya thha. (This was a very complex, layered character for me. I worked this hard on another series called *Powder*. In this project, I attempted to minimally use the regular tools an actor uses – the eyes, face, mannerisms, whether to speak firmly or softly – to see if I am able to communicate well or not. Since it was a small film, there was scope for experimenting, which the director was allowing. So I focused more on smaller details.)

AC: Let's see one more work which reached a lot of people.

(On playing Aatma Singh in *Newton*)

AC: First of all, tell me, how much was written and how much did you improvise?
PT: Iss scene mein I think maine kuch text improvise nahi kiya hai, khaali gesture improvise kiya hai. Batsman–bowler wala. Ye single take hai poora ka poora scene. Aur mujhe baat bhi karni thhi Raj se, aur mera path bhi decided thha ki iss raste pe chalna hai. Toh mujhe woh bhi dekhna thha. Ye jab script Amit ne bheji thhi, main padha jab toh Aatmaram ka kirdar bada arrogant, cynical laga, jaise ek aam army man jo humain lagta hai ki

bade sakht honge… (In this scene, I think I didn't improvise any text, only gestures. The batsman–bowler one. This whole scene was a single take. And I had to talk to Raj and pay attention while walking, to not stray from the decided track. In fact, when Amit had sent the script, Aatmaram's character felt very arrogant, cynical, like an ordinary army man whom we perceive as very tough…)

AC: Pankaj, I've heard that now filmmakers don't even direct you. That they say you can do whatever you feel is right. Is that true?
PT: Yes, zyaadatar cases mein true hai. Direction ki baat nahi, bharosa ki hai. Itna trust karte hai ki bole, 'Tum kar lo.' Haalanki main director ka actor hoon, main bahut improvise karta hoon, yes. Har film mein, har scene mein. Lekin mere improvisation mein maqsad ye nahi hota hai ki main apna alag dikhoon. Main hi hoon, doosra koi nahi – main uss theory pe nahi chalta. Ye scene aur achhe tareeke se nikharke aa jaaye, thoda entertaining bann jaaye. Kyunki mera maanna hai ki agar baat neeras hogi, toh audience bore ho jayegi. Toh thoda toh entertaining ho ki woh muskurate rahein aur humein jo baat kehni thhi woh bhi keh dein. (Yes, in most cases, that's true. It's not really about direction but about trust. Directors trust me so much that they say, 'Do it your way.' Even though I'm a director's actor, I improvise a lot. In every film, in every scene. But my goal is not to highlight myself. That it's all me and no one else – I don't subscribe to such a theory. I want the scene to shine better, to be more entertaining. Because I feel that if you do a sterile scene, the audience gets bored. So I want it to be entertaining to make them smile and also communicate what I intend to.)

AC: And in *Stree*, that Aadhaar card line is yours?
PT: Yes, of course it's mine. Kyunki mere mobile mein at least das dafa message aaye hain bank se, yahan se, wahan se, ki Aadhaar link karo. Mujhe laga jitne mobile ya bank account holder hain, unke paas bhi aise message aaye honge. Ye toh bohot contemporary baat hai. Ho sakta hai ki iss chudail ke paas bhi aise message jaate hon! (Because I get at least ten messages from banks, from all kinds of sources, to link my Aadhaar to them. I thought all the mobile users or bank account holders must have received such messages. This is a very contemporary thing. It is possible that witches and ghosts receive such messages, too!)

AC: She is a well-informed ghost.

PT: Haan. Kuch log bolte hain ki woh naye Bharat ki chudail hai. (Yes. Some people say she's a witch belonging to the new India.)

AC: You know, for Mr Mehmood, it was said that at one point he became so successful, and of course, he was so talented, that the heroes said, 'Don't cast him in the film.' You know, take anyone else, because at that time, it was very clear-cut that this is a hero, this is a comedian, this is a villain. Has this ever happened to you that people are now hesitating because you have become a scene stealer?

PT: Nahi, nahi. Mujhe jis din pata chalega katraa rahe hain, main turant average acting karne lagoonga. Dukaan bhi toh chalaani hai na? Acting ki dukan band ho jaye toh phir mujhe waapis gaon jana padega kheti karne. (No, no. The day I get to know that people are hesitating to work alongside me, I will start being an average actor. After all, don't I have to keep the shop running and earn my daily bread? If the acting shop closes, I will have to go back to the village to do farming.)

AC: No, no, that won't happen.

PT: Aisa nahi hoga kyunki mera maqsad hai ki koi bhi kirdaar karo, mera sirf aur sirf irada itna hi hai ki ye overall scene jo hai, jo writer ya director humaare kehna chah rahe hain, isko aur behtar tareeke se hum audience tak pahuncha dein. Mujhe Mahesh Bhatt sahab ne ek din phone kiya. Mere paas unka number bhi nahi thha. Toh unhone *Newton* ke baare mein bola ki, 'Out of focus main bhi tu truthful thha.' Aam taur pe abhineta ko malum hota hai ki, 'Accha, main out of focus hoon.' Toh woh focus pe dekh leta hai DOP ki taraf. Wide mein bhi, agar main bahut door bhi khada hoon, main apna kaam imaandari se karta hoon. (This won't happen because my sole aim, no matter the role, is to deliver in an enhanced manner what the writer or the director originally wanted to convey. Mahesh Bhatt Sir called me one day. I didn't even have his number. About *Newton*, he said, 'You were truthful even when you were out of focus.' Usually, an actor knows that he is in out of focus, so he looks at the DOP [director of photography or cinematographer] when in focus. Even in wide, or if I am standing far away in a shot, I do my work honestly.)

AC: This is so true. I had asked Nawazuddin Siddiqui if he ever gets angry that there are so many actors who are less talented, but have a lot of success, a lot of money, a lot of fame. He said to me, 'I used to get angry, but not anymore.' So do you ever get angry?

PT: Mujhe pehle bhi nahi aata thha, abhi bhi nahi aata. Haan, of course, matlab main bhi insaan hi hoon, koi devbhoomi se aaya hua aadmi toh hoon nahi. Saare emotions mere paas bhi hain. Kayin mashhoor, successful abhineta hain jo abhinay ke maamle mein kam honge, par unme dusri aur qualities hongi jiski wajah se log unhe pasand karte hain. Agar janta kisiko pasand karti hai, toh usme kuch baat toh hogi. Uski dusri baat hai ki woh seekhne laayak hai. Shuruat mein toh humein laga thha ki hum toh acting seekhke aaye hain drama school se, acting ka struggle karne aaye hain. Yahan ab samajh mein aata hai ki apart from acting, aapko aur dus cheezein aani chahiye. Aap bazaar mein khade ho, aapko khudko bechna aana chahiye. Ye toh humein maloom hi nahi thha. Humein toh drama school ne acting, motivation, truth, aur realism sikhaya. (I never used to get angry, and even now I don't. But, of course, I am also a human being, I have not descended from Heaven. I too have emotions. There are many famous, successful actors who are less talented when it comes to acting, but they may have ten other qualities because of which people like them. If the public likes someone, then there must be something in them. That also means that they're worth learning from. In the beginning, I used to think that I have studied acting at drama school and I am here to struggle as an actor. Now I know that, apart from acting, you need to know ten other things. You are a product in the market, and you need to know how to sell yourself. I didn't know this earlier. Drama school had just taught us acting, motivation, truth and realism.)

AC: Marketing is a big thing, yes.
PT: Haan, toh abhi bhi main seekhne ka prayaas kar raha hoon. End of the day, marketing ke saath saath aapke paas aapka craft bhi hona chahiye. Tabhi baaki cheezein kaam karengi. (Yes, I am still trying to learn. At the end of the day, apart from marketing, you should also have your craft. Only then will the other things work.)

AC: Your acting is your marketing. You don't need to learn anything.
PT: Aksar kayin log aa jaate hain photo ke liye. Main kayin baar chidhaane ke liye unko bolta hoon, 'Mera naam pata hai aapko?' Wo bolte hain, 'Nahi Sir, par bohot kamaal karte ho aap.' Main poochhta hoon, 'Phir kaaheko photo le rahe ho? Photo leke baadme naam pata karoge ki kaun hai ye?' Toh phir woh log bolte hain, 'Humein aapki acting pasand hai na, aapke naam se kya lena dena?' (Many people come to me for a photo, and I tease them by asking if they even know my name. They say, 'No Sir, but

your work is great.' I ask them, 'Then why are you taking a photo? Will you look up my name *after* taking the photo?' They say, 'We like your acting, what does it have to do with your name?')

AC: You have the same aim and ambition as well, right, that the characters should be memorable? Why do you dislike the label of a 'supporting actor'?
PT: Ek table ke chaar pair hote hain … unke bagair thodi tikega. Toh ye 'supporting' bolte hain na, ek secondary si feeling aati hai, ki do darze ke hain hum, ji ye 'supporting' hai. Kaahe ke 'supporting'? Actor toh actor hota hai yaar. Ye terms Hindustan mein bann gaye hain: 'supporting actor', 'comedian'. Mujhe 'comedian' se bhi chidh hoti hai. (A table has four legs, without which it can't stand. So when one labels us as 'supporting' actors, I get this feeling of being secondary, like we are second-class actors. Why do you call it 'supporting'? An actor is an actor. In India, we have these terms now: 'supporting actor', 'comedian'. I don't like the term 'comedian' either.)

AC: I read that you decided in tenth grade that you will have a love marriage, because up until then no one in the village had had a love marriage.
PT: Nahi, kisine ne nahi ki thhi. (Indeed, nobody in the village had gone for a love marriage.)

AC: So were you a rulebreaker from the beginning?
PT: Yeh abh ehsaas hota hai mujhe. Uss waqt nahi pata thha ki main rulebreaker hoon. (It's now that I realise I'm a rulebreaker. Back then, I didn't really know.)

AC: Thank you so much.
PT: Thank you, Anupama-ji. Main aksar aapki baatcheet dekhta hoon. Bada achha lagta hai, maza aata hai. (Thank you for inviting me, Anupama ma'am. I watch your interviews often, and enjoy them thoroughly.)

24 September 2018

5

Sandeep Reddy Vanga on Films, Processes, Beliefs

Anupama Chopra: Congratulations on the monster success of *Kabir Singh*. It's generated an avalanche of criticism. What have the last two weeks been like for you and what's in your head right now?
Sandeep Reddy Vanga: It was great when we started this film. I thought it will be a big success at the box office, but I never thought the rage will be repeated and multiplied four times. I never thought about being cult again. So that was surprising.

AC: Did you anticipate the criticism?
SRV: There's a part of the criticism that happened for *Arjun Reddy* but this was a little bizarre.

AC: Why bizarre?
SRV: I believe that when you question their belief system, people get angry. And it is not even healthy criticism; it's very pseudo.

AC: What do you mean? Here are some of the things I read – it's toxic masculinity. Female critics said they felt really uncomfortable because the men clapped when Kabir slapped Preeti.
SRV: When you are deeply connected with a woman or vice versa there's a lot of honesty in it. If you don't have the liberty of slapping each other, I don't see anything there. I feel this woman, whoever is talking about this, was never in love; probably never experienced it the right way.

AC: Perhaps they don't see this as love.
SRV: Yeah, that's too personal for them. I have seen a rage of criticism in Telugu but I enjoyed that.

AC: What was the difference?
SRV: They were criticising many aspects. But here they were only on the feminist side. They didn't speak about cinematography, production value,

background score, sound design, colour correction. Just writing, directing and editing because they hate me. I could clearly see they don't understand the difference between description and objectifying.

AC: But critics are here.
SRV: I don't even see them. Critics talk about a lot. One lady said that her dream got shattered because of *Kabir Singh*. She was enjoying films like *NH10* and said her dream of achieving better cinema got shattered because of *Kabir Singh*'s success. I feel a filmmaker's intellect is always directly proportional to the crowd.

AC: I really enjoyed *Arjun Reddy*. Vijay Deverakonda was terrific. *Kabir Singh*, I knew the beats. I had problems with the beginning of this love story. He's kissing her. He's putting his head in her lap. She says nothing. It's pure ownership. He instructs the juniors, 'Meri bandi hai (She is my girl).' And the film presents this as romance – not as a problematic man.
SRV: Mujhe toh kuchh galat nahi lagta usme (I don't find anything wrong in that). You call 2,000 people to your wedding and tie a knot. What are you trying to tell?

AC: Do you see this as a form of that?
SRV: Of course. It's a hundred-people classroom. You call 2,000 people and do nonsense.

AC: But she says nothing, Sandeep. She's like this mute cow.
SRV: There are girls who don't talk much. Has nothing to do with her intellect. She's not dumb.

AC: No, she isn't. But just that scene as romance, you don't think somewhere it'll give permission to men to say it's okay to kiss a woman without even asking?
SRV: No. I grew up watching *Gang Leader, Gharana Mogudu, Parinda, Ram Lakhan, Teja*, and me and my brother never became gangsters after watching *Parinda*.

AC: Of course. It's not a direct correlation but you are in a sense normalising that behaviour.
SRV: Normalising? See, it's between Preeti and Kabir. Why does it have to be generalised? I've seen so many girls saying that we need somebody like *Arjun Reddy* or *Kabir Singh* in life.

AC: For me, it was like two crazy people who can't live without each other. And I was seduced by it. You know?
SRV: He's a senior. She has seen him talking to the dean. And you are rescued from ragging just because his name is being used. Intimidation has its own charm, you know? Did you feel that Preeti was threatened when he was kissing her?

AC: It made me uncomfortable.
SRV: Discomfort. But why didn't she slap him then? And she slapped him couple of times in the film and nobody had a problem.

AC: Right, she slaps him later.
SRV: And she slapped him without a reason. Kabir has a reason. And if you can't slap, or touch your woman wherever you want and if you can't kiss, use cuss words – I don't see emotion there. Then it's all margins and papers. There's nothing unconditional about it. I personally feel like asking them, where do you get this energy from? Where are you deriving it from? What school you have been to? What colony did you live in? People have ridiculed *Arjun Reddy* in Telugu, but that was different. I never got this kind of criticism. Censor was also more open. No. It is narrower than South here. If these guys watch *Paruthiveeran*, I think they'll commit suicide. Have you watched *Paruthiveeran*?

AC: I haven't.
SRV: You have to. Priyamani won the National Award for that film. A film like *Paruthiveeran* can never be made now, because people would shed their pen when thinking about these critics. These guys should reinforce our work. They should not hamper it.

AC: No, but, Sandeep, critics never ever critique to hamper a film or to get in the way of a filmmaker. It's a comment on the movie.
SRV: Rajeev Masand gave 3.5 to *Sanju*. 'Sanju, where is my mangalsutra?' What happens after that? But everybody loved it. You know it's just 300-odd women he slept with. We all were cheering and whistling in the theatre. I never understood.

AC: That scene from the *Arjun Reddy* version, where Arjun and Shiva are talking about objectifying women, and Arjun is very strongly against it, why did you remove that?

SRV: Producers wanted the length to be crisp. When I was making *Arjun Reddy*, it was based on a script. *Kabir Singh* – we were making a film based on a film. We deleted twelve minutes. Those were hilarious scenes.

AC: Was it hard for you?
SRV: It was very hard. I wanted to keep it but a few regulations, you know, I have to follow.

AC: Okay, tell me about the sort of gaze on his crotch. He puts ice into his pants. We see him cut himself. We see him wet himself. Why was that important?
SRV: In childhood when riding a bicycle, kabhi kabhi, woh chain utar jaata hai (the chain comes off the ring). We try two or three times, with little fingers. If it doesn't work, we throw the bicycle and walk. It is like that. He tried – didn't happen. He thought putting ice would be a . . . . When you start watching *Kabir [Singh]*, we opened it this way. And then, you will be more interested to know what happened in his past.

AC: And why he is like this?
SRV: Yeah.

AC: Then he does cut himself. Then, he injects himself, wets himself. Why did we focus so much on his body?
SRV: Wetting himself was . . . you lose control of your bladder. A person like Kabir Singh is pissing his own pants – there is a lot of power in it, showing him so down. You see Kabir like that in the football ground in the Holi scene and then this...

AC: He has hit rock bottom.
SRV: Yeah. This is the beginning of the personal tragedy.

AC: Do you feel that as a character he suffered enough for the things he did?
SRV: Yeah, and maybe not till that interval but before the pre-climax. He loses his degree – he is proud of his professional career. So, I feel that's the biggest loss.

AC: So this is not a character who gets away easy.
SRV: That's what is pissing the critics. How can this guy be happy in the climax?

AC: Right.
SRV: They thought Kabir will die of liver cirrhosis or that Preeti will bear somebody else's child. Why so psychotic? Preeti is a very strong character. She gave up on the marriage after the third day. She says that she didn't let him touch her – and they didn't like it.

AC: Why is that important while Kabir Singh is sleeping with whoever he sees?
SRV: He doesn't sleep with anybody else.

AC: He doesn't? But in the opening, he is threatening that woman.
SRV: When Shiva asked him, 'Tujhe kya lagta hai woh "darling open the door" wala nahi aata, toh tu kuch karta tha usse (Do you think that if "darling open the door guy" wouldn't come, you would do something to her)?' Ye bolta hai, 'Haan (yes).' 'Ye sab karna band karo (Stop doing all this).'

AC: So, you are saying that he actually does not have sex with anybody.
SRV: Nobody.

AC: Right, because I didn't get that from this film. There has also been conversation about how much kissing there is in the film. Why was that necessary?
SRV: It's a love story. And there is no tongue. It was just a kiss. There is no pan right or pan left, tilt down, tilt up for the cleavage or a back shot. Even the putting ice – no close-up shot. We didn't want to underline it. I feel that is one of the major USPs of the film.

AC: Why do you think this character, complicated and so flawed, connected so well?
SRV: I feel that's because: in every person, there is a lot of Kabir inside. They don't express it for many reasons. When one falls in love, I think everybody has that honesty in them. That is the factor.

AC: So, does the massive box office success take away a bit from the sting of criticism?
SRV: Yeah, probably friends, family, probably 200 ka ticket gaya hoga (must've bought a ticket costing ₹200). Maybe 1,000 people or maybe 1,500. If this stopped at eighty crore rupees or ninety crore rupees, ye criticism multiply hota tha (This criticism would have multiplied).

AC: But Sandeep, as a filmmaker, does it make you think, maybe I should pay attention?
SRV: No, if you do that how can you write?

AC: No, not in a way where it hinders your creativity, but in a way where you're still listening to see, 'Okay, maybe I can see things in a different light.'
SRV: I'll give you an example. Sucharita Tyagi said that the first dialogue Preeti says is, 'Kabir, what do you like in me?' Kuch galat hai kya aisa puchne mai (Is there something wrong in asking this)?

AC: No, it just presents her as having no other life except this relationship, perhaps that's what she meant.
SRV: They were discussing anatomy, and the song took over.

AC: Sure. But it doesn't make you rethink?
SRV: No. When you see Preeti getting close after the Holi fight, cut to his feet getting cut and again to the boys' hostel and everything happens, – you see a big difference, but they don't talk. There is a huge jump in the relationship, which you could waste ten to fifteen minutes writing a scene for. That's a screenplay choice.

AC: So, you're saying that when you were writing *Arjun Reddy* in your head, none of the intentions that are being attributed to you were ever there? I mean this is a film that's been described as insulting to women, hateful to women.
SRV: No.

AC: You're seeing this as a great love story.
SRV: Yeah, that's it. I never felt that I'll face criticism. I always felt – I'm making my first film, I want it to be told in a different, engaging way. Keeping a dark mood in the film for more than hundred minutes, and yet to make a compelling story – that was a challenge.

AC: Where did this guy come from? I know some of it came from your own life, you've called yourself a 'love failure'.
SRV: I really don't know. First, whenever you're making something, you always compare it with the market. It's not like one point of inspiration. I took one year to write this.

AC: But it just kept coming.
SRV: Yeah. My first cut of *Arjun Reddy* was four hours twenty-two minutes.

AC: No way!
SRV: The first cut [of *Kabir*] was three hours thirty-five minutes, so the distributors rejected the film. Chopping down twenty-three minutes or whatever took a long time, more than one month.

AC: In your head, you were never objectifying women?
SRV: No. If that deleted scene was there, it would have been a little clearer.

AC: Because you have him say it.
SRV: Yeah, the air hostess scene. I want to put it on YouTube.

AC: And in your head do these guys live happily ever after?
SRV: Yeah.

AC: She lives with it or do his anger management issues get better?
SRV: Probably Kabir will be doing some research and will apply it after five years. After kids, people change.

AC: Do you think that films have a moral responsibility?
SRV: To some extent; that's why we have censors.

AC: Do you feel now that your cinema has to be responsible?
SRV: I don't know. I'll tell you probably after another film.

AC: What kind of cinema do you like?
SRV: I watch every film other than comedy.

AC: Are you an angry person yourself?
SRV: Uh, I don't think so.

AC: You connect with his [Kabir's] flaws, is that because you're also short-tempered yourself?
SRV: Yeah, I always take anger as purest emotion. And I feel like the more sincere you are, the angrier you are.

AC: So, you see him as pure, sincere, messed up.
SRV: Yeah.

AC: And how do you see Kabir?
SRV: He has problems. He doesn't know how to deal with himself because nobody mixes alcohol and morphine.

AC: How do you see Preeti?
SRV: I've seen women like Preeti in my life, in my college time. I feel Preeti is a very intelligent girl but she speaks less.

AC: Why?
SRV: Sticking to one man or a man sticking to one woman is going down.

AC: So, monogamy for both?
SRV: Yeah, monogamy is the right word.

AC: What's next for you?
SRV: I'm writing a story on crime.

AC: Do you want to make cinema in Hindi? In Telugu? What's in your head?
SRV: I want to finish what I started.

AC: But the crime story, do you have an idea what language?
SRV: I'm writing the treatment. I'll see how it goes.

AC: Are you a director who connects more easily with male characters? Like Rohit Shetty.
SRV: I really don't know. Judge me after two or three films.

AC: And now we're going to see a Tamil version?
SRV: Yeah.

AC: Is that very different? Do you get involved?
SRV: My first AD is directing it, so, I'm aware. I want to see it.

AC: Do you give notes?
SRV: No, no.

AC: And is it true that your son is named Arjun Reddy?
SRV: Yeah, he was born when I was shooting *Arjun Reddy*.

AC: I'm assuming you're hoping that he's not like Arjun Reddy.
SRV: Yeah. I remember asking my mom, 'Why didn't you name me Arjun?' I like that name.

AC: Anything to do with Arjun from the Mahabharata?
SRV: Just that Arjun sounds very sharp.

AC: What's the experience of being in Mumbai with a 200-crore-plus film?
SRV: I'm happy but I hope that when I do my next Hindi film, I want to start my office at 9 o'clock in the morning, nobody comes here before 12 o'clock. First day when I was in the office, jhaadu maarne wali (the cleaner) came at 10.30 a.m.

AC: Didn't anyone tell you?
SRV: No. After the first two or three days I asked my EP.... He said before 11.30 a.m. kuch nahi hota idhar (nothing happens here).

AC: That's a cultural difference. In Hyderabad, is everybody working at nine?
SRV: Yeah.

AC: Maybe you can instil some discipline in Mumbai, I would be personally very happy.
SRV: Half of the day is gone by twelve.

AC: Do you plan to set up base here?
SRV: Yeah, I'm thinking of it.

AC: What is exciting about the Hindi film industry?
SRV: There's more number of people watching. Kashmir to Kanyakumari – everywhere the film is released. This was released in Morocco.

AC: And this is Shahid's first 200-crore hit, what has his conversation with you been like?
SRV: Yesterday we met, he was very happy; but we didn't expect this rage, this love . . . that was shocking. People say that you can repeat the success, but you can't repeat a cult film. That was very satisfying.

AC: We look forward to seeing what you do next, hopefully it will generate less criticism.
SRV: It will be more. These guys are calling this film violent. I'll show them what a violent film will be.

AC: Surely that's not how you create?
SRV: It's not that. I'm curious as to how these guys are going to react. So we'll see and very big thanks to all the audience who loved the film.

6 July 2019

6

Deepika Padukone: The Best That Earth Has to Offer

Anupama Chopra: I'm really thrilled that we are celebrating turning one with an artist who is number one. Your co-star Vin Diesel said about you in *Time Magazine*, 'Deepika is the best earth has to offer.'
Deepika Padukone: Thank you!

AC: I want to start with our last conversation. The lockdown had just begun in April 2020, and you did all these interviews in front of one wallpaper.
DP: The famous wallpaper.

AC: You said, 'Truthfully, in my life I've been through the worst, so this is not really affecting me in a crushing way.' But it's been fifteen months. Have you changed fundamentally as an artist or a person?
DP: Oh, hundred per cent. Lockdown One was very different, trying to navigate our lives around this new way of living. Lockdown Two was different because everyone in my family including me had Covid at the same time. I think life after Covid changed for me because I was physically unrecognisable. The medication and the steroids. I don't know how many of you have had it, but you just feel like you've never felt before. Your body feels different, your mind feels different. I needed to take two months off from work because my mind wasn't working and so I think that phase for me was very, very difficult. My mother had different symptoms, and my husband came out of it very differently. I think it's changed a lot of things for a lot of people. I think that it's made us all more empathetic. I think I've become more empathetic; I've become more sensitive and also, that a life of purpose has become much larger for me today. I try and find meaning in everything that I do.

AC: So, she is doing one film *Fighter* with Hrithik Roshan, *Pathaan* with Shah Rukh Khan, going on to *Project K* with Prabhas. I've always tried to

dig out information, which has always been futile because she's very good at just smiling and saying no. But these are big movies. How do you ensure that the role that you're doing has enough depth, enough mileage?
DP: Today, directors with those kinds of roles don't even approach me. I think they're like, 'Don't even bother because she's going to say no.' But I'm like, 'Give me a shot, maybe?' I think I'm fortunate and I've worked hard to get to a place where I can give feedback and they're open to feedback. The kind of roles that are coming to me are pretty well written. Then I come in and add a little more depth to it and add layers to it and make it my own. The directors that I am working with have been open to that.

AC: Would you say that we're past that place where the women are just decoration?
DP: In my world, yes.

AC: That's just fantastic. Alongside, you're also doing a smaller intimate drama like Shakun Batra's film. I called him and I said, 'What is it like to work with Deepika?' and he described you to me as a school kid.
DP: Did he send you that picture?

AC: He sent me a picture. He said, 'She comes into the workshops with highlighters and a ruler and then she highlights in different colours, the dialogue.'
DP: It's colour for character based on what I think the colour represents. So, in some films, I could be green, and I'll give a character orange, and I'll give somebody else pink. I feel colours say a lot. So if I had to look at a snapshot of the scene, the colours define where the scene is going. I highlight the name of the character along with the dialogue in that colour.

AC: But not just your character?
DP: Not just my character.

AC: So, all your co-stars have a colour? And do they know this?
DP: That's my process. I don't care if they know or don't. On Shakun's film they all found it very amusing. So, it's a full pencil box, my colours are there, my rulers, sharpener, eraser, everything and then my script or the scene that we're studying is on a clipboard. Some writers are very married to the dialogues that they write and you cannot change anything. And then you have Kabir, and people like Shakun or Bhansali, who are very

open to making the dialogues your own as long as you get the essence, emotion of the scene and what you're trying to convey and communicate. I take a pencil and mark out the words that don't feel natural and write it on the side.

AC: So, he said, 'She has the mind of a student', and I thought that was just fascinating and admirable for a superstar.
DP: Wow, that's a huge compliment, thank you. I've never thought of myself like that. That's just been my process, I have figured it out along the way. I started when I didn't have command over the language, and I used to learn my dialogues by heart. Over time, with the experience and the criticism that I got, I found different processes and figured out this process that works for me.

AC: I think to be a lifelong student is the best any of us can do.
DP: I try and apply that to as many aspects of my life as possible. I feel like you need to be flexible in order to be able to allow new experiences, to make mistakes and then to learn from that. If you're stuck in your ways of doing things, then I feel like you're not allowing energy and not allowing yourself to grow.

AC: Shakun said he wants to only work with actors who worked with Bhansali because you are perfectly good with doing twenty takes.
DP: Yes, Shakun does forty-five and he's still not happy.

AC: Are you serious? He does forty-five?
DP: He's in denial but I started saying now that it's actually the other way around. If you work with Shakun Batra, you can work on a Sanjay Leela Bhansali film because he's just not happy. I'm joking about the complaining part, but I love his process because it's exhausting. From the time you reach set till the time you leave, actors are on their feet the whole time, except maybe for a twenty-minute lunch break. Even that, the AD is like, 'Guys, today if you can do it quickly na?' and I'm like, 'What do you mean today? We've been doing it for the last one and a half years; I've been eating lunch in like ten minutes!' But his process on this film was all handheld and like, 'Okay, can we try this? Can you start this from here? Can you walk in from here?' We were all extremely nimble and therefore – all the more reason to know our dialogues so well that it didn't matter what you were doing. To know the scene inside out and so well that I still

felt confident and had command over the scene, versus feeling like the scene has control over me.

AC: You've told me before that you don't like to talk about your craft, but I'm curious, how do you find emotional truth or authenticity on take twenty?
DP: I don't know, I guess it's just trial and error. You just keep going. And somewhere in forty-five takes we must have got something right. Otherwise, we wouldn't be having this conversation today, right? I wouldn't be here. Just the way he works – a style very different from Sanjay Sir. Sanjay Sir likes the beginning to end to be perfect – or he won't use it. Shakun might use a moment from this take and a moment from somewhere else and stitch it together. When you're constantly on your feet, something new will keep coming up.

AC: I saw a conversation you did with Abhinav Bindra for the 'Live Love Laugh Foundation' lecture series, and you asked him, 'When does something you do go from being pleasurable to being pressurised?' I want to ask you the same question. Does what you do ever become pressurising?
DP: I think it can. It's where I draw the line in my schedule. That's the only place I could start feeling like I'm not enjoying what I'm doing. The only other time was when I was experiencing depression, but that was very different. Many years ago I realised that I had to find this work-life balance. I don't intend to burn out, I'm not going anywhere. Somehow in our country it is considered unprofessional – just wanting time for yourself. It has this connotation of being not driven enough, and I disagree. You can be all of those things and still make time for yourself. How are you going to replenish? How are you going to put good energy back into the work? Especially as an actor I think you need to have life experiences. I do everything on my own, it keeps me grounded.

AC: What do you mean everything on your own?
DP: Running the home – absolutely everything.

AC: Really?
DP: Yeah, everything. Sometimes, booking my flight tickets or booking a seat. And I'm having to articulate this because there is a sense that 'superstars' or 'celebrities' don't do a lot of things and maybe others don't, but I do, because that's the way I've been brought up, and they keep me

grounded, in touch with reality. It gives me things to do outside of my work. I need to do other things; I need to potter around the house. I keep changing things…

AC: Are you still cleaning your cupboards?
DP: 100 per cent. As I speak, I'm halfway through.

AC: Last time we spoke, you had thrown your back and Ranveer told you to rest, but he went down to the gym and then came up to do a spot inspection, and you were back at the cupboard!
DP: Yeah. (laughs)

AC: You said you'd organise your kitchen.
DP: Yes, I'm organising the kitchen, the cupboard, I'm ordering things online. I'm ordering fruits and vegetables for the kitchen, whatever it is! Even if there's nothing, I'll find something to do. I'm watering plants or removing dried leaves, just doing things all the time.

AC: This is part of the finding balance?
DP: Yes, yes, very much. Even at home in Bangalore, I wake up, I make my own bed. Find that hard to believe?

AC: I do. I don't make my own bed, for sure.
DP: I do. My husband has a lot of catching up to do, but…

AC: I'm sure he doesn't make his own bed.
DP: No way! Does he look like the kind who makes his own bed? It's just basic things. You finish your meal, and you pick up your plate and put it in the sink. These are basic things which a lot of people around me don't do. For me, it's important.

AC: You said somewhere that it's important for artists to be able to nurture their creative fertility. Is this part of that?
DP: Yes, all of these little things. It's not just about travelling. It can range right from doing different classes and courses and meeting different kinds of people and travelling, that's a part of it. But let's not forget that life is also happening and this is life. All of the things that you do, your routine – you can't forget that. Maybe somewhere in 2014, I forgot that. I think I forgot who I was. And I think today I'm able to differentiate between me

the creative person, the actor, the professional versus Deepika the human, the daughter, the sister, the friend, the wife and nurture that side of me.

AC: And that's what's keeping the balance?
DP: For me, yes.

AC: I want to talk a little bit about you as producer. Your company is called Ka, which means soul in Egyptian, specifically the part of your soul that you leave behind after you're gone, and you said that you would like to leave behind a body of work that people can keep coming back to. Are the things you're interested in as a producer different from those as an actor?
DP: The place where it comes from is the same, which is my gut. *83* for example, I got the narration, and they were pitching it to me for Romi Dev's part and I said, 'I want to produce this film.' The choices come from the same place, but the roles vary, whether I'm playing actor or playing producer or both the roles at the same time. But primarily it's always been my gut, and that process has always been very, very sacred for me. I don't experiment with that because you can have twenty other people telling you something else but deep down inside, you know. That voice deep down inside is always guiding us. The payoff for that may be two days later, two years later or twenty years later. And even if it's wrong, at least you know you listen to yourself and I think then you're able to process that better and say, 'Okay, I think I made a mistake here.' And you're able to make wiser choices moving forward.

AC: It's a fantastic trailer.
DP: Aah, thank you!

AC: I just got all emotional watching it and I'm not even a cricket fan.
DP: That's the reaction we got from a lot of women saying, 'We don't even understand cricket but it moved us, it did something.' Goosebumps, you know.

AC: And he's so damn good, man.
DP: Who? Kabir or Ranveer? The man I married? Yes.

AC: The man you married.
DP: He is. He is special. Husband appreciation post. I should put up some post, no? My fans would be very happy with that.

AC: As a producer, what are some of the things you want to see done differently in the film industry?

DP: I think to begin with – the hours that we work. I think especially for the crew, that there is this sort of sense that, 'Make people work extra and work overtime and work continuously and you'll kind of get the work done faster.' And my thinking is actually completely the opposite. I feel like people need to be given enough downtime or rest. You come back with better energy and that anyway makes you not just faster, the quality of the output is far better. Step number one would be to streamline the hours of work. Make it a Monday-to-Friday week. You keep your Saturdays for prep or discussions. On Sunday, nobody calls – no message, nothing. Even your call time for Monday comes in on Saturday. Step number two is to be compensated for extra hours. If the agreement is twelve hours for actors or crew ... actors still feel like, 'You know what? It's my film at the end of the day,' and they're going to walk away with the rewards, right? The awards, the rewards, the directors and everyone above board. But the crew, they come in much earlier, they leave much later. There could be days where you do go over, but I think we need to find a mechanism where they're at least compensated for that hourly. Number three – the kind of food that the crew is served; nutritious food needs to be served; it's a very small thing. If you keep the crew happy and just feed them well, they'll go out of their way. I'd like to also have a mental health expert on set for anybody – it could be for a technician, it could be for an actor, it could be for an actor in a volatile role. Even if it's not a full-time professional, even if it's some helpline numbers or a counsellor or somebody the team can reach out to if required. These are some of the things that I would want to change when I get into it full steam.

AC: That's one of the things that our friend Shakun told me.
DP: I've been spending too much time with Shakun.

AC: He said that you actually are extremely mindful of how people are being taken care of on the set.
DP: It's very, very important.

AC: Is that because, as one of the powerful people on set, you also set the tone?
DP: Very much, but I also think it's just about being sensitive to the people around you. They're as much a part of this process as we are. I've

never understood why there's a separate A catering and B catering. What does that even mean? Food is food. Everyone should have access to good, nutritious food.

AC: So that almost suggests if you get paid less you should eat—
DP: —different. I think it also comes with being a complete outsider and having a fresh perspective to being on set and watching what is happening at one end of the spectrum, and at the other. It's not rocket science, it just needs a little observation and it's pretty blatant, it's there. It's the choice you make – you can either say, 'It's not my problem, I don't care, I'm getting paid,' and move on or you say, 'When I have the power to do something, I will,' and maybe I'm there. And if these small things can make a difference to somebody's entire work experience – you're spending six months or a year together, so if you can make it a pleasurable experience, everything else is secondary. The success of the film, the box office, the numbers – all secondary. The memories that you take are the experiences that you've had on set every single day.

AC: And that's also all you control.
DP: And that's the only thing you can control. Come on to set every morning, see happy people, people working because they want to work not because they have to, and I think you already have a winner.

AC: How do you gauge success? Is the box office a measure? Do you have other barometers? And two actors in a partnership, how do you handle failure?
DP: We've had three very successful movies.

AC: Not to nazar lagao (cast an evil eye).
DP: Yeah, but I watched an interview with you some years ago and remember saying the numbers don't concern me. I've changed my mind about that. I think it is important because somebody has put their money in it. They need to make their money, they've had that faith. What is equally important is the impact that you have on the audience, on society, on people. I think I measure success like that. If you're able to shift the needle, impact people's lives in a positive way, bring about change, have people think or see differently. I think today that, for me, is success.

AC: And what about failure? Aamir said that he needs to mourn his failures, he says, 'I literally cry them out.' Is there a process?
DP: I think it's internal, and maybe that's the athlete in me. When you lose a match, you're trained to do it differently. You pick yourself up. It's not to say that you're not . . . . It's a lot of reflection.

AC: So, you don't show it?
DP: No.

AC: Expression nahi badalta (Expression doesn't change)?
DP: No, it's internal. I'm sure in my own time, when I'm in my room alone or . . . . It's just processing. If I've played a badminton match and I've lost, you're relaying the match in your head, thinking about the different strokes that you played and mistakes and what you could have done differently, and I think that I pretty much apply that over here.

AC: You relay the film in your head?
DP: I would relay the film, the experience. Did I approach it in a way that was not correct? Even the prep. 'Was there a disconnect between me and my director? Was it execution or something that I could have done differently?'

AC: But it doesn't crush you.
DP: No. Failure has never crushed me. I've never felt, like, broken. I don't think I have that in me, at least not yet. I think my nature is to say, 'How can I do this differently and what are my learnings from this?'

AC: It's also the smarter way to handle it.
DP: I don't know any other way.

AC: A couple of weeks ago you and Ranveer posted lovely pictures of your wedding anniversary. How do you decide what is private, what is public?
DP: Communication. One of the best things that we have is that we communicate a lot. We might agree and we might disagree, but when you communicate, it kind of makes a marriage much easier. There are battles where he will 'win' and I will have to say, 'Okay, fine, take this one.'

AC: Win in what way?
DP: Win the battle, na. It's like, 'I said then you said'. And there are times when I might be very, very firm about my belief and he might say,

'I disagree with you but, okay.' This holiday we wanted to share some part of our life. My fans kept messaging me saying, 'Post something!' We spoke about it and said, 'They would be disappointed if we didn't put anything out.' Luckily, we agreed on which pictures and how many pictures.

AC: Is that also an argument sometimes?
DP: I won't say it's an argument. Of course, there are two people, two personalities, two careers. Both of us have to be sensitive. Most often we find that mid-path. We give some, both of us take some and eventually find what works best for both of us.

AC: My sense is he wants to be flamboyant and you're always holding him back. Would that be correct?
DP: You want to guess? Yes, I'm always trying to put a leash on him and being like, 'Um, maybe…'

AC: Reeling him in.
DP: But he understands. And I've also wrapped my head around the fact that that just gives him joy and that's who he is and I don't think I can or should change that.

AC: Deepika, next year is fifteen years of *Om Shanti Om*.
DP: Yes!

AC: Fifteen years! How does that make you feel? Are you very different as an actor than that girl?
DP: Oh, very much. I'm different as an actor, I'm different as a person. I've evolved, I hope. And I think that's how the journey ought to be. Today when I think about *Om Shanti Om*, I'm like, 'How?! How did they even think that I was good for that movie?' There are times when I'm like, 'Oh my god, if I just knew everything that I knew today, I could have done that so differently, I could have done so much more.' But I guess that is the journey.

AC: It doesn't feel like fifteen years at all.
DP: Every time there's a film anniversary my fans keep reminding me. I need to do that more often, just stop and pause and look back at the journey and say, 'Hey! Not bad, you've done a pretty good job.' But yes, I

still feel like there's so much more to do. The craft is evolving, the world is evolving, the kind of stories that we're telling, the kind of platforms that these films are releasing on, so much is changing. There's so much evolution that it's very, very exciting. There's so much more to do!

AC: So, I also spoke to Nag Ashwin. And of course, he would not tell me what the 'K' stands for in 'Project K', the Prabhas movie, but I asked him why he cast you and he said, 'As an actor and as a personality she makes my life easier.'
DP: Oh my god!

AC: You know, what a lovely compliment! You said that you're going straight into it, right? You're going to shoot now.
DP: Yes.

AC: First film with Prabhas – how are you feeling? Is it exciting? What is your headspace right now?
DP: I'm nervous.

AC: Why?
DP: When the camera rolls, it will feel like familiar territory, but I've not worked with Prabhas before, or Nagi. I'm going to also have to do this in a different language apart from Hindi. Plus, it's such a VFX-heavy film. The character, the world, all of it is so new. So, I'm just curious and excited and nervous. I'm excited because there's this new journey that we're kind of embarking on, I'm nervous because it's unknown. I leave day after.

AC: I have to warn you, at least in interviews, Prabhas is a man of very few words.
DP: So, between him and me there's going to be no conversation.

AC: Are you quiet on sets usually?
DP: I'm a relatively quiet person; not just on set, just generally in life. I'd like to think that I listen, I watch, I observe. I don't enjoy talking too much.

AC: I'm reading Will Smith's autobiography right now, it's called *Will* and he says, his mom used to say, 'Only speak when it improves on the silence.'
DP: I agree!

From the floor: Q&A

Rohil: Which two things would you choose out of these three options: your dream cast, a great script, and a great director?

DP: Script, number one. Script is the most important thing. You can have a substandard director, and you can have substandard actors, but if you have a great script, I think you still have a decent film on hand. My second priority would be a great director, because I think a great director can then do justice to that great script and can also make actors act. I've seen directors who are actually able to draw performances from actors or edit in a way where performances come out strong. So, that would be kind of the least important thing.

Shantanu: Are great actors born or made?

DP: I think a bit of both. I don't think people considered me a born actor. Anu still doesn't think I'm a good actor, but she still keeps calling me back for Front Row. (laughs)

AC: This is not true, at all! But I think it would be a bit of both, no?

DP: It's a craft that you can keep learning. At the same time, I know a lot of born-talented actors who either take their talent for granted or don't continue honing their craft. I think you've got to work hard anyway. Maybe for those who don't know how to act, maybe it's a slightly tougher journey. I don't think that people who can't act can never be actors. I think it is possible.

AC: Was there a moment when you felt, 'I've got it'?

DP: Yeah, your ex-colleague Rajeev said that he started seeing it in *Break ke Baad*. And I would have to agree. I started feeling like, 'Okay! I mean, I'm actually now beginning to enjoy this.'

AC: For me it was *Cocktail*.

DP: I was completely a blank slate and just allowed Homi to do whatever he needed to.

Aditya: How do you manage to remain calm with all of the media attention?

DP: It's not new to me. And I have a father who has seen some sort of limelight in his time and continues to. He keeps saying that it's so different now, but at least I had him to advise me every now and then. 'Be honest in interviews or don't react instantly.' You know? A large part of it is also the way we've been brought up, a huge factor in the way that I'm able to deal with it. Maybe my personality as well.

AC: So, you don't get flustered?
DP: How bad can it be? I think that you've got to keep focusing on the things that matter to you the most and not lose sight of your vision. Everything else kind of comes and goes, like clouds. Khushi.

Audience member: Thank you. Cinema has been telling different kind of stories lately, what genre of movies do you see yourself doing more of later?
DP: The possibilities are endless today. There used to be a time when one had a wish list, romantic movie, action movie. But I think we're pretty much beyond those genres now. I'm just really open to doing all kinds of characters and roles and movies.

AC: Villain?
DP: Sure, why not? Gone are those days where mainstream actors would shy away. Look at Ranveer, when he did Khilji, people were saying, 'Don't do it. . .'

AC: It was dark. Without any redeeming features.
DP: I think for an actor like him to take a role like that or when Shah Rukh did *Darr*, these are examples that show how those taboos are changing today. Audience today is able to differentiate between person and role. The audience's evolution allows actors to have choices.

13 December 2021

7

Ranveer Singh: The Human Chameleon

Anupama Chopra: Many years ago, I read that Javier Bardem said that what he wants most when he's old and retired is to have all the characters he's played get inside a room and have anything to say to each other because they're so different. And I think that if there's any actor in Hindi cinema who aspires to that, it is actor and chameleon Ranveer Singh!
Ranveer Singh: Bajirao loves you too. I'm so happy to be here, Ma'am. I've always wanted to do this!

AC: I'm so happy you're here.
RS: Dusre movie stars ka dekhke maine bhi socha, 'Yaar, kitna achha hoga mujhe bhi bula lein kabhi (After seeing the other movie stars, I thought it would be great if they call me too).'

AC: Achha?
RS: I'm such a good conversationalist, you know. I'm always looking to have these deep intellectual conversations about craft and stuff.

AC: I know.
RS: Otherwise, it's all like, 'Aapke koi plans hain, future plans? Aapki picture mein aapko beti chahiye, aapko life mein kya chahiye? (Do you have any future plans? In your movie, you want a daughter, so what do you want in life?)' Anybody asks me that again, I'm gonna (pretends to spill drink over someone).

AC: Thankfully, I'm far enough away from you. *Jayeshbhai Jordaar* is the first film you're doing with a debutante director after *Band Baaja Baaraat* in 2010. What are the qualities that only a first-time director has?
RS: They have a very different energy from accomplished makers, senior makers. They have a kinetic, effervescent, bubbling energy. It's on you as a performer to harness that energy for an effective performance. Divyang is always moving and like me, he comes from no background. So, this is

like make or break. World Cup penalty kick. So they just put so much of themselves, their emotion, they're completely involved – all makers are, but there's a difference. Senior makers are more anchored, manipulating the energy flow, making their vision come to life. The new directors are desperate – without any kind of negative context.

AC: It's a good desperation.
RS: He's so invested. You've got to watch Divyang at the monitor, he's so invested in his characters, in the world of his film, and is a writer, actor, director. He watches it like this (comes very close to screen). He's performing with you, crying with you. He can't even call cut, somebody else does. He's so immersed, it's beautiful and so infectious and that attracted me. Adi and Manish designed this project and said, 'You and Ratna and Boman are probably the only people on this set with experience.' The AD was a first-timer, the director was a first-timer. All of this fresh energy, unique and original. I'm happy to see it has worked.

AC: At the trailer launch, Divyang said he could see you had surrendered completely to him. Tell me as a superstar about surrendering to a person who is raw and new.
RS: There is a small component in your head, 'You, as the experienced person in this dynamic, should look out,' but mostly, I just respect that he is the director and it is his vision we're bringing to life. I never breach that protocol. They've lived this material longer than I have. They're way more invested in the world of the film. So, you know your place as the actor. I just need to be the best clay possible – fluid, liquid, be like water. If there is a creative disagreement ever with any director, senior, newcomer, whatever, they are always right. They are the storyteller, you are a vehicle.

AC: I read this brilliant piece in *Film Comment* about Cate Blanchett. Her public persona is very poised, very elegant, but the word she uses very often in her interviews is 'chaos'. And this dissonance makes her such a charismatic and compelling actor. I was wondering if the same is true for you. Because look at you jumping into the audience! And yet we know that you're such a serious actor who gives in to the process, who inhabits his character. Is this a correct thesis?
RS: You may be right. I don't think this projection or persona you perceive is not me.

AC: Right, it's one version.
RS: It's one version. Me at work is another version, me at home, me with friends, all of them are me. For Khilji, I had to tap into a part of me that has a darkness within. Jayesh is very sensitive, Bittu is happy-go-lucky. I have all these facets to my personality. Which one do you amp up for that context? I have this belief that life is suffering. Life is very difficult for everybody. I'm sitting in front of you today, very grateful, but I'm fighting battles I don't speak about. You are fighting your own. Make no mistake, everybody is! It's not all roses. And so, in life, I like to be light-footed.

AC: Walk lightly.
RS: We all know the inevitable destination and this journey is very difficult. There's adversity around every corner. I believe this timeline is the Kalyug, it's the worst it's ever been for humans. Just existing in the world today is agonising. And so I like to joke, keep it light, do stupid, silly things just to make a person smile. I'll tell you a joke, a story. I'll sing you a song, I'll do a dance, entertain you on this journey we are on together. There's no effort, I like to keep things light, lowbrow and slapstick. There should be humour, a lightness of being, and sunshine. I reserve the darkness for myself. We play different roles in life. I'm not the same in my house with my folks, and with my close pals. Even on set, if I'm shooting *Cirkus* with Rohit Shetty, we're laughing our heads off all day. But on *Padmaavat*, we're shooting a very serious scene, and I carry that energy.

AC: Well, I'm just grateful I'm not your bodyguard.
RS: I'm pretty sure they think I'm psycho. Mildly schizophrenic. Karan Johar said, 'You have so many people inside you, you just don't know which one we're going to get on any particular day!' It helps me at work, so!

AC: Shah Rukh told me, Javed sahab once walked up to Gauri and said, 'How are they?' Because there's so many people inside.
RS: He's true greatness, that man. An absolute pioneer. He's the king for a reason. Inhone jo mall banaya hai, usme hum apni choti dukaan chala rahe hain (In the mall he built, we're running our small shop). He's a pioneer, he's made Indian entertainment what it is. I can't wait to see him back on screen.

AC: Yeah, absolutely! So, I asked Maneesh how you've changed between *Band Baaja Baaraat* and *Jayeshbhai*. He said, 'Before the release of *Band*

Baaja Baaraat, post the screening I asked him "Kaisi lagi (How did you like it)?", and Ranveer said very non-committally, "It's not my kind of genre. As an actor, bade issues hain mere mein, picture kaisi hai pata nahi (As an actor, there are many issues in me, I don't know how the film is)". He came to *Band Baaja Baaraat* with the intent of excelling at craft and he continues to do that. From day one, he's hit the bullseye. As a person, Ranveer has stayed super grounded and super lazy. People see him as an energizer bunny, but the moment he's by himself, he's a couch potato watching football or playing video games.'
RS: Wow! That's spot on.

AC: But you knew that you have lots to work on and that was your aim, not what this film was about or what it could do for you?
RS: Any actor who tells you they watched the *film*, they're lying. They only watched themselves on the first watch. You're only counting pimples. And making notes. God's honest truth. Second time, you're only watching yourself in isolation. Third, fourth time. Then after a year, two years, maybe you can watch it as a film. I think it's just a natural thing.

AC: Are you very critical of yourself?
RS: Not anymore.

AC: What changed?
RS: I'm just kinder to myself in general. I used to be overtly critical. My ambition wasn't helping me at all. So, instead I try and see the merit. At least I know deep down, I tried my best. So, it's fine. Try again and even then you do your best. I manage my expectations of myself. I try and achieve a work-life balance. I'm obsessed by my work. I don't even see it as work, most times I see it as play. But now, with your close relationships, you realise that life is a shared experience and a collection of memories. So, you try and spend more time with the people you love. We only have time and how we spend our time matters. Now I spend time with my wife, my friends, my family and it's lovely. And all credit to my wife, she's the reason I'm able to have this personal evolution. She's experienced a burnout and she doesn't want me to go down that same unpleasant path. She's now sharing this realisation with me. She sits with my calendar and manages my day. It's really lovely, Jai Jhulelal, I'm very lucky, very happy.

AC: But I suspect that you were having fun from day one.
RS: Yeah, yeah.

AC: I want us to see a clip I found.

(Clip from Kishore Namit Kapoor Acting School plays)

RS: But see the end! So serious!

AC: But you're *in* it.
RS: Yeah, even in acting class I used to be very sincere. Even when I was a copywriter or a struggling actor or in acting class in university, I'd go all out. I remember once, this was the first day of acting class and this exercise was demonstrating how things get lost in communication. Later we'd analyse. Like a Chinese whispers game – you show the action to somebody, they render it. I was the last person. This is after thirty people miscommunicating – the action actually was standing in front of a cupboard, opening the cupboard, choosing a shirt, putting on the shirt, buttoning it up, getting ready. I love that kid. I don't know who it is anymore, but I have a soft spot. Those are my best days.

AC: I also asked Karan what he was most surprised by in *Rocky aur Rani*. Let's listen to what Karan said.

Karan Johar (audio): What surprised me is that he's an outstanding dialogue writer. He'll improve a scene, and I've never quite worked with an actor who's ever done that. He physically writes it all down himself.

AC: I'm fascinated. You're a dialogue writer?
RS: Yes!

AC: Always?
RS: Probably the best in the business. I am a closet writer and when this acting thing felt too far-fetched, you know, mera kya chance lagega (where will I get a chance), I was actively pursuing writing. I went to the States to do media studies. I thought I'd get a copywriting job in New York or Chicago. I had done two internships and excelled. One fateful day in university I happened to take an acting class, and I was like, 'Man, this is it. Why am I compromising with my whole life? This is what I want

to do!' But the writer is there and *Ram-Leela* is where it started. Sanjay Leela Bhansali – I can't express what that man has done for me as an artist, overhauled my thinking about the craft, art, about performance art, shattered all these constructs and made me realise art is limitless. Performance art is limitless. There are no rules. You make them, you break them, do whatever you want!

AC: He let you write?
RS: So, he'd be very collaborative in the blocking and staging process, he loves that. His writers are there on set every single day. He's creating there. It's not like he's in some other space, sitting with his writer, writing the scene. I've worked with filmmakers who have that process. But not Bhansali. He loves to play. I crave it. I crave it. There are no rules for him, right? Even if this scene is on paper, you don't have to do it. 'Say do what you feel. It's your character now. I gave it to you, you tell me what your character would say, would do.' It's so palpable, that creative energy. He can turn a four-page scene into one line. Be prepared for that. Often actors come in and get thrown off.

AC: You're the Bhansali veteran.
RS: On that set. He's like, 'You tell me, what do you want to do?' I was like, 'Sir, I feel like catching him and putting him up against the wall and saying, you…' Can't say it. And he's like, 'I love it, do that.' 'Then what do you want to do?' Then he'll come up with an idea. I absolutely love him.

AC: But this is where the writer started?
RS: I'll live a hundred times and always be indebted to him for teaching me everything that he has. He wholeheartedly allows me to blossom as an artist and that has really spiked my growth as a performer. So, on *Ram-Leela* when this fluid creative process is happening, I love to play with language, accents. I love to pepper the stuff that I've picked up developing the character and during research, which writers love. Touch wood, I've only worked with writers who are excited to have input. So, Siddharth-Garima, Vijay Maurya in *Gully Boy*, Prakash-ji in the other Bhansali movies, even Rohit Sir. They'll be so collaborative. I was like, 'Wow, yeah, this is great!' because some of the best stuff came from that. Saying instinctively what you want to say; try it again; and now I feel more confident. And when you have somebody like Karan, ever so collaborative, you make more suggestions and it builds. About the writing part, it's funny he mentions

it. I didn't expect him to notice it, but I do that very deliberately. When I'm reading the scene, there's a rhythm to the scene. So, I take what's typed and re-write it by hand, in the rhythm that I have interpreted.

AC: You're hand-writing this?
RS: I have a little compass box with highlighters and pencil, pen, rubber.

AC: You know your wife does exactly the same thing?
RS: She's another beast altogether, a good student.

AC: And so are you?
RS: I'm not disciplined like her at all. But I rewrite it and everything will be in my interpreted language, for me. If it was in a hushed tone, I'd write it very small but if I was yelling it, I'd write it in big, bold text, with exclamation points.

AC: Your cues. That's amazing! Coming back to *Jayeshbhai*, the general flavour right now seems to be very larger-than-life hyper-masculine heroes.
RS: Tell me about it!

AC: You played a version of that in *Simmba*. Jayeshbhai is sensitive, vulnerable, he's timid, very lovable. Do you think this wave of testosterone is going to alter the Hindi film hero?
RS: How about me coming with an oestrogen film in the wave of testosterone?

AC: I would love it!
RS: I was going over this Karan thing...

AC: It's still in your head.
RS: It's been a delight working with Karan, it's like comedy circus all day long. We're making a light, happy vintage Karan Johar family drama with romance and colour and song. It's been party time on *Rocky Aur Rani Kii Prem Kahaani*. He is the first to say, 'I'll give you additional dialogue credit for all the writing.'

AC: Really?
RS: I was like, 'Nahi, nahi yaar (No, no bro). Yehi toh humara farz hota hai na as actors (Man, isn't this our duty as actors)?' If you can't better it then what are you doing there as a creative contributor?

AC: Absolutely, yeah!
RS: I don't want additional dialogue credit.

AC: Achha, testosterone ki baat karein (Okay, let's talk about testosterone)?
RS: Arre! Phoot-phootke nikalta hai mere andar se. Mera har zarra testosterone se bhara hua hai! (Oh! It comes out of me in oodles. My every cell is filled with testosterone!)

AC: We have no doubt!
RS: Lloyd Stevens, my trainer for *Ram-Leela* – it was the first time I created that kind of physique in my life – he was expensive! He trained Tarak for *RRR*, as well. He has a scientific approach, you do all these tests and you want to see how much testosterone you have in case you need some supplements. And the reports said I have too much!

AC: Okay, we have no doubt!
RS: I can spare some!

AC: But we love that you're Jayeshbhai in the middle of all of this.
RS: So I'll still do those movies. That is where it all started. Before I wanted to become an actor, I wanted to become a hero. I started off watching Arnold Schwarzenegger, Sylvester Stallone. I used to watch them shirtless. This is what I wanted to be. I was very upset when Tiger said he'd do *Rambo*. Big muscles, big guns, shooting, save the day! That's my default. Even the great Amitabh Bachchan, he's my original hero. *Ajooba, Toofan, Jaadugar, Shahenshah.* Same guy who's done *Kaala Patthar.*

AC: *Deewaar, Sholay.*
RS: That's my default, I'll be very honest. When I watch *KGF*, I'm like, 'Yes, kill him, Yash!' I love that cinema; that's my first love. I'm watching alone in bed, at night, and cheering and hooting. I saw *RRR* recently. *Simmba* deserves a reprise, right? He's one of my favourite guys. And yeah *Simmba* actually, to be honest, was always designed to be a franchise. And one of my favourite movies and favourite performances of my own. So, I love it and I will do it. As I grew older, I started watching all kinds of cinema. Very late, I was about eighteen or nineteen when I started consuming non-mainstream cinema, if you would like to term it as that. Grew up on like Karan Johar and Yash Raj movies.

AC: Govinda, of course, your big love.
RS: I had a turning point at, I think, age eighteen; first class in university and I was supposed to write a four-page analysis of *Taxi Driver*. And I was in the library watching this movie, and sometimes you have that moment, like a 360 degree turn of the character. I was like, 'Yaar, picture aise bhi ho sakti hai (Man, cinema can be like this too)? It's not always a happy ending!' And I was ravenous for movies. I took a job in the movie library of the university, a far-flung place in the campus, so hardly anybody ever used to come. I used to just watch movies – movies – movies, all kinds. It called upon another aspect of me as a performer – you can live different lives. You can take different parts and pour that into your art. But the default is low angle, blaring background music, slow motion.

AC: High speed.
RS: Larger than life. I love watching that being a part of that cinema. I'm waiting for the next opportunity. I think it will be with the great Shankar!

AC: Very exciting!
RS: I would credit Maneesh, Vikram, Zoya . . . all of these directors who taught me how to . . . . Actually it was *Lootera* where . . . *Ladies vs Ricky Bahl* hadn't done well, I was full of angst. I was like, 'I'm gonna prove a point.' To myself. That I wasn't one dimensional. In *Lootera* I realised that I have that potential, and I took it forward in *Dil Dhadakne Do* and then *Gully Boy*. So, I'm also just learning as I go and experimenting. Something works, something doesn't, but I'm learning with every filmmaker. I watched *Jayeshbhai*, I was like, 'Okay, the toolkit seems to be pretty set now.' You're just acquiring tools. Now I'm adept at using it also. Earlier it used to be like (imitates taking stuff out of tool belt), 'Haan, ye uske liye kya chahiye, haan kahan tha (Yes, for that what do I need, where is it)?' It's been ten years!

AC: Yeah!
RS: I made it, completed a decade! So, now I feel like I've acquired tools and I'm able to easily bridge myself to where I need to be emotionally with less effort. In *Lootera*, I was doing crazy shit.

AC: You stapled your stomach.
RS: It was just experimentation. How do I achieve that effect? You try different things. Now I can achieve the emotional effect without causing too much physical, mental, emotional harm to myself. Also, to be able to

detach. *Padmaavat* was one dark year for me. I was inhabiting this mental and emotional space that was hating on everybody. I'm more efficient now.

AC: I remember the first time we talked to each other, in 2014, you told me that and you'd been working for three or four years. And you said that bad experiences in the business had hardened you a little. As an actor, your job is to be open and vulnerable, but it is a brutal business. How do you stop your heart from hardening?
RS: I don't even know that guy anymore.

AC: Really?
RS: I'm like, 'Fool, you don't even know the half of it!' I mean, bade-bade talks de raha hai bhaiyya 2013 to 2014 mein (Bro's using big words and doing big talks between 2013 and 2014). Oh, I've become hardened and all. I've come a long way from there.

AC: But the heart is not hardened?
RS: It is as cold as it gets!

AC: Really?
RS: It's not a heart, it's a patthar (stone). Patthar wala dil ho gaya hai mera (I've become stone-hearted).

AC: Kyun (Why)?
RS: Ho gaya hai madam, abhi main kya bataun? Ye life hain, madam! (It's done madam, what do I tell you? This is life, madam!)

AC: Okay, but how?
RS: Thokar kha-khaake loha bann gaya hoon main, loha (With all the punches, I've become like iron)!

AC: But in a good way?
RS: *Simmba 2* laga, shot laga (set up the shot, set it up)!

AC: Is this good?
RS: No, how can it be good, ma'am? You should always have a soft heart.

AC: Yeah.

RS: But what do you do now? In the Kalyug, this is going to happen! Let's say I have one chamber in my heart that's still pure and thinks everything is great, everyone is good, that we live in this utopian society, and there is only love in this world to share. But yeah, it's only gotten—

AC: Harder?
RS: My belief in goodness has consistently waned.

AC: But that's not impacting on your work?
RS: Fortunately, I have been able to protect the side of me that is empathetic and compassionate. I fiercely protect that side of me. I'm very happy that I've got some angels around me – my mother, sister, my wife, my best friends, my team – who protect me, protect my heart. Otherwise, that good soft boy is always under attack. But yeah, I've grown up only to realise that it's not all roses. I've become a hard guy now, but I don't judge myself for it. You live, you learn, you grow, you evolve. It has to become a conscious effort to protect that.

AC: Yeah.
RS: And it sometimes takes a concentrated effort to just believe. Take that leap of faith. Still keep that romance with life alive. But other than that, it's just been more of the same. I'm a hardened criminal now.

AC: You know, one of the things I really like about you is how much you celebrate your wife's success. You're very proud of her. I love it! I love that you're so happy—
RS: My jaan (My life)!

AC: —when she is successful. How are we feeling about Deepika Padukone on the Main Competition Jury of the Cannes Film Festival?
RS: (Gets up and dances)

AC: Isn't it amazing?
RS: I was like, 'Waah yaar, baby waah yaar (Wow, baby wow)! People want you to be the person who decides which is the better film!' That's huge!

AC: It is huge.
RS: I mean, I thought to myself, 'Yaar, mera kabhi number aayega kya? Mujhe kabhi bithayenge kya jury-wury pe? (Man, will I ever get this chance?

Will they ever make me part of a jury?)' Aaj tak kisine bulaya nahi (To this day nobody has ever called me). But Cannes! Baby is like deciding from the best films in the world at the time, which is the better one! It's so crazy. 'Wow!' That was my reaction. I'm very proud of everything that she achieves every time. I'm her designated cheerleader. She does stuff that is just unprecedented for mainstream leading women from Indian cinema; forging her own path. And I hugely admire her, she works so hard. I am extremely proud of her, she makes me glow!

AC: You are probably the best cheerleader a woman can have.
RS: Yeah, plus she's gorgeous!

AC: It helps!
RS: You should see the reactions when she walks into a room! She has that aura. I love it! I walk into a space hand in hand with her, and I just love to see people's reactions to her!

9 May 2022

8

Stage Queens: Zeenat Aman & Shabana Azmi

Sneha Menon Desai: Shabana ma'am and Zeenat ma'am, thank you for allowing me on the sets of *Bun Tikki*. There's joy in immersing yourself in the madness and the magic on a film set and in speaking to actors while they are marinating in it. Each set has its own energy. So, how would you best describe the energy of *Bun Tikki*?

Zeenat Aman: I think the project is very charming, very sweet. It's about relationships and there is a deeper undercurrent. What I will take away is the joy of working with the entire team, Shabana, Manish who's been a wonderful producer, Faraz.

Shabana Azmi: I think she's put it absolutely perfectly. I'm working with her after a very long time. This was something that I was really looking forward to. Manish is a dear friend, and I am so amazed that he's such a mainstream person and he's chosen to launch his career as a producer with three tiny films. I applaud the courage. And Faraz, of course, I've had a delightful experience with, because I did his short film called *Sheer Qorma*. And the little boy is really good. We were in this beautiful hotel in Simla, one of my favourite. It was luxurious for a small film.

SMD: You look amazing as Manish Malhotra heroines, both of you.

SA: She's just been styled really extraordinarily, glamorous.

ZA: Manish has done an amazing job with the look for my character Sitara. I was never a saree person, but he's reintroduced me to sarees. I had a birthday on set. It was so difficult to locate flowers in Shimla. And he sent me a bouquet that was almost as large as myself. I was so touched.

SMD: What are your memories of working together as thirty-year-olds?

SA: Zeenat was a big star when we first did *Ishk Ishk Ishk*. I had just started. And she had no starry airs. She was extremely accessible, very warm. That really put Zarina [Wahab] and me and others at complete ease. We were staying at this fishtail lodge in Pokhara, it was fun. Then we did a completely mad film called *Ashanti*.

ZA: We did a Lavani, which is a Maharashtrian style dance. Shabana sat down and wept. 'I am not a dancer.'

SA: I said, 'Listen, you have to give me rehearsals.' P.L. Raj was strict. I said, 'You cannot scream. You cannot yell at me.' He would want to beat me up because I was not getting it. And then also go on patiently. And Mithun Chakraborty, who's the dancer among us, was just doing dhol (drum). I was also amused, 'Ghar jaake bohot pitayi karta hoga apne bachchon ki (He must really be beating his kids up at home).'

ZA: It was a lot of fun.

SMD: You posted a picture from *Bun Tikki*, looking glamorous as Sitara Jaan and captioned it, 'Life has come full circle.' Do you feel it's a better time to be a heroine today?

ZA: One thing that stands out today is the paycheck. Look at the crores these girls charge. We never charged that. And the technicality has changed. You can look at a monitor and improve your shot and so on. This whole thing was a fun experience. I have minimal screen time, but I'm definitely a part of the heartbeat of the project.

SA: I envy the intensive workshops that younger actors get the time to do. By the time they reach set, they're pros.

ZA: True.

SA: In Zoya's film *Archies*, Suhana looks as if she was born to skate – and she had never stood on a skate before that. So, the kind of confidence with which the newcomers come is really enviable.

SMD: So, can you talk to me a little bit about the capacity in which we can see the two of you in *Bun Tikki*?

SA: I don't know how much of it I'm supposed to reveal. But suffice it to say that it is an interesting pairing. First you see them as friends. Zeenat's character is more quiet, more gentle, god-fearing. Mine is, because I'm a lawyer, much more outspoken. And then you wonder, what is this relationship?

ZA: What is the dynamic?

SA: And then, when you actually see it, you feel, 'Oh, we should have noticed all the way!' But it's not sensationalised, that's what is most interesting.

SMD: Ma'am, you come out of such a delightful performance in *Rocky Aur Rani Kii Prem Kahaani*, despite the 'bold scenes'. How liberating is it to make choices that would have stereotyped you earlier? Do you feel like there is more acceptance? How do you choose your scripts today?

SA: When I first hear the script, there is an instinct that this is something that interests me, that I would like to explore. Dialogue is very important. Do they sound truthful? Do they fit the environment? And then, do I feel challenged? I've been in the industry for fifty years. I have absolutely no qualms about doing a small part. Sometimes it's just the money. So different reasons, but something about the script and the director. I believe that if ever I've been credited with a good performance, the director must take the credit.

SMD: I had a little chat with Faraz. He met you at a hotel in Bombay and started narrating the script. And five minutes in, you held his hand and said, 'I'm doing it.'

ZA: Yes, I love the thought, the narrative. His vision, it was just charming and quaint and so positive. It's basically a father–son story. Just to be part of it made me very happy. As the grandmother's plus one.

SMD: And like you mentioned, fifty years of doing what you do so amazingly. I know that you are shooting a pivotal scene, the climax. Have you identified what works for you right before a shot?

ZA: I don't really know about this particular project because the climax is based on two other characters. And we are part of it, but it's not based on us.

I have to understand my character. I have to know her backstory, whether it is shown or not. I have to know who she is, where she comes from, what makes her resonate and what is happening. And that's what propels me forward. I love to collaborate with my director and my co-stars. If there are several of us in the scene, you feed off each other. This lady here, she's a queen of performance. I had such a time watching her, just watching her work.

SA: For me, I'm a trained actor, my professor used to say, 'Be in the moment.' For me, being in the moment matlab sur mein dhal jaana (means to immerse yourself in the music). Even if it is a disparate shot, you don't have the whole scene in front of you, par aap agar usme dhal gaye, toh phir woh sacchai nikal kar aati hai. Aur main kabhi apne expressions nahi plan karti. Jo nikal gaya, woh nikal gaya (but if you are immersed in it, then the truthfulness comes out. And I never plan my expressions. What comes out, comes out). It has to be truthful and in the moment. But I must read the scene over and over again, to know it.

SMD: I asked Naseeruddin Shah this once. You have this very well-deserved stature of just being legends. But I'm pretty sure no good comes from co-actors being intimidated by your presence. What do you do to ensure that isn't the energy on set?

ZA: Any actor worth his salt would put that personal aspect aside. It happened to me when Rajesh Khanna was the phenomenon. I had mugged up all my lines. I was totally intimidated by him. But did I show it? No. I performed and I said, 'Oh wow, I just gave a shot with a superstar.' So, that's the attitude to have.

SMD: But do you find yourself doing anything to make people ease up?

SA: If I'm with younger actors, it's very important to let them feel okay. The thing that I hear from them which makes me very happy is, 'Oh, she's really cool.' I don't understand the difference between cool and hot. Ultimately, you are reacting off the co-star. I don't feel like challenging my co-star in my life. And I cannot bear tension on the set. I like it to be nice so that everybody's relaxed and gives off their best.

ZA: It's teamwork. The more relaxed you are, the better you perform. You complement each other. And the scene turns out truthfully.

SMD: Neena Gupta, a few years ago, took to Twitter to announce that she's looking for work. Have you ever had a moment of frustration at any point in your careers?

SA: Not me. I was very lucky. I was at the Film Institute till 30th of April, got the Best Actor Gold Medal. Within three days, I was working on my first film. But I have never had qualms about going up to a director. I went to Mrinal Sen and said, 'Mrinal-da, you have to cast me in your film. Otherwise, I'll come and do dharna (protest/sit-in).' I'm also giving the director something, na. I don't say, 'Arre yaar woh role mujhe mil jata (Oh man, I wish I'd got that role).' Aisa kabhi nahi hua hai (That has never happened).

ZA: No, I've never really felt like that. After children, I took a hiatus from work. If I really want something, I will reach out for it. I think the world is now reaching out to me, which is a lovely place to be.

SA: But Zeenat, how unprepared were you for what came your way with these Instagram posts?

SMD: I was going to talk about that!

SA: She was forced to do it by her son. And she said, 'No, this is not me.' She felt overwhelmed.

SMD: We cannot not acknowledge the collective joy that you have given us over Instagram. Are you having fun with it?

ZA: Absolutely! I was initially very reluctant to do it because I was not aware of the technicalities of it. So, my son and his partner said, 'Just do it. We'll help.' It became like an exercise to remember, to write, to think, to post. And I love it because it gives me a voice. I have always been talked about and looked at from other people's perspective. And I have been definitely overwhelmed by it. I'm very grateful.

SMD: How do you make sure that it fuels you and doesn't feed off you?

ZA: Because I choose to write what I want to write. I have no complaints about Instagram.

SA: Touch wood.

SMD: Ratna Pathak Shah told me how unfortunately long it took her to realise she wanted to be an actress for the rest of her life and her face had nothing to do with it. Do you feel we are just beginning to able to see actresses for who they are today?

SA: I think so. And it's largely due to OTT. Earlier, at thirty-five, you were finished. And then you could be a bhabhi (sister-in-law) or a mother jiske haath se thali girti thi aur 'Nahi!' iss tarah se karein (who used to drop a plate and yell 'No!' like this). Stereotypical roles. Today so many different things are available.

ZA: Very true, very true.

SA: I'm really fortunate. And you don't have the consideration ki agar nahi chali toh? Iski wajeh se aisa nahi hoga ki aapko agli film nahi milegi (what if it doesn't work? It won't happen that you won't get the next film because of this or they won't consider). We are free from that rat race. That's very liberating.

SMD: And there's possibly an entire generation made up of Gen Z and millennials who are just discovering your work. So, what is a piece of your work that you hope that they find and watch?

ZA: Oh, this is very difficult. No, Shabana?

SA: Very.

ZA: It's difficult because for me, it was a journey. I was a teenager and I came in cold. No knowledge of the language, of acting, of classical India. I learnt with every film and I grew. That's why in twenty, thirty, forty, fifty years, you know the craft. How do you choose one? I was part of commercial cinema. When you think of *Don*, or *Qurbani*, or *Satyam Shivam Sundaram*, or *Hare Rama Hare Krishna*.

SA: Oh, but they remember all of that, Zeenat, everybody.

ZA: I never had the opportunity to work in the kind of projects that Shabana worked in.

SMD: You had your own journey.

ZA: It's difficult to choose one.

SMD: I say find them all. Ma'am, for you?

SA: Films that people remember today are different. Earlier, they used to talk about *Ankur*, then a huge, huge section started talking about *Arth*, it was iconic for its times. A certain generation of women come and talk to me about *Arth* even now. Then there is *Fire*. *Masoom*, because of its songs. But now they remember me because of *Makdi*. I want to tell them, 'I'm not only like *Makdi*.' So, you don't know which thing that you hold dear is going to appeal to whom. I can't think of a performance where I'll say, universally from a child to an older person, I will be able to . . . . I really hope that that film is still to come.

SMD: What a magical career the both of you have had, and people are just going to keep discovering it forever.

5 July 2024

9

'We're Not Damsels': Ratna Pathak Shah & Ayesha Jhulka

Sneha Menon Desai: What wonderful women to be able to celebrate Women's Day with. We see you; we value you. Collectively, the two of you have seen a large part of the evolution of the Hindi film actress. So today, when you go on a set like *Happy Family, Conditions Apply*, is there a sense of excitement and validation?

Ratna Pathak Shah: Yes, hundred per cent. I don't think actresses have had as good a time before this. My mother, an absolutely wonderful actress, never got a chance to do what she was capable of on film. On stage, she did a lot. Fortunately, we're breaking out of the typical moulds for female performers. And I'm very happy I'm around when that's happening.

Ayesha Jhulka: So, I did not feel like I fit into all that. And then came OTT. I feel that when we were there on the set of *Happy Family, Conditions Apply*, instantly, there was a connect with senior artists like her, with Raj-ji.

RPS: And the younger ones!

AJ: The younger ones were newcomers also. You learn from them as well. We didn't have mobiles, computers, you know, we had to learn everything.

RPS: Worst of all, we didn't have role models. And that is what, now, hopefully will change. I find many role models among the younger girls. They are so sharp, focused.

AJ: Prepared!

SMD: What have you learnt from them?

RPS: The ability to take risks. I grew up at a time when a female actor focused entirely on her looks. Maybe a little dance would be welcome. I found it a terrible strain. I'm average-looking, but I had something else. That's why I was here in this business.

SMD: You could act!

RPS: It was just not part of the deal. And the way it tells on actors, I've seen that. Actresses do nothing except look at the mirror. Before the shot, no lines, characterisation. This younger generation is not so self-obsessed.

SMD: You felt limited being the typical heroine. And you, ma'am, talked about how you never fit the mould of the typical heroine. So these are opposing problems, but at the root, it's both of you pushing back against being boxed into the typical heroine.

RPS: Exactly, yes.

SMD: I love this line I heard you say in an interview, 'Jawaani mein bore hue, ab budhape mein maze le rahi hoon (I was bored in my youth, so I'm enjoying myself in my old age).'

RPS: Best way. The whole system has turned upside down. How wonderful.

AJ: That gives me confidence. When I am at her age, probably I'll also enjoy.

RPS: Absolutely!

SMD: Is there a tinge of regret at not being utilised better, sooner?

RPS: Of course. I would have liked to do some more challenging work when I was younger – on film. I did plenty on stage. So mera dil bhar gaya. Kisi ne dekha nahi wo alag baat hai, maine kar liya. Maine bahut seekha usme. (So, I did it to my heart's content. The fact that nobody watched is a different topic, but I did it. I learnt a lot.) So, no real regret. I am just happy that this is possible.

AJ: For me, I can never say regret because I took very conscious decisions. I came to the industry at a very young age. I wanted to work.

When you are just sixteen, you do not realise or think that mujhe aise career ko aage le jaana hai (I want to take my career forward like this). I did so many films. I was lucky they were hits. And at the time, I had to do the dancing and the romantic films. Then came *Dalaal* and all these other films which are a little more mature. And at that point, I made a conscious decision to step back. The same kind of stuff was coming my way. I want to do something which has some meat in it. I did a play called *Purush*, and Vijaya Mehta was my director, and I realised what acting is all about. And all the years that I worked, those twenty to twenty-two years, I felt I did nothing.

SMD: I'm reminded of the scene from *Khiladi* where Akshay gives you the white rose. If you were to manifest your second innings, what would it look like for you?

AJ: I would like *Jo Jeeta Wohi Sikandar* and *Khiladi* ka sequel to be made with the same cast.

SMD: So would we!

AJ: And I told Mansoor that, a couple of months back.

SMD: I see you living your best life, really with *Lipstick (Under My Burkha)* and *Trial By Fire* and *Unpaused*. It's a welcome change. But what is it that has caused this shift in the gaze through which we see women?

RPS: Oh, how we see women in general? Oh, my. Lots of things. We have a much more educated audience today. Almost everyone that you meet has at least been to school. Audiences are now seeing so many more things. The internet has opened up the world. No more can you copy or steal as easily as we used to do. People want something fresh. The old-fashioned rubbish that used to pass because it had a star in it is not working anymore. Focus on the script has been a much-needed game changer.

SMD: Well, your writer Aatish Kapadia was also with you in *Sarabhai vs Sarabhai*. Will we see flavours of that in *Happy Family*? Or do we have to wait for a season three of *Sarabhai*?

RPS: You'll have to wait for season three of *Sarabhai*.

SMD: Are you giving us a date?

RPS: I wish I could. You have traces of Aatish.

AJ: *Happy Family* ke teen season aap zarur dekhenge (You'll definitely see three seasons of *Happy Family*).

RPS: Inshallah (God willing). It is Aatish-driven. We are there as vessels to pass those ideas on. But like *Sarabhai* and *Khichdi*, this show is also Aatish-driven. It's *his* zany humour. It's *his* wittiness. It's *his* crazy take on this crazy world of ours.

SMD: Personally speaking, in your own happy families, what are the conditions that apply to ensure that it's happy?

RPS: Open channels of communication. We talk, not quite about everything, of course, but mostly everything. It was difficult but it has paid off. I think we trust each other.

AJ: For me, I feel there is a little Pallavi in Ayesha.

RPS: Yeah, I've seen that.

AJ: We are open with certain family members – we can say anything. But then the elders do not understand the language that I'm trying to speak. And so, I have to become Pallavi. There is no other choice. I don't want to hurt them or shake them. The balance is very important.

RPS: Ideally, the whole family should understand.

AJ: But that doesn't happen.

RPS: Unfortunately. I'm looking ahead. There's nothing much we can do about people who have been brought up in a different style.

AJ: Yes, exactly.

RPS: Woh toh apna waisa hi karenge (They will do what they want and what they've learnt).

AJ: Hopefully, they will get better.

RPS: At least more open.

AJ: Communicating doesn't help completely, you have to understand also.

RPS: That's another thing. Hindustani tendency, bhakti karo (Indian tendency, to worship). Papa is always right. And it's much worse for the boys in the family, I've noticed.

AJ: Yes.

RPS: The men suffer. Women are much smarter, instinctively. We find our way. The men get stuck.

AJ: I think *Happy Family, Conditions Apply* is going to be a very welcome change for OTT also. With Prime Video taking on this so-called experiment.

RPS: Yes, I've got my fingers crossed. But I do feel there's always a risk with comedy. It has to land.

SMD: Of course. You've often talked about how comedy saved you.

RPS: Absolutely. I was on my way to becoming a great tragic actress. And thankfully, *Idhar Udhar* happened. And I was relieved of this weight. And it gave me a chance to learn a skill. Acting is skill-dependent. Good speech, an expressive body. I had very few of those skills. And comedy gave me the chance to acquire those skills. So, I'm very thankful, deeply grateful to Anand Mahendroo, he was the first person who thought I was capable. It has helped me as a serious actor also. I don't focus on myself so much; I focus on what has to be done. That's the trouble with acting.

SMD: It's a trap.

AJ: It is, it is.

RPS: You become so full of yourself. And comedy mein woh kar hi nahi sakte hain aap (And in comedy it is not possible at all).

AJ: Give and take.

SMD: Making sure it lands.

RPS: Exactly. You're playing off somebody. You've got to time it. You've got to be part of the whole.

SMD: And speaking of your happy family, when we have the finest actors – Naseeruddin Shah, Ratna Pathak, Supriya Pathak, Pankaj Kapur. What are dinner table conversations like?

AJ: And now we have Sanah also.

RPS: Sanah. Not to mention my three children. Everyone's an actor. It's about acting mainly. Or theatre, film, gossip. Definitely focused around the work.

SMD: That inevitably happens?

RPS: Yes. I know Supri says that about her family too. And it's other things also. If work is fun, what else do you want?

SMD: What's an emotion that you struggle to play on screen?

RPS: Laughter. I'm much more comfortable now. But to start with, laughing is a technical thing. I've got waterworks. Any time you want. I believe that was all a Hindustani actress had to do. Fortunately, comedy saved me.

AJ: Earlier, I thought I could never do this crying business easily, without glycerine. Then somehow, I learnt the technique. I give a lot of credit to Vijaya Mehta for this, because I was playing a rape victim on stage – to get tears on stage without any glycerine, every show. So, I got through that. But one thing I can never do, I could never do is, 'Aah, bachao (Aah, save me)!'

SMD: Can you do it?

RPS: I've never had to do it!

AJ: I had to do it in practically every film.

SMD: With conviction.

AJ: Gunde aa rahe hain ghode pe, ya waise, ya kuch. Aur pakad rahe hain, 'Aah, bachao!' (The goons are coming on horses, or something else. They are grabbing hold of me, 'Aah, save me!')

RPS: I would find that hard.

AJ: At home, my family would actually see me screaming, 'Bachao, bachao (Save me, save me).' My mother came in once, 'What happened?!' It just doesn't come from within.

SMD: We are not the damsels!

AJ: Yeah.

SMD: Ma'am, in your fortieth year in cinema, I'm just very curious to know, what's the secret behind staying passionate and professional over time?

RPS: The fact that I had to do less work. I didn't have to do 'Bachao!' too many times. I got more interesting work, thanks to the theatre. That gave me a chance to develop my mind. I've heard, 'Actors don't need to be educated.' I disagree entirely.

SMD: Why?

RPS: It's a stupid idea.

AJ: It's really stupid.

RPS: The more you understand about the world around you, the better you are as an actor. You can be self-educated. You've got to be. You cannot experience every emotion in the world, but you may be asked to play it. So you read about it, you talk to others. You have to connect with that character. Actors need to be highly intelligent.

AJ: Exactly! Observing a character.

RPS: I got time to develop my mind as well as my skills as an actor.

SMD: Is there a price to being outspoken as a woman in cinema or being a woman in general?

AJ: Always. I just speak my mind. I don't care who's listening or what they're thinking of me. At one point of time, I was tagged as the most controversial newcomer. If I have to put my foot down on anything, I would do it. And initially, when you're new, you—

RPS: Don't know how. That's one of the things in our happy families. Various people say things which are sometimes intelligent.

AJ: Correct.

RPS: And yet they are said in a way that's not hurtful. Except for Hemlata. She says the first thing that comes into her head without—

AJ: Mincing words.

RPS: Or being diplomatic. But everyone else is. And that is the point the show is trying to make. Family is a very important institution in India. But it's not sacrosanct or perfect. It needs change like every institution.

SMD: Is there a price to being outspoken?

RPS: Yeah, but who doesn't pay that price? Outspoken man also pays a price. In our country, we are great conformists. We want to do what Papa told us. Across everything. Papa knows best. Don't question papa. Woh family mein badlaav aayaga, kyunki abhi young log nahi hain, jaise pehele ke thhe (And that change will come in the family. Because young people are not like they used to be). Everyone has to be ready for the new challenge of living together.

SMD: Absolutely. What's a piece of advice that you'd give your twenty-year-old self, or an actress looking to break into films today?

RPS: She broke into films at twenty. I didn't. So go on, tell us.

AJ: I broke into films much earlier.

SMD: What do you wish you had known then?

AJ: Sometimes when I see these new people coming in with so much preparation, they are so focused, and they come in as if they've done some twenty years of work. And I have observed that, often, if there is some senior actor trying to help—

RPS: She calls it helping, but not everyone thinks that.

AJ: That's what. And the person was like, 'What are you trying to teach me? I mean, you?'

RPS: 'Who are you?'

AJ: That confidence, they have today. And confidence, we also had a lot. But I like the way we were not prepared for all things. When people say, 'Oh, you are very relatable. You have that girl-next-door feel,' I wasn't so manja hua, tarasha hua (cleaned and polished) before entering. Maybe that innocence was intact. But today, I don't think that'll work. In today's times, you have to be prepared. You have to be more confident and more organised. In those times, we never walked in with a big team or managers.

RPS: That is one thing I wish we could dump.

AJ: Really.

RPS: I really can't stand this. And what does it do except make you self-absorbed?

SMD: The size of your entourage determines your star power.

RPS: What does it do to your head? I've seen actors on a plane, coffee is brought by assistant. Assistant opens the cup. What are you, a three-month-old child?

AJ: It is scary.

RPS: Constantly, 'Mera makeup, mera makeup, mera makeup, mera makeup (My makeup, my makeup, my makeup, my makeup).' I find that so dangerous. And I've seen good actors affected by this entourage business.

SMD: Is there a way to be outside of this, do you think?

AJ: When we entered the industry, we were not focused with all this. We had our staff.

RPS: Hair and makeup! Cooks! Workout ki team ja rahi hain aapki, aapka saara gym equipment ja rahi hain (Your whole workout team is going with you, your gym equipment). How much money is that film earning after all the gym equipment and caterers and chefs? Did the film make the money that was put into it? It's very silly.

AJ: That's how it works. But earlier, we didn't focus so much on that. There are some really good things that have happened. We didn't have vanities. We always needed somebody to help us change.

RPS: Yeah! To hold the pardah (curtain).

AJ: So, I can adjust without a lot of things. But you see newcomers, 'Where is my vanity?' And I was shooting on another set where the artist walked off because his vanity was not there. We waited for four hours. Because he was asked to adjust for vanity with another actor.

SMD: For someone just breaking into films, what can they learn from your experience?

RPS: Focus on your craft. That's the one thing that will stand you in good stead. Work on your skills.

9 March 2023

10

Hrithik Roshan: In Search of New Experiences

Anupama Chopra: Hrithik, it has been twenty years since *Kaho Naa… Pyaar Hai*.
Hrithik Roshan: Has it?

AC: Exactly twenty years.
HR: Why does this always happen? That when you look back you say to yourself, 'What the hell was I thinking? Was I thinking this is cool?' Oh my God. I forgive myself.

AC: Nobody has matched this debut.
HR: Yeah, it doesn't get any better.

AC: I remember the national meltdown. That *India Today* cover: 'Heartthrob Hrithik'. And here we are, twenty years later. *The Times of India* says you were the most profitable star of 2019. What does it take to have that kind of longevity?
HR: I have no idea. I think it takes a whole lot of vacuum. If I may say so, I think what we set out to do in the world is, in some way, trying to fill ourselves up from inside. So, there's something lacking and we're trying to fill it up. The larger the hole or the vacuum inside you, the harder you work to fill that up. That's your addiction then. I'm not saying it in a negative way, but if you are going through struggles and pains, that really is your first chapter. I have experienced that trajectory in my life. If you had a very strict father like I did – nothing was good enough – and you had to be perfect, that kind of conditioning puts you on this marathon.

AC: And pushes you.
HR: Of course, that's one aspect of it. It's also a whole load of fun. It's like riding that roller coaster, which is scary, but you're like, 'Aaahhh, this is fun!' You have to be okay with the fear to be able to last. Otherwise, you'll

burn out. And you keep changing. I'm at a juncture right now where some change is about to happen.

AC: Changing choices?
HR: I don't know. I'm an adventurer. That's what I like to say, but I'm really going to put it into practice now. I want to experience something new. I don't know what I'm going to do, what kind of film, if it's going to be a film. I'm at a very crazy place in my head.

AC: Is that scary or exciting?
HR: Both. What's scary is just the uncertainty. And the path to growth is through uncertainty.

AC: And where is *Krrish 4* in all of this?
HR: That's there waiting to happen. Maybe I'll give it another twist. Or do something strange.

AC: Are you feeling reckless?
HR: Probably not a bad word to articulate what I'm feeling. In a good way.

AC: That's very exciting for an actor.
HR: Exciting for someone who has actually tried to be very safe all his life. Not in films, but in life. I've had to be. I'm very careful not to stumble while talking, for instance, because I've struggled all my life. And now suddenly I'm saying, 'Let me see what happens.'

AC: You said your struggle becomes a driving force. You've handled brain surgery, your father surviving cancer, bullets, extreme success, extreme failure, divorce, legal war with a co-star. How have you done all of this?
HR: Yes. I think most of the things that you mentioned actually prompted the best out of me, nudged me to be the best version of myself.

AC: How?
HR: If there is a problem to solve and I have my eyes on the truth, it gives me meaning. And now, I've done *War* and both my films are successful. I'm sitting down and thinking, 'Something is missing.' I've just been so used to challenge after challenge after challenge. So now, I don't know how to be. Too much of a good thing. So, I'm going to be a bit reckless and see where that takes me.

AC: Are you enjoying this downtime?
HR: I am trying.

AC: Why does that sound like a chore?
HR: It's strange. The mistake some of us make is making our lives entirely about the goal. We need to build in our lives a system that keeps you going every single day. My father, grandfather, they wake up in the morning, they get dressed and they go to the office. Whether there's work or not.

AC: It's the discipline.
HR: That's the system. In the past two or three years, I was just trying to get both these films done and there was a lot of chaos. Now I'm like, where's it gone?

AC: So, what's your most enduring memory of *Kaho Naa... Pyaar Hai*?
HR: The working relationship between my father and me was amazing. And since then, I've always tried and succeeded most of the time to duplicate that with every director.

AC: In what way?
HR: Complete transparency in communication. Audacity to say what you feel. To be aligned towards a goal. There was this boat that we were shooting on and I was wearing a ganji and a shirt and he wanted me to be only wearing the ganji. I was very transparently showing my displeasure, and he lost it. In front of everyone he shouted the hell out of me. And I did the shot with the ganji. Five minutes later, it was all about the next shot and we had forgotten completely about what had transpired. Absolutely fine.

AC: But how wonderful.
HR: Yeah. Which is why I have always tried to maintain that kind of openness with all the filmmakers that I work with and it is so relaxing. You feel safe. There's no hiding.

AC: And it's not personal.
HR: Exactly. It's towards that common goal.

AC: Just before *War* released, you talked about the freedom you feel now as an actor and you said, 'I'm more interested in being authentic than popular.' So, what are you doing differently now?

HR: I was doing *Kaabil*, and I'm quite aware of my abilities and weaknesses. I was taking out shots from a tool kit, stock expressions. And I said, I don't want to do that. So, I called an acting coach, Vinod, and I sat him down and I said, 'You're going to make sure that I don't repeat any of my stock shots.'

AC: So, he would stop you?
HR: He would completely stop me. He would say, 'You've got to go back right now and give one more take.' I said, 'Commerical hai thoda (it's commercial).' He said, 'Why don't you just do one more take? If it's not good then we will not use it.'

AC: You had somebody just looking at your expressions.
HR: Somebody who knew whether this is authentic or a stock expression. It was a big risk because I had to step into areas where I could really falter. And it slowly it became a lot of fun. Acting is a very lonely job. I say, 'Why can't actors come together and like just help each other?' It doesn't happen. But it happens in a class, in a community. That's what prompted me to find a coach. I was very scared. But slowly, I allowed my body to lead and my mind to follow.

AC: What do you mean?
HR: Well, when you're emoting, there is a part of your mind which knows where you want to reach. I think it's your prefrontal lobe, constantly watching. And you need to hit a note and your body knows that to hit that note your body needs to turn or move a certain way or something. And your body keeps following your mind, because your mind is taking you there. This is a little abstract – the mind wants to experience that peak, and the body is doing whatever it can to reach that peak. But ever since *Kaabil*, there was a shift in my system. I knew where my mind wanted to go but if my body didn't want to go there, I didn't go. And if my body wanted to do something, I allowed it to do it. So, I allowed my body to move and my mind followed.

AC: So, it's more instinctive.
HR: Exactly. There are actors who are born like that. But I am coming from the other end of the spectrum, so, for me that was amazing. And then I got more curious and wanted more. Luckily, *Super 30* had filmmaker Vikas who was exactly what I needed at the time to grow. He used to set up a shot and I would say, 'I don't know what I am going to do.' I have

seen other actors doing this and I used to think, 'What fools! They have not worked hard.'

AC: But why?
HR: 'There is no prep.' There is a scene in *Super 30* where Anand gets the Cambridge admission and he is on the terrace and then he walks, sits down and breaks down – very happy. Vikas asked me, 'What are you going to do?' I said, 'Can I just show you my extreme? I might go there and mostly I will be here.' This is something that I never did earlier.

AC: You would map out your performance?
HR: Just to be safe. And other actors have been doing this all their lives and I used to think less of them. And I used to get praised, 'Kitna hard work karta hai! Sab pata hai usko, kaunsa take hai, kaunsa ye hai, kahan jaana hai, kahaan mark pakadna hai, sab pata hai usko (He works so hard! He knows everything, which take it is, where to go, where to hold the mark, he knows everything).' But I think finally you have to come to a point where the art overcomes the skill.

AC: That's lovely.
HR: So, I told them where I would go. I will go to that edge but I will not jump off. They had to do use a steady cam. That was the only way to get that shot. I really did not know what I was going to do. So, that's the composure I was talking about. I am finally experiencing the flight of an actor and I hope it lasts. Otherwise, I am feeling so lazy right now.

AC: In *War*, Hrithik, you decided to keep your greys. Siddharth Anand, the director, was not happy—
HR: He is pretty amazing.

AC: I read that Siddharth said you might lose some fans
HR: It's on camera. So, Aalim was cutting my hair and I was telling Sid, 'I think I should enhance my greys. These two patches.' He said, 'Your female fans, you will lose them. No, you can't!' I said, 'Wait, let me show you.' So, I got into the look and . . . this reminds me so strangely, the last film and my first film had this in common. I had to convince my dad that Raj, in the second half of the film, should be clean shaven and wear glasses, and the first guy, who was a simpleton, will have stubble and long hair. And he was like, 'Kya? Kyun? (What? Why?)' Because

only the heroes had the stubble and the geeky nerds are clean-shaven with glasses.

AC: That's the stereotype!
HR: That's the stereotype. I had to get all my friends, mostly girls, to come home casually one day to convince him. I just need to be true to the character. Whether that makes me look good, bad, fat, slim, sexy or not, it doesn't matter.

AC: This is an industry where fifty-five-year-old men are working with twenty-year-old women.
HR: That's good, why not?

AC: We will debate that. But how do you come to a point where you're comfortable letting your greys show?
HR: Because I don't fear it. It really is too much of a burden to be in pretence. To try and be your authentic self is just so simple. You will be liked by a few; you will not be liked by a few. Before *Kaabil*, I was constantly pretending. I have no qualms with saying, 'That's not me.' My characters are crafted and then I finally give it off to the world and come back to who I am.

AC: What a bummer.
HR: I'm causing mass disappointments all over the world.

AC: You are!
HR: When *Kaho Naa... Pyaar Hai* released, my first public appearance was at a place called Crossroads. They were screaming my name. And I came on stage and they didn't recognise me.

AC: No!
HR: They were refusing to believe it. I went in my chappals, I had a shirt on, and a cap which was turned around. I almost apologised, 'That's how I am in real life. I'm sorry!' I have met people at airports and stuff after my first film. One guy who must have been seven feet tall, he comes really close to me and he says, 'Dude! Fuck, I'm taller than Hrithik Roshan!' I said, 'Dude, you're a giant. You're taller than 90 per cent of the world!' But he was happy that he was taller than Hrithik Roshan on screen . . . . I've experienced that time and again, after *Kaho Naa... Pyaar Hai*, *Dhoom*

2, *Bang Bang*, now *War*. I might not be completely him, but I am maybe 60 per cent. That's not bad.

AC: What's amazing to me is that you do this, and you also do a film which is diametrically opposite – *Super 30*. I want us to look at my favourite scene from the film, where I think you just found an emotional honesty. Tell us how you did this.

(A clip from *Super 30* plays. Audience applauds)

HR: I felt so strongly about this film. I could dedicate this film to the eleven-year-old me. I am lucky I'm getting to do films that I really feel something for. This becomes easy acting – you have a connection with the emotion. I was very nervous that day. It was raining and you're wondering if maybe school will be shut. Shall I have my bath? You're hoping. It was raining that day and half of me was like, 'I can relax if the shooting stops.'

AC: Were you afraid of the scene?
HR: Because there was something there that I could do. Will it come out? Everything boils down to this moment. I said, 'Okay. Just stay with the emotion.' Anand Sir was supposed to come to the set, and I told them, 'Anand Sir should not come on set until I have done this shot.' That was my nervousness. Nandish was really amazing. That really helps because I am always only as good as the actors I am working with. First take, the camera made a mistake. It was a steady cam, they didn't know where I was going. There is no reaction as such. I didn't want to rush the emotion, to experience and express it. I said, 'If I don't break down, I am okay with it, but let me see where this takes me.' There was one take in which I was feeling it. I was like, 'This is going to be the best shot ever!' And the camera guy said, 'Cut.' I didn't know what to do. 'Should I kill him?' Once you get that displaced, then it becomes really hard to get back. I can share a secret – at times like this when there is chaos and noise, I think about death.

AC: Really?
HR: It really relaxes me.

AC: Your own death?
HR: Hundred years from now, nobody will know me, or think about me. None of this will matter, whether I did good or bad on this day. And that

sets me back to zero and I begin again. And that's the shot that happened after going through this.

AC: How many takes?
HR: About five.

AC: Can you repeat what you do?
HR: There's only one authentic way. You can hit the same peak again, but with a different stimulus. If you begin with the same stimulus again, the mind will know where it's going. Any shift will start another authentic journey. Continuity can get you stuck. Find another little cheat. After this, do this. And you'll form another authentic . . . . I'm talking as if I know acting. I'm an aspiring actor. We're all the same. I'm still learning.

AC: You say that a lot. You call yourself a mazdoor (labourer).
HR: Yeah, man, I work so hard. I want to stop. Can you help me please? How much is enough? Why am I constantly searching for some truth? I should have been a scientist or an astronaut. It's the same urge – you want to find out the truth.

AC: About the universe.
HR: Existential questions. It's the same search that drives us. I really want to find out whether I can relax now. Can I let go of that and just live?

AC: Be able to relax.
HR: Being able to relax and just act. That's also a beautiful skill. Just act it. People do it.

AC: This struggle you talk about, things that come to other actors organically and you have to work at it – does it get easier with experience?
HR: Yeah, it does. I'm a little tentative, though. In a lot of ways, it gets easier. All the peripherals, the frivolous stuff becomes easy because they don't matter.

AC: Like what?
HR: A hero has no mould, I'm just exploring. Peripheral is when you feel a hero can only sit like this. There's a lot of posturing that we have grown up watching. I found out it's unnecessary. In *War*, it's not posturing. I've got the same postures but it's thought through.

AC: It's organic swag.
HR: It's not just put on. It's like, something is stimulating that kind of a walk. What was the question?

AC: Is it easier?
HR: Yeah, so, a lot of the peripherals go out the window. You start looking at the larger picture. Discovering parts of the character. Kabir, when he was written, he was a straightforward guy. A good guy taking revenge. What we did was . . . sorry, I'm digressing.

AC: Please go on!
HR: This is the first day of *War*, okay? We are in a place called Lake Como or some place in Italy. Shit, Sid is going to kill me. Reckless, right? So, Sid comes to my room excited. 'Day after we are starting…' I had a double slipped disc in my back. Adi had padded this schedule so that I will be comfortable. I can't move, I'm in terrible pain. I said, 'Sid, what am I doing in this film?' He said, 'Ay Hrithik, what are you saying?' I said, 'I love the screenplay of the film. But I'm doing nothing in this film.' 'Okay, relax. We'll discuss.' Adi had told me, 'I need you to be my rock in this schedule.' Sid's like, 'What do you mean?' So we sat down. Vinod was there. I said, 'I need to do something with this guy. Go research and pick out eccentric characters.' Vinod came back with bits of *Taxi Driver*. I asked Sid, 'Sid, can I play him drunk?' He said, 'Do whatever you want to do.' He was like, 'Yeah, yeah, okay.' Sid said, 'Adi will collapse, we'll keep it between you and me.' So, I took a lot of these little instances and created a character that was not predictable. I chatted with Tiger as well. He told me, 'We are all doing this. You just be honest.' I took that advice and it worked. So, I told Tiger, 'I am doing all of this. You do nothing. You will shine.' That's what happens in equations in our films, in our Hindi films. If one actor is doing something good, the other actor tries to beat it. Arnold Schwarzenegger and his best friend Franco. When Arnold was towering, Franco would go down on the floor and do it down. I told Tiger, 'Just be real.' And he was beautiful. So, in that first scene, when I walk up to him and say something mean – you are seeing two authentic characters and there is unpredictability, mystery. I have completely forgotten the question.

AC: Fascinating story! What are you like on set? You are the most powerful there.

HR: I just want to add – to be flexible as a director, as a filmmaker, listen to your actor, that is something that is really important. So full credit to Sid for having that flexibility, tolerance, patience.

AC: When you have the power and the clout that you do, how do you conduct yourself on set? Are you a screamer?
HR: No.

AC: Do you sulk?
HR: No. I really miss people teaching me what to do. I want to work with people where I can be a student again. I want to be wide-eyed. I had a lot of those moments in my last two films. But yeah, I use the power sometimes.

AC: To do what?
HR: To make my work easier when I'm in pain. I'll just say, 'Listen, I'm going to be late.' And that's okay.

AC: You're the bridge between the Khan generation and the Ranbir-Ranveer generation.
HR: I'm the bridge, I'm connecting them.

AC: What has changed the most for the Hindi film hero?
HR: What a Hindi film hero was supposed to be and what he is now. It's a big relief. Otherwise, that posturing would have just continued. Today if somebody wants to be an actor, he doesn't necessarily have to do dancing, fighting – all those things. It's good if you can, it frees your body. Films are becoming a good reflection of reality. All heroes don't know how to dance. We'll have a lot more kinds of films, of stars. Every star will not fit into one mould, which is so boring. In the West, for one Tom Cruise, you'll find hundreds. I think we're heading there slow and steady, but we'll get there.

AC: What is the ambition now?
HR: I was hoping you won't ask me any question about the future, because frankly, I don't know, and I think that's very interesting. For the first time. Do I want more of what I have? Or to explore something new? I don't know. Ambition is what? Number one, money, biggest house? I'm not ambitious. Ambition or money or fame goes along with happiness up to

a point only. Is more of what I have gotten making me happy? That's the question that I'm living with right now. I might become a singer. Or I might start my film in January or February. It's nice to have the luxury of choice. I have gratitude for that. All the hard work has brought me to a point where at least I have a choice.

From the Floor: Q&A

Audience Member: Were you ever asked to play a character that you found to be really difficult? Do you have a method for something like that?
HR: Yeah, and I failed terribly. There was a film that I did called *Main Prem Ki Diwani Hoon*. (audience laughs) I was not mature enough to understand that side of me. A very happy, very uppity character doesn't come very naturally to me and at that point of time, I wasn't aware of the fact that there are some things that are not natural to your state.

Audience Member: When you're preparing for a role, for 6–7 months, does that character show up in your real life too? I had a crazy time with my family while I was doing one character.
HR: Yeah. It happens all the time. I think it's a great thing.

AC: Like you'll be sitting and suddenly Kabir appears?
HR: His thought process will appear.

AC: So, you'll start being mean or cool?
HR: So, I can bet that if I sign a comedy film right now, my next six months will be spent in more laughter. I start thinking how that guy will think, in my life. So, my decisions, my instincts, all start becoming very fresh and new. I love to do that but not with all characters. When I was playing a Bihari character I was constantly talking in that accent. I had quite a few laughs. It's fun for me. I hope it's fun for you.

Audience Member: My mom says, 'You're behaving weirdly.' And my sister too. And I had to accept it but as soon as that thing was done, Sir, I was back to normal and now they are loving me more than anything.
HR: Try and be that character without anybody finding out. So, it will become more you. And then slowly let it diffuse into the room. Don't shift so much that it's too much.

AC: So, it's the character behaving like you.

HR: Yeah, actually. Yeah, try that.

Audience Member: I have a two-legged question. Before *Kaabil* there were movies like *Koi... Mil Gaya* and *Guzaarish* where your character was not the typical Hindi film hero character. How was the process like there? And second, any plans for the reckless future?

HR: Man, when you say it, it sounds scary. Your reckless future!

Audience Member: Do you want to take a dab at direction as well?

HR: I'll answer the second question first, I keep hearing this a lot – that I will finally direct. But I don't feel it in my bones. I'm happy that I'm surviving as an actor. When it shuts down, I'll think. The other part of your question: when I see *Koi... Mil Gaya* there are parts of the film that I could have done so much better. But I was lucky. Rohit's character was one that . . . . I had those experiences in my life as a child. Films like *Koi... Mil Gaya*, *Super 30*, etc. have been my easiest. Up until *Kaabil*, I was doing well, it's not that I was not. But there is a composure since *Kaabil*, that perhaps you will find in *Koi... Mil Gaya* – because that character I was very comfortable with.

Audience Member: What is your most creatively satisfying moment, on camera?

HR: It'll take me another twenty years to answer that. The characters which I have rejoiced in are the ones where I've found the most flow. I didn't have that in my life because of my speech. Coincidentally, the two characters in which I found my maximum flow were in my last two films, Kabir and Anand. There was just, I mean, I could speak Bihari for the rest of my life. It's got such a nice flow. I must have been born Bihari in my past life. It all boils down to finding that flow in front of the camera.

6 January 2020

11

'I Marry the Director's Mind': Ranbir Kapoor

Anupama Chopra: You're here to promote *Sanju*, and I can't actually talk about *Sanju* because of conflict of interest. My husband is a co-producer. But we have this audience of acting students, film lovers, film students. Let's talk about acting.
Ranbir Kapoor: Absolutely. I'm tired of talking about *Sanju*. When you do a film, there is this marketing period. And you're trying to sell the film to people, trying to get them into the audience. It's the most tiring process. You know, you may do like films like *Gandhi* and *The Last of the Mohicans*, which can tire you as an actor. But those five days of promotions can just kill you.

AC: So, Deepika always says, 'Don't ask me about my acting process.' Are you able to tell us how you transform into other people? Are there rituals you follow?
RK: Yes. I would like to share. Every character comes with its own method, a new set of procedures that you have to follow. And I forget.

AC: You forget what you use?
RK: Yeah, that's an old you. You're just constantly evolving, trying to better your own self, your craft, your skill. But it gets boring if you have one fixed method for every film.

AC: Let's talk about *Jagga Jasoos*. I thought you were just so lovely in that movie.
RK: Yeah, it broke my heart and my bank. But see, Anurag Basu is from a very different species of directors. On *Barfi!*, there was no script. No blueprint of where the story was going. But we all knew the story. Dada always improvised. Because of the good experience we had on *Barfi!*, it lent itself to the making of *Jagga Jasoos*. Character is pretty simple and it's pretty basic, but a lot of complications went into making it look that simple and basic. We had taken too much on our plate. It was a detective film. The

character stammers. It's a musical. He's finding his father. There is a love story. It's episodic. So, it was very hard. And I'm not good with dialogues, so, I was happy. I think the challenge in this film was how not to make the stammering sound irritating. And when you sing the songs, it was meant to be like dialogue. Very real.

AC: I've felt that about you always. From *Saawariya*, you just lit up the frame as dark as that film was. And I can't see you acting, I think it makes you so amazing.

RK: Thank you. What you finally see on the screen is, of course, the magic of cinema, and there are so many people behind it. But my method is very basic. Two things I always follow are – one is to marry the director's mind. I am that Bandra boy who's lived a very luxurious life, travelled all around the world. But I don't know my own country, my people, my characters. So, I always have to steal their personalities. That love story between me and the director is very important. He has to fall deeply in love with me and I have to be deeply in love with him. Then comes that trust. You want to give yourself to this guy and he's taking and giving. And that's an amazing relationship. And second, to understand the text, what's written. We read a scene and we see it superficially. But there's so many things that a writer and director go through, creating every beat. What is the other person saying? How to add a sense of truth to everything? Once you know the director's space, and you understand the text, then your job becomes easy. But courting the director in the beginning is harder than courting a girl. But I really enjoy that. And then I do stupid, superficial things like, use one perfume for one character.

AC: Vidya Balan said she does the same.

RK: That's great. I'm in good company. My sense of smell is very strong. Any sense, touch, smell, feel, if it can remind you of that character, it helps. I was doing *Wake Up Sid* and *Ajab Prem Ki Ghazab Kahani* simultaneously – ten days here, twelve days there. Perfume helped. When I put it on and stepped out of my trailer van, it kind of put things into perspective, 'Okay, I'm this guy right now.' Shoes – I like particular shoes for different characters. Now this is all pseudo-intellectual stuff, you know, we're not saving the world. Once you know that, then it's just presence of mind while being on set. Not coming with set notions but coming in and making a mistake, making a fool of yourself and being honest to the moment.

AC: Can you tell when a shot is not authentic enough?

RK: I've stopped looking at myself in the monitor because I started cringing, I started becoming too aware of myself. Whenever I've gone home and said, 'Aaj maine kamaal ka shot diya (I gave a great shot today)', that's never good. It's always when I've come home in confusion or trying to rethink – that confusion state is like really being alive as an actor. That has always yielded better results.

AC: You said creative energy comes from isolation, nature and sacrifice. What did you mean?

RK: I think isolation is very important for every human being, it's very important that you love yourself. You don't need another person to feel alive. In isolation, you go deeper within. Nature – as an actor, you're consuming nature. Once you can take in nature, that world will represent through you. It also keeps me peaceful, balanced, makes me understand my value in this big universe. And third is sacrifice. I learnt a lot from Sanjay Leela Bhansali. He instilled this value that you need to sacrifice something that stardom will give you, because otherwise it'll take away from a certain deep empathy you'll feel for your characters.

AC: Can you put your finger on what you've sacrificed?

RK: I've sacrificed a lot of friendship. My school gang, I meet them once a month. They meet each other three times, four times a week. You're kind of lost in the conversation, lagging behind, there are new beats of laughter. Small things like this. I don't want to sound like a crybaby. I've only sacrificed that because I have benefitted.

AC: I was chatting with Aamir. He said he can consistently choose great narratives because he looks at a project as a producer and not as an actor, not just his part in it. If that is the case, then can we assume that you made some really terrible choices because you were too focused on your part?

RK: Maybe. Since *Saawariya*, every choice has been mine. I'm responsible for every success, for every failure that I've had. I can't take a third perspective on the script. 'Do you like it? Should I do it?' If I'm not connected to the material or the character, I won't be able to do anything. I don't have that skill set that Aamir Sir has, and that's why he is who he is today. It's something that you develop with experience, years of understanding your audience. And I'm okay with it. I don't think *Bombay Velvet* or *Jagga Jasoos* or *Barfi!* or *Wake Up Sid* were experimental films. I liked them.

AC: But these are all also worthy experiments. I'm talking more about films like *Besharam*.
RK: Well, *Besharam* was the only 'masala' film. I use this word masala not in a negative way. Masala means that a large audience will see your film. It's the hardest genre. You know, you can make a nice story, say *Wake Up Sid* or *Rocket Singh*, and there are very few chances of you going wrong. Commercially, yes, but there'll be audience that will like your film. But to get the great super hits, that is the hardest genre. And sometimes that comes out of the blue. You know, Shah Rukh Khan used to tell me that he never saw the potential in *Dilwale Dulhania Le Jayenge*.

AC: Right. It's a silly love story.
RK: And then see what that film did.

AC: Still running.
RK: Yeah. When I did *Rocket Singh: Salesman of the Year*, I thought, 'Yaar, this is my *Munna Bhai M.B.B.S.* You know, I'm set for life.' When I did *Ajab Prem Ki Ghazab Kahani*, I thought I was screwed. So, you don't have the formula.

AC: So, nobody knows anything.
RK: Nobody knows, and that's the magic.

AC: Ranbir, you said that the next few years of your career are going to be spent entertaining the audience and not proving your acting chops. Are these two necessarily different things?
RK: For me, yes. When I do a film like *Tamasha* or *Jagga Jasoos*, I'm first looking at my character and not necessarily at the larger picture. You need to go to an extreme long shot like Aamir Sir says and understand what value your film is talking about, who it's talking to, what the budget is. Filmmaking is expensive. You can't do things solely because this is your passion project. And I learnt that from Raju Sir. He has this desire to entertain, not bore or force down moral opinions. His film may have a moral value but he wants to entertain you, make you laugh, cry. And to understand, don't take yourself so seriously; you're not saving the world. Then your choices also change, it becomes more about the film. I'm doing Rajkumar Hirani's film. I haven't chosen, he's chosen me. Anybody would do a Hirani film. So, if *Sanju* is a commercial success, I can't take credit. But if *Jagga Jasoos* was a success, then maybe I could. Alas, it was not.

AC: A director said that your problem is that you're the prince of Bollywood. You are Rishi Kapoor's son. And you're perhaps not hungry in the same way that Ranveer is. So, you won't do a two-hero film. Right?

RK: Absolutely not. Yes, I don't need to work to feed myself and put a roof over my head, but I've always been extremely passionate about movies. Because you're born in a film family, they say, 'Oh, he got it easy.' Yes, I agree, but I've worked really hard these last ten years. I've not taken my job for granted. So, my hunger is there. I did *Raajneeti*, which had so many heroes. I'm not insecure. I've never been offered a two-hero film that I and the other person have liked. Also, when you do a two-hero film, your job is much easier because you're sharing the burden of success and failure. So, I'm looking forward to one.

AC: But you said that you are too insecure to audition.

RK: I'm not that confident. I am low on confidence. Today, thankfully, I have a body of work. But if you send me to Hollywood and say, 'Audition for this filmmaker', I don't know if I'll be good at it. So, I think it's a confidence issue. And now I'm spoilt. People have my films to see me. But yes, I am shy about auditioning.

AC: But you're Ranbir Kapoor. Why low on confidence?

RK: That's my glamour image that's out there.

AC: You're supremely talented.

RK: I don't regard myself as such. That's why I have to work hard. I know my shortcomings. I've been terrible in a couple of my films, where I have probably not given my 100 per cent.

AC: What is a terrible performance?

RK: Like *Besharam*, *Anjaana Anjaani*.

AC: *Besharam* is a bad film!

RK: I always maintain that I'm as good as my film. If the director is good, it's not because of me that a film works. Like in *Rockstar*, if you took out Imtiaz Ali and I directed that film, I would be terrible in it. It was his energy. I'm very insecure. Every day I go to set, I have anxiety: 'Okay, will I be able to do this shot well? Will I be able to surprise my director? Oh God, he's asking for the sixth take. It's so embarrassing.' This stuff goes on in my mind every day. I'm not really happy with what I've achieved. I have lots more to do. That insecurity creates that drive. And if that dies, I will die as an actor.

AC: What's the most takes you've ever done?
RK: I started with Sanjay Leela Bhansali, he doesn't do anything in fewer than forty-five takes.

AC: Are you serious?
RK: Even if I had to just turn my head this way, I'll probably have to give fifty takes. There was a shot in this so-called towel song 'Jab Se Tere Naina' where I had to roll back on this chair and fall down. And the towel had to fall in a certain way with my leg showing. One shot, lying down laughing, then get up and sing a song. And he's particular about what beat you catch, he's a very musical director. I did like some forty-five or fifty takes one day and my back really broke. And the next morning he said, 'No, I've not got it,' and I had to do another seventy takes. So, now eight to ten takes is nothing.

AC: In *GQ* magazine you said, 'I'm nothing more than the characters I've played, the books I've read and the women I've dated.' What did you mean?
RK: Exactly what I said. These are the experiences. Today will probably add to my tomorrow. I've only said books and relationships or characters, but so much adds up to who you are.

AC: Gender parity is one big topic. This is the era of #MeToo and Time's Up. And I have to ask you this.
RK: You don't have to, you know that, right?

AC: No, I have to. (To the audience) Because after this, he disappears, okay, guys? This is not somebody who's going to do press now again until *Brahmāstra: Part One - Shiva* releases.
RK: Yes, thank God.

AC: You're doing a film with Luv Ranjan, who is a successful director. But his films are steeped in misogyny. Do you worry or think about the images and the art you're putting out there?
RK: Okay, how do you pronounce this word, misogyny?

AC: Misogyny.
RK: And misogynistic, right? I have not been a part of those films. Yeah, so I'm working with a director who, according to you, has made misogynistic films, but I'm quite conscious about the parts I do. If it's something

belittling society, belittling something which I feel is unfair, I wouldn't do it. I have to represent a certain value system that I want to express. So, the film with Luv Ranjan is not that.

AC: Okay, good to know. Benedict Cumberbatch recently said that he's not going to do a project unless he knows what the female actor is getting. He said it's important that men in the industry take a stand to make the place more equitable for women. In India, will the men in positions of power, like yourself, take these positions?
RK: I think somebody just has to do it. Then it's like a domino effect. But in our industry, nobody reveals what they really get paid, I guess because of income tax purposes.

AC: So, not the men and not the women.
RK: No, but my contemporaries, Deepika or Katrina or Priyanka Chopra, I think they're right up there. You know, it's not that they're getting paid less than what I'm getting. There is a perception that an actor gets X amount of crores. Today, I think there is much awareness of market value. This is a market-based industry. If your films are doing well, you will get the money. If not, you won't. But Benedict and his take, I think that somebody has to do it. If I'm on a project and I say, 'Okay, there is Deepika. And Deepika is as big or a bigger star than me, then there has to be equality.' But somebody has to do it.

AC: Who will that somebody be?
RK: I don't know. We'll wait and see.

AC: Is there anything that makes you uncomfortable as an actor?
RK: I don't think so. I dropped the towel in my first film.

AC: What else is left to do, right?
RK: But being physically naked is not that hard, being emotionally naked is harder. To really get attached to a moment, feel real, a sense of truth. But there are certain things like, what's the word?

AC: Misogynistic.
RK: You have to be aware of who you are as a person. What do you stand for? Films are a representation of you as an artist, what you're standing for. Your films have to reflect that. But beyond that, I'll do it all.

AC: Two years ago, you wanted three children, and you said, 'I'll fall deeply, madly, passionately in love.' You seem to fall in love a lot. Does it complicate the craft ever?
RK: Falling in love?

AC: Yeah.
RK: Falling in love is the greatest thing in the world. Everything is great. Water tastes like sherbet.

AC: So, we're in the water-like-sherbet moment?
RK: Yeah, and you seem like Uma Thurman to me.

AC: I love it!
RK: You feel great. Who doesn't want to be in love?

AC: But what does it do to you as an actor?
RK: It does things to me as a human being. Acting is my profession, but if I feel good about myself, it's only because life is great and love makes your life great, right?

AC: Can you look at your performances and say, 'That was a beautiful moment in my life'?
RK: No, I don't remember per se what I was feeling on that particular day. But I can tell that's a beautiful moment on screen. Your entire day is consumed to get that particular moment right on screen. But I have bad memory, I don't remember things.

AC: You just put it behind?
RK: I don't remember myself at fifteen, and before that. I think that entire life of mine has been wiped out.

AC: Really?
RK: Yeah, some bizarre thing.

AC: No memories at all?
RK: I think it is because I was trying to give up smoking and I went to this place in Germany to get these injections in my ears because your nicotine receptors are there, and I feel that's really messed with my memory.

AC: So, you quit smoking?
RK: Yes.

AC: Oh, well, memory loss and quitting.
RK: Yeah, smoking kills you more than memory.

AC: I was with Vinod and Raju, when they showed the *Sanju* promo to your dad and he got tears in his eyes. What does that feel like?
RK: He never really expresses what he feels about my work.

AC: Yeah, I can't imagine this happens often.
RK: Never. I'll tell you. When he saw *Rockstar*, and he usually sees the films three or four days before release and I'm really tense, because he's so honest with his opinion. He said, 'Haan, woh last mein heroine mar gayi thi ke wapas aagayi (In the end, did the heroine die or come back)?' So, I said, 'No, she died and it was a soul which came on stage.' 'Yeah, okay, bye.' And he cut the phone. When he saw *Barfi!*, he said, 'Yeah, tu acting-wacting theek toh kar leta hai but stop doing these arty-warty films (Yeah, you're decent at acting, but stop doing these arty films).' He's hard to . . . impress. So, when Raju Sir sent this video to me . . . it feels great, when your parents are proud of you.

AC: But do you ever talk about it? Will he tell you in person?
RK: Never.

AC: No? That's not gonna happen?
RK: Post that video he's not mentioned anything.

AC: Ranbir, last year was your tenth year in the movies. What do you know now that you could have told your younger self?
RK: If I can call this a journey, it's been phenomenal. I would like my younger self to discover this journey again. I've grown up in a film family, I know what success can do to your head and what failure can do to your heart. I was well-equipped. Gratitude, that's something I've learnt. The fact that I'm sitting on this chair in front of all these amazing people, talking about my craft and talking about my life. I like to credit that to myself. Not to being born with a silver spoon, because I worked really hard. I feel immense gratitude.

20 June 2018

12

Celebrating *All We Imagine as Light*: Payal Kapadia & Ranabir Das

Anupama Chopra: Payal and Ranabir, thank you for doing this. I've accosted you. You had no plans to give an interview. I first came to this festival in 1999 when Murali Nair won the Caméra d'Or for *Marana Simhasanam* and since then it's been thirty years and nothing has happened. So what you guys have accomplished is just so incredible and we're all so proud. I couldn't let you go without this.
Payal Kapadia: Thank you.
Ranabir Das: Thank you.

AC: *All We Imagine as Light* is a really evocative and moving film and you layer it and build it piece by piece. I started crying when Chhaya Kadam's character says, 'Ki vo tower pe tower bana rahe hai, uncha aur uncha kar rahe hai, shayad unko lagta hai voh ek din khud hi bhagwan ban jayenge (They are building tower upon tower, they're making it taller and taller. Maybe one day they think they'll become God).' It said so much about Mumbai. I know this has been marinating for years. Where does this script come from?
PK: It's been a long time that we've been working on it together. Although Ranabir is the cameraman, we work together on everything. As with my previous film, we work like a team. As time goes by you write and you change and the film also keeps changing. The starting point was me meeting a nurse — we became friends and spent a lot of time together. The profession itself is so difficult. So that was the starting point, but the film grew into something which is also looking at the city and the people and how it's a place where a lot of people can find work, but it's also a very cruel space and all the contradictions. These contradictions are what interested me. And also the film is about friendship, somewhere. When you leave home it's your friends who become your family and friendship is a relationship that has no

definition. It is what you two decide you want it to be. I hope these ideas came together.

AC: What struck me was the visual language, the way that you portrayed the city. It's such a cliché to say that the city is a character, but I think what you capture is just how crushing it is, and also a grim beauty about it. What were the conversations that the two of you had?

RD: We shot in Mumbai in the monsoon. And in the monsoon, it is very different. We wanted to capture the season – how fast it is. You rarely have time to stop and think about things.

AC: It's relentless.

RD: Yeah, and we wanted it to feel real – the crowds and everything always moving.

PK: The monsoon light can be beautiful and horrific. Monsoon can be a relief from summer .... But the water can flood your house and it can be awful to get to work every day. That contradiction – romantic but also unpleasant. For people to go to work every day in the rain it's not romantic. It's really difficult.

AC: You don't have boundaries – fiction, documentary, hybrid animation. You've got illustration. In *A Night of Knowing Nothing*, there is found footage, there are fictional love letters. This is your first narrative fiction; did you find that constricting?

PK: Fiction is a whole different ball game – a lot more people involved, a lot of planning. Non-fiction, you can just go with your camera and shoot, and it might be a complete failure. You can't do that in fiction, it employs people, there's a lot of money on the line. So we find that restrictive. To counter that, we shot in different schedules. We shot, took a break, edited a bit, then went into the second shoot – which is closer to the non-fiction process: shoot, edit, reflect, and then see what you need.

AC: So your edit would shape what was to come? No bound script?

PK: There was a bound script but—

AC: But this would still have impact on what you would do next.

PK: Yeah. We realised that these actors are so amazing. There was camaraderie between them, which I hadn't expected. We worked together, we did workshops and spent a lot of time together, it was like a family. I changed the script a bit for the second half to accommodate something that I'd learnt.

AC: I just spoke with the actors. They said that all the improvisation was actually in those rehearsals, and so when you guys went to set, there was a very precise mapping of the performance. Tell me about this.
PK: It was a big learning for me. Even in FTII, I didn't get to work so closely with actors. The workshop was a learning process. I don't speak the language, and it's difficult to understand what is being spoken, even when it becomes internalised by the actors. So the workshops really helped. They really made the characters their own.

AC: They're lovely.
PK: They are the best. The time and commitment they gave – it's really a delight to work with people like this.

AC: Love is such a recurring theme in the films that the two of you make.
PK: We are at an age where people around us are getting married or in very serious relationships. And in our country love is extremely political. Caste or religion – it's been difficult. We are all having these conversations. I'm also a very big romantic so...

AC: You can see that in the movies. And here you are going up against Coppola and Cronenberg. What does that feel like?
PK: It's a bit overwhelming. These are filmmakers we really looked up to. So it's just really an honour. I'm really excited about Miguel Gomes. I wrote my thesis about him, I'm a fangirl. So it's like being in a candy shop, but also I'm nervous.

AC: What a year for FTII.
PK: It is great.

AC: From La Cinef to ACID, you guys are in the main competition now. What do you think a year like this can do for FTII?
RD: I don't think it's about what a year like this can do. It's a testament to the space and to what has been happening for many years now. It's a space that has given opportunity to a lot of us to grow and make films.
PK: The people we met – Maisam is my batch-mate and his film is also here, Raghu who was in the editing batch – we all grew up together. FTII changed how we think about the world and ourselves. Filmmaking is a very long process, and you need to find people who you can work with and who understand you. FTII gives the space to experiment . . . . And

that carries on even later. We need spaces like FTII and more, which are publicly funded in all states, so that everybody gets the opportunity. It's really expensive to become a filmmaker. You need to be able to not have a job and make films. So it would be nice for everybody to have an opportunity.

AC: Absolutely. I'm married to an FTII grad. I read that Janus Films has picked up *All We Imagine as Light* for US distribution. Do you have plans for India?
PK: Yeah, we are planning a release, and in Kerala. I think Kerala audiences really appreciate different kinds of cinema, and they have so many interesting filmmakers. It is really incredible. They also have a state fund supporting filmmakers. So I think that it would be great to start there and then also go to the rest of the country.
RD: I hope so.
AC: Well, I can't wait to see it. We are rooting for you.

25 May 2024

13

The Versatile Fahadh Faasil

Anupama Chopra: I want to start with your very singular ability to create menace on screen, right? You're not a physically imposing man. But on screen, you're terrifying. Shammi was terrifying; that repressed rage in *Joji*; in *Maamannan*, you're beating a dog to death. Of course, the cop in *Pushpa*. Even Ranga with *Aavesham* – charming and charismatic, but there's a sliver of danger. What are you tapping into to summon that unhinged intensity?

Fahadh Faasil: This is how I see it. And I don't think of it as a singular effort. If a different lensing was used for Shammi, I don't think it would have been this impactful . . . If my wife and sister on screen didn't react the way they did, or even without Sushin's background. Shammi speaks in a very measured manner, thanks to Syam. I cannot do this alone.

AC: Of course.
FF: With *Maamannan*, I had a big debate with Mari. Till the release of the film, I kept telling him, 'Nothing would change if you take off that killing-the-dog scene. The character would still be the same.'

AC: So even you didn't want to kill a dog?
FF: No, I don't like to do such things. Another time I have done this is in *Pushpa 1*, in the ending. For *Maamannan*, I honestly wanted it out. I am a dog-lover. So, to avoid all these contradictions, that's why I talk less.

AC: Do you ever scare yourself when you do a scene like that?
FF: No. I smell ketchup when I do all that because they put ketchup on my face, and I know it's not a dog.

AC: You are never like, 'Holy shit, what's inside me…'
FF: I asked that after giving the peeping shot for Shammi. That was the only time I actually judged something. Otherwise, I see it at the edit table and that's the end of it. I don't see the finished film.

AC: You don't watch your own movies?

FF: I watch much later. I watched *Trance* a few months back. When I see the final edit, that's when I can judge the film the best. I remember after Shammi, that shot, everyone was excited. I went to Syam, 'Are you happy?' I have read reviews, Ranga reminded them of Shammi – they don't even talk the same way or behave the same way. I've been hearing that for a long time, about Shammi in my characters. Shammi was so powerful. I've heard this about the actor who did *Psycho*, he could never come out of it.

AC: Ranga – I could happily hang out with. My favourite thing was the towel dance. Not a shred of vanity. You're in a towel and you're just jiving all over the room, no abs or muscles, which is normal where I come from. How do you let go of vanity completely?

FF: I don't know. I don't want to depend on any external factors to pull off a performance. When you work internally, everything changes, the way he walks, behaves. And I'm very comfortable with that. My wife said, 'You're taking off your shirt, just look presentable.' It was a celebration of the character. It was even wilder. What Jithu wanted to do was—

AC: Did you do it?

FF: No. Time was a factor. Jithu was always worried about that, and wanted to pack things in the first half. There are a couple of interesting scenes we took off. There are scenes we didn't shoot. That character itself was so wild, you could come up with any scene and somehow make it work.

AC: Yeah, yeah.

FF: In fact, I was talking to Jithu and a few other friends, it's Munnabhai.

AC: Munnabhai and Circuit. How good was he? How good was Ambaan?

FF: I know. I don't know if you've seen him earlier in *Romancham*.

AC: Yes, of course.

FF: Very interesting actor. I think he internalises. I've never spoken to him about how we're going to do it. He's never asked me anything. We were ready all the time. I was so comfortable with him. The only reason I wish to do a second part is to do more scenes with him. I love working with him.

AC: You talked earlier about how directors give you a phrase or a descriptor. Did Jithu give you anything for *Aavesham*?

FF: The character is loosely based on someone Jithu met when he was in college in Bangalore. He told me certain things about the character which I found very interesting. The first two weeks of shooting, he told me, 'If two people are talking, he'll observe. And he'll smile.' And that was very weird. 'He's not even in the conversation, and he smiles,' and he kept telling me that. Evidently, it's not used in any part of the film, but Ranga is like that.

AC: He's just happy to be alive. My favourite was when he said he doesn't get enough likes on Instagram.
FF: He wanted to be an actor. These are all backstories.

AC: He's a failed actor?
FF: Yes. We had a scene that shows he was a major fan of a particular kind of actor. Too much information.

AC: What a banner year for Malayalam cinema. You've got *Manjummel Boys*, *Premalu* – you are a co-producer; *Bramayugam*, *Aadujeevitham*, *Aavesham*. But in most of these films, women are not even supporting actors. They're almost not there.
FF: But the presence of mother is very strong in *Aavesham*, right? You don't see it, you feel it.

AC: Is it just a coincidence?
FF: With me, it's an absolute coincidence. I don't start or finish my films on time. Otherwise, I would have had Althaf's film releasing earlier this year. For *Aavesham*, I kept asking Jithu, 'I want a scene with my mom.' He'd say, 'That's old. Who would shoot flashbacks now?' I crave to bring in such emotions on screen, but I go in a very unplanned manner. My next film has a lot of women in it and women will love it.

AC: Women love *Aavesham*, too. You are credited with redefining the hero in Malayalam cinema. Shammi was the symbol of poisonous patriarchy, but you've also played ordinary men, broken men. Some called you Malayalam cinema's first metrosexual actor. Is it intentional?
FF: These are all reflections of things I've felt over the years. The life I've seen, the people I've met. The decisions I make now to do a film, it's because of who I am and the things I believe. I've never been fascinated by how good-looking the hero is or his ability to pull off something the

villain cannot. I wanted things to be as real as looking out of the window. But, you see, performance gives you a high. And it's different for each actor. I pick up on something.... But the idea is to do what you believe in, and make it entertaining. I just want the audience to watch it and just leave it there. The film will find them if it's truly haunting and all that. I want to do what I've seen growing up.

AC: Fahadh, every time you've given interviews, when I said that you're a pan-Indian star, you've always deflected it. I want to share a story with you. About two years ago, we set up this actors' roundtable. This big Bollywood actor said yes. And two days before the roundtable, I got a call from the manager saying, 'He's not going to show up.' I met him about a month later on a flight. He said, 'I didn't come because I thought you were going to put me in a room with Fahadh Faasil, and you didn't.' So, that's the impact you have. But especially post-*Pushpa* do you ever think you're huge, even beyond Kerala?

FF: No. I don't think *Pushpa* has done anything for me. I have to be very honest. No disrespect to anything. I don't think people expect magic from me, from seeing *Pushpa*. It's pure collaboration, and love for Suku Sir. My stuff is here. I and my friends believe Vicky Kaushal is the find of the decade. Rajkummar Rao, one of the finest. Ranveer, best actor in the country. I was surprised people are watching *Kumbalangi* and *Trance*. I kept wondering, what is the connect? What is it that they're identifying with? And even now it's the art form, the setting up, the honesty in the narrative. It started around 2018–2019. But now, there are non-Malayalam-speaking families who watch Malayalam releases. Very exciting.

AC: But do you believe you're a pan-Indian star?
FF: No. I'm just an actor here. Films do business, that's secondary. But the films I do here, I can never do anywhere else. I can easily set up a film in Tamil, Hindi, but everything would fall in place except the idea.

AC: So, the freedom here is what you treasure the most?
FF: Yeah.

AC: What it gives you is what nourishes you?
FF: And it's okay if I don't promote, the audience understands. I'm not saying it's a good thing not to promote your films. I just want to

interact after people see it. I spent a year making this film and now for me to come and explain? I don't think it's fair. It's much better to discuss after the audience has also discovered what you were trying to attempt. I spoke to Karan after he watched *Aavesham*. He loved it. He called me after watching *Trance* and *Kumbalangi*. Very sweet. I speak to Vicky after every release of his. And Rajkummar. I love that pan-India interacting with your friends. Absolutely brilliant guys. Nothing beyond that.

AC: And no Hindi film has appealed to you yet?
FF: I had said yes to the first script that came, Vishal Sir's, five or six years back. And I don't know, he couldn't put it in place. Then I moved on. Nothing serious has come since. I messaged Imtiaz Ali last night.

AC: Did you see *Chamkila*?
FF: I loved it. I've been hearing about *Chamkila* for the last two years. When *Malayankunju* was in Rahman Sir's studio, *Chamkila* was also there. I was waiting for this film and I loved it. I spoke to Imtiaz. The right film has not come. I understand very little Hindi, so I have to play a South Indian who speaks Hindi in Kashmir or something.

AC: It's fine, we'll take it. I don't have a problem, just do it!
FF: Let's see. I am open to it. I've done Telugu, Tamil films.

AC: Speaking of *Pushpa*, there's a lot of chatter about how you are Indian cinema's highest-paid villain. Does money factor into your choices?
FF: Money is, of course, a factor, but money is not the only factor. Something has to excite me for me to leave my house and it's not money. I love interacting with Suku Sir. So, I go there with that understanding and my sensibilities. And there's happiness around working, with everyone there. But I don't know if I'm the highest-paid villain.

AC: Well, it would be nice.
FF: I don't know.

AC: You know, Fahadh—
FF: Sorry, before I met B.R. Baradwaj Rangan, he had reviewed one of my Tamil films, I won't say which one, where I played a villain. And he said I did it for some foreign car or something.

AC: It was the paycheck!
FF: Yeah, it was on the review, and I was like, 'Oh my God!'

AC: So, you've never done a film for the money ever?
FF: No. I've made lots of money, with *Kumbalangi Nights*, *Trance*. I don't have to depend on that. I belong to a family who did cinema for over forty years, and I know how unstable this business is. All that I wish for is financial stability. I wish I stay stable, regardless of my films doing bad or good.

AC: Yeah. It's a tough one.
FF: Everything is a bonus. I came here for a holiday. My visa renewal didn't happen. Mom was asking, 'What are you doing?' – every day. One day I said, 'I'm going to write a film.' Then she gave me three or four months off. I was not doing anything, just fooling around. Then I met director Ranjith, and he put me up with Uday and that's how my first comeback happened. Then I thought, I'll do one more and go back. And then *Chaappa Kurishu* happened.

AC: So, if that visa had come through...?
FF: I would have gone!

AC: Are you serious?!
FF: I loved that country. I landed when I was eighteen, I was there till I was twenty-six.

AC: How do you stay grounded despite success? You said that one morning, there was no milk in the house, and you went down and got the milk. Can you still do that, Fahadh?
FF: Yeah, I still do that.

AC: And you don't get mobbed?
FF: They look at me and smile, and that's enough for me. The moment they ask me for a selfie, I run. The most I expect from all that I do is just an acknowledgement, nothing more. I tell openly, 'Don't watch my bad films. Watch it only if it's good.' There is a freedom I get here, to go out. I am enjoying that. I don't like to be photographed, especially when I am out with my mom and my wife.

AC: So, you don't want fans coming up to you and saying—
FF: I don't want anyone, not just fans. I would never use the term fans. Just smile at me, man, it's the best you can give me. A lot of people do that. They are beautiful.

AC: I have just started reading Ed Zwick's book. He talks about the complexity of success and the nobility of failure. After two decades, Fahadh, do you see that?
FF: Today, I structure my films in a way that even if it doesn't do magic in the box office, everyone involved is covered. Still, people see me upset when stuff goes wrong. They ask me, 'What is it?' There is nothing to be worried about.' When you are doing a film, it is the result of your thoughts, belief system, the society, your observations. When a film fails, what hurts the most is that my thoughts were wrong; the way I looked at things. That's very disturbing and happens only through failures. I have learnt more from things not working more than films that work. Before *Trance* was released, everyone knew that the second half of the film had an issue. We tried to address it but there was no way to conclude the film the way we wanted to. Or we had to change the entire narrative of the second half. We were prepared.

AC: Has the experience made it easier to deal with failure?
FF: My wife says, 'You've been doing it for twelve years, man. Chill!' It doesn't affect me like it used to, I move on fast now. You could be right or wrong, but never be in a position where you're doubtful. The most important thing is the film I'm shooting at the moment.

AC: I've seen your ads. You're selling ice cream.
FF: 'Penthouse, this is a penthouse! There's a Porsche!'

AC: Many actors speak about themselves as a brand. Do you?
FF: No. Then all my films should work right? I strongly don't think I'm a brand. I endorse primarily because *they* believe that, not because I do. I did an ice cream ad with my wife, we totally enjoyed.

AC: That looked like fun.
FF: They would send us ice cream every weekend.

AC: So, you did it for the ice cream?
FF: Yeah, every flavour they had would come home. Even new ones.

AC: Okay, so, we can basically seduce you with ice cream, that's it?
FF: Ice cream is also one factor, yeah.

AC: Despite all the accolades, you still speak of yourself as a very insecure actor. You talk about going to the monitor, talking about lenses with the DOPs. When I started this conversation, you immediately gave credit to everybody else. Do you think insecurity fuels you?
FF: I don't know if it's insecurity or that I don't know anything about cinematography, music, audiography. So, I feel that I can always ask. I can honestly ask, 'How would this look in eighty-five?' And Shyju has laughed, 'No one would shoot that in eighty-five, man!' Sometimes Shyju gets sparked, like, 'Let's try that.' For me, it's a trial-and-error process, and this interaction is also basically to explore. I'm sure, in whatever small way, I've challenged Shyju, Jithu. One individual, I don't think, can do anything.

AC: No, absolutely. Especially with cinema. But do you have a sense, Fahadh, when you do a shot, 'Okay, I nailed it'?
FF: I've gotten happy a couple of times.

AC: Couple of shots?
FF: No, some seven or eight shots...

AC: In your entire filmography, seven or eight shots that you were happy with?
FF: I think, yeah.

AC: And the rest?
FF: I see it as the film or the scene, whether it's actually working, taking the screenplay ahead. But there are certain scenes where I have to be really good. So, yeah, there are times I'm really happy with my work.

AC: You're not on social, but we see you on Nazriya's Instagram. Does she have to run this by you?
FF: Absolutely not. She's a star herself, she's an individual.

AC: Of course, she is! But are you conscious about what is going out there about you?
FF: No, my wife is putting it, right?

AC: You don't care?
FF: I don't care. If I'm bad, the blame goes to her. Someone asked me . . . . So, Nazriya sang in *Aavesham*. I had no clue she sang in *Aavesham*. She never told me that. We give total freedom to each other. We love the way we function. She can do whatever she wants with her life. And her life is also me now.

AC: And she's never tried to convince you to go get on Instagram?
FF: She knows it's impossible. I have never turned on the camera on my phone. Except for a wildlife trip or something. I'm not that exciting as an individual, I'm quite boring.

AC: Does she still give you instructions?
FF: My answer will never be to the point, it will just go around, but the answer will be somewhere there – it's up to the listener. She's always worried about that. It's good that she sees me as just I am. She sees all my weakness, my insecurities. I'm very fortunate that way. I think that makes a lot of difference in the life you're living.

AC: And we are fortunate to have you as an actor.
FF: Thank you, ma'am.

6 May 2024

14

Priyanka Chopra Jonas: Redefining 'Bold'

Anupama Chopra: Priyanka, you said, 'Good girls don't make history, bold girls make history.' You've been bold for as long as I can remember. This year is your twentieth year in Hindi cinema. *The Hero* released in 2003. Our first interview was two years after that for a story in the *New York Times* about Hindi film heroines becoming bad on screen.
Priyanka Chopra: Oh, when I did *Aitraaz*.

AC: You played this sexual predator. You were bold then. You are bold now. What does it take to be a consistent disruptor?
PC: I was lucky to have an upbringing where my parents gave me a sense of self and the ability to make my own choices. A lot of girls don't get that. Once a girl stands on her own feet, she takes her family, community, and country forward. Women are 50 per cent of the world's population and have always had to step back. It's our responsibility – men, women, communities – to empower girls. I was four years old when my father encouraged my opinions. He came from a middle-class background, so did my mom. But he took my voice seriously. In military houses, nameplates say who's staying there. My dad was a major, my mom a captain. I saw the nameplate and asked, 'Do I live here?' He said yes. I said, 'Why isn't my name on it?' He changed it to say 'Priyanka Mimi Chopra KGB', for Kindergarten B. That's what I mean – taking children seriously. As a new parent, I know how important it is to invest in our girls.

AC: I think you've redefined bold.
PC: In a good way?

AC: In a good way. Pehele kehte the, badi bold hai (before they used to say, she's very bold).
PC: Mujhe voh bhi kaha tha (They even said that to me). I converted it into a good thing.

AC: You are now headlining *Citadel*. First Indian actor to headline a global spy series. 200 million dollars, upward of 1,600 crore rupees.
PC: Mujhe toh maths nahi aati (I don't know math). I can't convert between rupees and dollars.

AC: Bahot paise hain (It's a lot of money).
PC: It's above my pay grade.

AC: What do you want it to do for yourself, for others?
PC: I started looking for work in Hollywood in 2013. It's been ten years. For immigrant actors, it takes perseverance. When I began, there were four or five South Asians. We all knew each other. Our goal – Mindy, Aziz, Kal Penn, me – was to open the door for others. I believe in hard work. I made a showreel, walked into meetings, did auditions, got small roles and grew them. I have a first-look deal with Amazon Prime, producing stories about South Asia and our diaspora. I started that four years ago. I'm proud to work with a streamer invested in Indian stories. I'm working with incredible new writers, like I did with Purple Pebble in India when I started making regional movies. Regional movies, first-time writers and directors – I work with new voices now too. No one opened doors for me when I started. I want to be the shoulders that others can jump off of.

AC: That's wonderful, thank you.
PC: There's one show that Purple Pebble was presenting, and they'd been knocking on all these doors. We got them in at Prime. She gave me a hug, and said, 'To be able to just know that I have someone I can call and say, hey, I'm from your part of the world, can you connect me to someone? Can you show me the way?' To be able to be that conduit really gives me so much satisfaction.

AC: Priyanka, you've been famous for most of your adult life. Now the fame is outsized, right? Eighty-five million followers on Instagram. It's insane. But your job is to make us forget about Priyanka and enter a character. Does that get harder?
PC: Fame is a by-product, not what I was seeking. I wanted people to like my work and take me seriously. I'm creative. I protect myself so I can protect my characters. I've never played myself. Like Nadia – she has no sense of humour. I'm goofy and funny. She's serious and tough. I cry easily and share openly. That keeps me sane and rooted. On *Citadel*, Richard and

I relied on each other. The show is non-linear, so we worked closely with writers to make sure everything made sense. We worked as a unit, which helped us be honest to the characters.

AC: So when you you're in front of the camera on set, you are fully able to disconnect from the noise.
PC: That's what I do. That's my job. It's between action and cut. I have been trained in Bollywood movies. I've been in the middle of Trafalgar Square, with 500 people around me, dancing in front of a horse. Nothing shakes you after that.

AC: When we look at you, we see this woman in charge – 23,000 square-foot home, rock star husband, a gorgeous daughter. But you talked about how tough it's been – politics, bullying, trolling. When your daughter was born, all sorts of comments were passed. How do you disconnect from that?
PC: I came to terms with fame very early. I realised that women, specifically, are more written about. About everything else but their achievements, how they fell on a stage, who's her boyfriend. I took a decision to keep my private life very private. I've never spoken about it. I'm a public figure. You can talk about me, I can't stop you. You can sit with your grandparents and say, 'Achha usne to yeh pehna tha (Well, she wore this).' I can't come into your houses and do that. So I have to make peace with the fact that that's going to happen. I did that very early. I started protecting myself by creating a really tight circle of people that I trust. My team, my family, my friends. I can count twenty people in my life that have been consistent for years. I recommend that to all young people. We live in the world of social media, which is kind of like being famous anyway. It's kind of the same thing. You are always looking for validation on the internet. We're all looking at comments. We're trying to find the best angle. And on social media, including me, we put out the best versions of ourselves, right? I don't have that luxury as a public person. You can literally lip-read and say that I said something and that will become an article. I made peace with that a very long time ago. When I wrap up work – usually 7 o'clock, I sit with my family and my friends and have time for myself to enrich my soul. I didn't do that in my twenties. And I burnt myself out. I went through a really, really dark phase where I was working too much. I didn't know how to emotionally feel. I was dealing with a lot of loss and grief and changes. I had to step

back and take time out and prioritise what was important. And I'm very clear about my priorities today. And I'm the most content and happy I've ever been.

AC: Well, you look it! Coming back to what you had talked about, specifically about the politics or the bullying, what can we do?
PC: I think conversation is very important. We get caught up in pointing fingers, playing blame games. Cancel culture is so prevalent right now that people think that's the solution to everything. I completely disagree. It is never one or two persons' fault. It is a society and a community that perpetuates that. We need to think about how we create opportunities, a positive workspace, make space for others instead of having a smaller and smaller table. How does your table become larger? How do you give more people a seat? I have incredible friends, amazing filmmakers, but certain cliques always do that. That'll happen in every profession. Creating more space for people is very important in every job. To create a good, positive working environment – with transparency, with respect. Respect cannot be demanded. It has to be commanded. When you walk into a room, you have to walk in with a sense of self. That's very hard when you're young, new, and scared. I always encourage young people, especially young girls, in this world of information – misinformation, fake, or correct – you have to really take time to see what affects you, what moves you, what you care about, what is important. The noise just kind of goes away. And when the noise goes away, you find that self-confidence. That's what I tried to do. Of course I was intimidated. Of course I was weak in the knees and terrified. But I tried to cut the noise out and I took my next step. I didn't think about the large picture. I knew if I take one step and make it excellent, then take the next and make it excellent, hopefully my journey will be excellent. And here we are now.

AC: *Citadel* started as a conversation you had with Amazon studio head Jennifer Salke years ago.
PC: Five years ago. Crazy.

AC: The fact that she's in charge has some role to play also in the fact that this is the first time in your life that you've got pay parity. So a woman in the position of power really makes a difference.
PC: Absolutely.

AC: *Film Companion* does a report with Amazon and with Ormax called *O Womaniya*, an annual report on women in entertainment. And last year, the report found that if a woman is heading any project, it even impacts the talk time that women have in trailers. It's 35 per cent if there's a woman in charge, it's 22 per cent if there's a man in charge.
PC: Wow.

AC: The sad thing is, in the projects that we looked at in the Hindi film industry, only 10 per cent of the HODs were women. So how do we change this?
PC: We are already changing it. We are already changing it. I'm so proud of the women of my generation – female actors, directors, and a few amazing men – who have taken it upon themselves to create more opportunities for women in the industry, in front of and behind the camera. We have Aparna sitting here who heads the India side of this studio. She's formidable and pulling up other women. Jen set that top-down tone. The more women there are in positions of power, the more we'll see women in decision-making, and then impact on communities – on men and women alike. Women have been deprived of opportunity for such a long time. Especially in positions of power, we have to work four times harder than men to get there. When a woman is in charge, she's 'tough'. There are derogatory words used. If a man were the same, we'd say he's 'impressive'. We get intimidated. That conversation needs to change. We have to normalise wanting women in power, respecting women in power. We pray to goddesses. We believe in Durga. We believe in the power of dadis and moms. Why can't we take that outside of our homes? Why can't the conversation about equity also be inside our homes? Durga is relevant to all of us, and we really have to go back and remind ourselves that, you know, women are what make our families. We are matriarchal as well. We believe in the power of dadis and nanis and moms, and we always go back to that. My grandmother had four daughters. My grandfather was sure they'd all be educated, and they were. Then they changed the lives of their daughters. Their daughters are changing lives now. I think it's very important to raise our sons respecting our daughters.

AC: You're absolutely right, Priyanka, because I've done this for twenty-five years. And when I started, women didn't talk about these things.
PC: You're not supposed to talk about it.

AC: We all accepted that as the norm. None of us questioned it. No female actor would talk about pay parity.

PC: I also didn't expect it when my agents told me, 'You're playing a co-lead, let us go and talk to Amazon about getting you parity.' I was like, 'Okay, it's never going to happen.' Even I didn't believe it, because for so many years, I fought that fight. I never asked for parity, I only asked for a little bit more. So I just gave up the fight. I was so jaded. I was like, 'That's not going to happen.' I have to give a shout-out to my agents, UTA. They were like, 'Let's have that conversation.' And then Amazon, which said, 'That's fair, and that's how the show is going to be. They're both co-leads, they'll get the same parity, same perks.' I was shocked. I popped champagne, my family was celebrating. I've had a twenty-two-year career, one step at a time. One win at a time. And then you look back, and your life is a win.

AC: Prime also runs Maitri, headed by Smriti Kiran. It's a collective for women in entertainment. Do you think these perpetuate the change faster?

PC: Absolutely. When women are surrounded by each other, there's magic. For the longest time, women were pitted against each other. The most beautiful girl gets the job, or the boy. Actresses can't be friends. They have catfights. Nobody talked about that with boys – it's a bromance.

AC: We always heard, ki do heroine hai toh ladhai toh hogi (if there are two heroines, there will be a fight).

PC: Of course. And that was perpetuated. I'm so proud of my generation of women, not just in entertainment – all of you who have created a sisterhood. We can be friends, support each other. In fact, we can do business together. We can make money together, create opportunities for other women. Now I know that the next generation will not inherit that problem.

AC: You said, you're the happiest you've ever been, right?
PC: Content.

AC: Content. Is there anything you wish you had done differently?
PC: I wish I hadn't shed as many tears as I did, beaten myself up as much as I did.

AC: Why did you beat yourself up?
PC: Because that's what we are taught to do. When you're young, you feel like one failure is the end of your life. Or one breakup. Or one friendship. Or one fight. You feel like you can never come back from that. And I am a very intense person, very sentimental, emotional. Energies affect me. If I've hurt someone, it affects me. So, I think, I used to really beat myself up when something went wrong. I used to say it's my fault. And I would like to tell my younger self, life is all hills and valleys. It's never going to be a smooth road. When it's down, you will go up. So, when you're up, be prepared for a down. And it's okay. Surround yourself by people who are genuinely happy for you. Not all the followers. But the ones that pick up your phone call at two in the morning. That will sit with you for hours, overnight. Those are the ones you keep for the rest of your life, the biggest riches in the world. And I had that when I was 20. I just ignored it because I thought my new life and this industry and my career was the most important thing. And having a support system that makes you want to step forward every single day. Have the right people in your life.

AC: You know, as long as I've known you it's always been world domination plans – always, I want everything. Which is wonderful. Has that changed at all?
PC: I think so. There's always a glass ceiling that is set up for women. I just don't like a glass ceiling. My dad told me this. There are glass ceilings set for everyone – girls, minorities, immigrants. People will have all kinds of opinions and noise that will turn your personality into what they think you are. Yes – age, maturity, motherhood, battles and overcoming, reaching a plateau. Getting to that place required a journey. Being kind to yourself, which I didn't do a lot of times, which I do now, is crucial.

AC: What does that mean?
PC: I'm an ambitious girl. I want everything that's bigger and better. But there were times where I forgot to sleep, forgot to eat, forgot birthdays, wasn't home for Diwali, worked on Christmas. My mom used to say, 'You have so many stamps on your passport but you've never really been anywhere.' And it's true. Hotel room to set, set to hotel. I took my first holiday almost ten or twelve years after I started working. Now I've invested in myself. I'm trying to find things I like outside of work. I haven't found it yet. I'm a really bad painter, I found that out. Shouldn't have bought that easel.

AC: What are you painting?
PC: I don't know. I had a really ambitious . . . . I found this beautiful billboard in black and red. And I bought a black easel and I said, 'Yeh toh easy hai (This is easy).' It ended up looking like watercolours by a two-year-old. It was so embarrassing, I decided painting was not the thing. I've tried knitting, I'm going to try pottery.

AC: You're knitting?
PC: I knitted a scarf. It was nine feet long, because I don't know how to do corners.

AC: Matlab voh end hi nahi hota (That means it never really ends).
PC: Chalta hi gaya (It just kept going). Angry knitting.

AC: You're competitive in your knitting as well?
PC: All my emotions have been poured into the scarf. Now I take time for myself. I'll take a holiday, spend time with my friends, laugh a little. I don't always live in work. I think we're told that for a very long time, that if you stop working, somebody else will get that opportunity. Don't stop working, but have a work-life balance. If you invest in yourself and you're really good at what you do and you find your rhythm and your strengths, it just becomes so much better. You're inspired, you're excited and that's how I'm being kind to myself.

AC: I remember a conversation we had five years ago, before your marriage – I asked, what have you given to your career, and you said, my life.
PC: Completely, I did not have my twenties. I don't remember anything except being on set or on trailers or my team. In my thirties, I started going to America. And I was having a little bit of a two-second music career and I had a great time. I love music. Musicians are incredible. Musicians and writers, people that can create from air. As actors, we lean on other people's words, direction – we are given way too much credit. But writers, people who conceptualise, come up with ideas, whether that's for music, books, art – I'm a big admirer. When I started doing music, I was in the room with these people that I'd grown up admiring, will.i.am, Pitbull, RedOne and I suddenly started doing stuff that I liked. Honestly after I heard my first song I was like, 'Oh I don't know if this is going to be long-term,' but I was enjoying it too much. I realised that I really have fun when

I hang out with my team after work. We find a new restaurant or go to the theatre. Those were things I just never did and maybe because I had a little bit of anonymity in America. I started doing stuff like that and it shifted my mindset. I started looking for like-minded people to collaborate with, making friends that like similar things, taking time out. Going away for a weekend? It was such a new novel concept.

AC: Here's the thing I don't get, despite the incredible fame, you are able to look at that music career and honestly say it was two seconds.
PC: In my twenty-two-year career, it was two seconds only. There are literally four singles.

AC: But you're able to see it objectively and say, 'Maybe I wasn't so good at this.' There's not a lot of famous people who can do that.
PC: I come from a place of honesty. I think it's just easier to be authentic and transparent. Tell me what you really feel so we can all talk about it. It's all on my timeline. I don't have a sense of ego when I walk into a room. I know when my films haven't done well. I know when they have done well. I don't rest on my laurels. I'm looking for the next thing – how I can beat what I just did. I can be very honest and say, 'Okay, that was bad,' cry and I dust myself off. Failure is going to happen to all of us.

AC: That deserves a round of applause. Are you good with failure?
PC: No, it takes a lot of dramatics before it comes out of my system. Overeating, over-thinking, over-crying, watching movies for five days and not talking to anyone. It sucks when you fail, any dent hurts when you work really hard. Especially in my job. My job is so inconsistent. I don't know where my next cheque is coming from till I sign my next film. It's really a terrifying thought to build a twenty-two-year career with that kind of inconsistency. I think it's easier for me when I'm more realistic about it. To be able to be better, I cannot be deluded. I don't like being deluded and I don't like deluded people.

AC: You said, 'I don't like to sit in the shit.'
PC: I don't, it stinks. It'll stink. You'll stink. Go have a shower, get out of here.

AC: What do you do? Practically, to not sit in the shit?
PC: Lots of tissue paper. I picked a really solid metaphor. Life throws stuff at you, and sometimes it feels like quicksand. You can't see hope. We've

all been through that. You should mourn what you're feeling. I believe in talking about it – find a person you trust. When you're alone, fear becomes big. But when you talk to someone – family, loved one, therapist – the power goes away from it. So what I do is – diffuse it. Say I have an issue with you – next time I meet you, I'll talk to you about it. We talk for five minutes, it's over. I don't carry that baggage. Life is easier when you let it go. You're so heavy, you're never going to rise above the water. I like breathing fresh, clean air.

AC: I deeply admire how much you get done in a day, okay. We also work together on the Jio MAMI Mumbai Film Festival and it's unbelievable that you sit on it with the kind of detail that you do. How do you do it?
PC: If I can't do it, I won't take it on. You called me and said, 'I want you to be chairperson this year, I want us to go in a different direction, how can we do it?' I thought about it, I talked to my team and I was like, 'All right, I want to be able to prioritise this.' I think MAMI is such an incredible destination for filmmakers pan-India. That excited me. When I take any responsibility on, I divide the time in my life and it really helps to have an excellent team, I could not have done this alone. My team is my greatest strength. I don't have to sit on scheduling, the minutia, I can actually be the creative that I am. But I also do like multitasking. I'm greedy, I don't like to give up opportunities. In twenty-four hours, if I want to sleep for eight hours, ten hours of my life will be dedicated to all the various things that I have to do. I am so productive because I've figured out my priorities. It's like Jenga, you kind of have to fit it in and pull it out and hope it doesn't fall.

From the Floor: Q&A

Audience member: What was the most challenging part of making *Citadel*?
PC: It was a year and a half of shooting, and I'm used to sixty to ninety days. This was a year and a half for six episodes, it was a lot of work. It's a complex show, timelines jump, characters jump. Also we shot it during Covid. As actors on a set, we're the only ones that take off our masks so it was very scary. While everyone was in PPE . . . I went back to work in October of 2020 for *The Matrix Resurrections*. We were filming in Berlin and I remember crying and I was scared, I didn't want to talk to anyone. So filmmaking is not rocket science, we're not saving lives or anything, we're just making movies – so it's fun, it should be fun. This was tough because of the emotional setbacks, the physical demands. I think being able to

work with an amazing team helped and keeping friends and family close. And my dogs were with me.

Audience member: What is the greatest life lesson you learnt in your journey of success?
PC: I think the greatest life lesson that I have learnt in my journey so far is to really find the reason you go to work everyday. Don't just be a zombie. I'm lucky because I go from project to project, I know there are many people who have one job for a long time, and that's hard. Have a sense of passion for whatever, whether it's your job, your life, your hobby – to have a sense of passion gives you a sense of purpose.

Audience Member: What's next for you? Would you love to direct or write?
PC: I don't think it'll be fun, it'll be terrifying. Yes, I do aim to evolve. I've been offered opportunities to direct, which I declined. I prepare and immerse myself. If I had to direct, I'd disappear for six months. So I tell my team, 'When will you give me six months off?' But I want to do it. I hope it's in my future. I want to build a career in America like I did in India. I've worked with the best talent in India, I've done a variety of genres. I haven't done that in Hollywood yet. I want to explore more roles. *Love Again* is coming out on 12 May – it's a romantic comedy, the opposite of *Citadel*. I want to be surprising there like I was here.

Audience Member: What is more difficult – to get into the psyche of that character, or to get out after the project?
PC: To get into it. I'm not very method. It only happened to me once where my mother was like, 'Snap out of it if you're going to come into my house…' I used to walk in slowly, talk deliberately, I'd pick up my coffee cup like this, look at you slowly. My mother was like, 'Hello koi camera nahi hai (There is no camera).' I was working with Kareena and Akshay at that time. They were big movie stars. My mother took a video of me talking to somebody once and showed it to me, and I was so embarrassed that I quickly realised that I have to leave my characters on set. When I read a script I like to familiarise myself with the character – she's like my best friend or someone that I've known for years. Before I go on to set, I throw my script away. I come in completely unprepared. I know my lines but I don't think about how I'm going to do the scene. If I know my character, I know exactly how she will react. It gives me the ability to create magic. I don't benefit from too much practice, I become very robotic.

Audience Member: As an actress and as a viewer, what is one genre which you will never get tired of?

PC: Real-life crime dramas. Murder documentaries. I can watch reruns of *SVU* and *Law & Order* and all of that. Another one – I think good romantic comedies. I love having tears in my eyes because my heart is full. I love walking out with a skip in my step because the hero and the heroine found each other. I watched *Jerry Maguire* recently. It reminded me of my teenage years. At the time, it was my favourite movie.

19 April 2023

15

Imran Khan: Planning the Comeback

Anupama Chopra: Imran, it is so, so good to see you. I want to start with the question that's on everyone's mind. You've said that you're reading scripts. You don't have a plan.
Imran Khan: Yeah.

AC: But you said this about six to five months ago?
IK: Yeah, that was in October.

AC: So have you seen anything you liked?
IK: I'm still grappling with the whole thing. This whole thing has been sudden and unplanned. I wasn't quite prepared for the idea of, 'Okay, I'm going to re-engage with public life, with the film industry, restart work.' Since then, I have slowly started to re-engage with the film industry. I've started to have those creative conversations. What am I interested in? I've read a couple of things that I've liked. I'm sitting with these folks to try and develop it. I have not been offered anything that is absolutely ready to go, that I have connected with. Things that resonated are a little more kaccha (raw), that's the stage that I'm at.

AC: You're baking.
IK: I'm baking, cooking. I'm in pre-pre-production.

AC: In the interview that you did with *Vogue*, you talked about how in your twenties, you gravitated towards characters who were where you were.
IK: Yeah.

AC: Rats in *Jaane Tu... Ya Jaane Na* or Jay in *I Hate Luv Storys* or Rahul in *Ek Main Aur Ekk Tu*.
IK: Boys finding their way into manhood.

AC: You said, 'Now I have a child. I've been through a divorce. I've had a career setback. So I have to find things that speak to where I am in life.' Where are you in life?

IK: So my last film release was *Katti Batti*, which released when I was thirty-one. Today I am forty-one. I spent my twenties building a career that ended up being not the thing that I felt like focusing on in my thirties. These past ten years I have spent kind of grappling with larger questions of who am I? What do I want to do? And having started a film career at a very young age, it would seem logical that that's just what you follow through with. A series of life circumstances led me to a place where I was not getting the fulfilment that I was seeking. And I guess somewhere I was unafraid of the idea of saying, 'If not this, what if something else entirely?' It has been my tremendous privilege and good fortune that I was financially secure. But I said, 'Okay, I don't have to worry about money. My family, my needs, the roof over my head are taken care of. What else? How do I want to approach my life?' That was not coming from the film industry.

AC: So did you fall out of love with films or the industry?

IK: Working professionally in the film industry, you exist within an ecosystem, And everyone who exists within that ecosystem is primed to consider everything from a monetary perspective. And I started to buy into it more and more. So the only value system then becomes bottom dollar. And that was never the reason that I was interested in films. I grew up enamoured with cinema. As a maker, I love every part of it. I love to write. I love pre-production. I love sitting with set designers, costume designers, being on set. And somewhere I started to buy into the notion that if you don't earn this many dollars, there is no value to it. Ultimately it took the joy out of it for me.

AC: You've said that it broke your heart when *Katti Batti* didn't work. So was failure the immediate trigger?

IK: Yes. At that moment, I didn't consider it that way. That on this day, I quit. It was kind of a process of a week becoming a month, becoming a year or two, where I said, 'Okay my heart's not in it.' So I was attached to at least one project being developed, after *Katti Batti*. But my heart disconnected and said, 'I can't do this thing.' It was wanting to not engage with something that didn't feel absolutely right. And as time has gone on, I've been re-looking at the films.

AC: And posting about it.

IK: Looking at them through the eyes of an audience. And someone will message me today and say they saw *Break Ke Baad*, a fifteen-year-old movie. A commercial disappointment, but someone remembers it today. It holds meaning for someone. And that reminds me, that's the point. You don't measure it by weekend box office. You measure it by emotional resonance over time.

AC: You also talked about how you felt a little damaged inside. In March 2017 you said that you sought out therapy.

IK: 13 March.

AC: And you've kept it four times a week?

IK: I've missed, uh—

AC: A few?

IK: It's part of the process. You have setbacks and you get back on.

AC: What role has therapy played in your life?

IK: I have never had the stigma. My mother is a working psychoanalyst. From early on, I was exposed to the world of mental health. And it was normalised and destigmatised. Like any kind of medicine. So I did not have a hurdle to overcome. The hurdle, in fact, that most people have, is recognising, 'Oh, am I stuck in a pattern without realising it?' To catch that is tricky. But having become cognizant of that, how do I address this? And where do I prioritize this within my life? If someone were to have a physical health scare, a heart attack at a young age, you drop everything and you change your lifestyle.

AC: Whatever it takes.

IK: Same also for mental health. That's basically how I approached it. I had a mental health scare and I reached a place where I said, 'I'm not okay.' And there is a mental self-image that you have. And I realised that I was not that, I was much more fearful, scared, anxious. But in my head, I see myself as a capable, strong, confident person, but I was not actually engaging with the world in that way. That disconnect is finally what kind of led me to make that my priority. And I said, 'I can put my work down for now. It is not my job to be an actor. Fixing myself is not optional.'

AC: But those years, Imran, post the film, you almost completely disappeared. You made the short film *Mission Mars: Keep Walking India* in 2018. And then until last year when you resurfaced on Instagram, there was no sign of you. What were those years like? How did you cope?

IK: There were many deeply challenging days. I removed myself from the film industry and this world because I was not able to engage with any part of that. The trappings and the baggage associated with that life, it's difficult to navigate at the best of times.

AC: Yeah.

IK: The strongest, healthiest, well-balanced individual will still face hurdles navigating this world. It's complicated. I was able to recognize that I'm not in a condition to engage with that. I dropped all parts of it. I said, 'I am not that person anymore.' Any of the trappings associated with that, I shed. I still continue to engage in that way. I don't have PR people, agents, managers. I didn't want to engage through that lens. What are the things that you actually need in your life? What are the things that are valuable to you? What can you do without? And once you know they don't hold power over you, it's a lot easier then.

AC: But Imran, it's such a seductive space. Was walking away hard?
IK: No, not at all.

AC: When you were done, you were just done.
IK: I've never been enamoured with it.

AC: The peripherals is not what brought you there in the first place.
IK: I've never been very impressed with stardom. I've never been impressed with myself. I have never valued all of these ephemeral parts. it's just that – it's dust. It's the way the wind blows, you're hot, you're cold. But I'm still me. The week before *Jaane Tu... Ya Jaane Na* released, nobody cared if I walked down the street. The week after, suddenly there are people chasing my car. A film doesn't do well, and the same industry people think you're out of season. The actual value is the thing that you believe in, the thing that you love doing. I love to make movies. I love to tell stories. And I've been fortunate to make stories that have resonated with people. And because people will still tell me, 'I love that film of yours.' That is the value.

AC: Did you miss being on set?
IK: Yeah.

AC: But never enough to say, 'Let me give it a shot'?
IK: Not in those years. I was just not capable of doing these things. I was barely functioning. When you're tackling deep and severe depression, just getting up in the morning and brushing your teeth, then taking a shower is a monumental task. That's where analysis helped, because I had steady appointments. If I did not have that, there are many days that I would not have gotten out of bed. Sunrise to sunset, you can just stay in bed – but I had to go to analysis. It got me out of bed, out of the house. It kept me moving. And for a long time, that was as much as I was capable of. I would go to analysis and come back. I was wiped out. Bit by bit, I have become stronger and more capable of engaging with life. But I couldn't have done it back then.

AC: What has this re-engaging been like? The film industry is a very different place. Even in just ten years. What's it been like to slowly just come back?
IK: It's not all that different. What's the thing you say? Same, same, but different.

AC: Ha. Yes.
IK: Sure, we've got Netflix and Amazon and all this digital space. And it's awesome the way that they have thrown the doors open to all manner of content creators. But the core of the thing is still – who's hot today? How much money can I get for this? They dress it up a little differently,

AC: You said that you're amazed at how much people still love you, talk about your films. I mean, there are people who come to our office only because you're here.
IK: Because there is this conventional wisdom – you're out of sight, out of mind.

AC: But you're not.
IK: That's what I'm saying. And at the time that I was working, everything was still largely dominated by legacy media, television channels. So we had television, we had newspapers and magazines. And as social media has started to come in, everyone has their own little soapbox to stand on. So much content.

AC: Look at me.
IK: 'Hi guys, you can watch me do push-ups now.' So within that world, one assumes that you will just disappear. And I did my best, genuinely. I did not engage via those threads. You know how desperately people cling on to the spotlight?

AC: Yeah.
IK: I did exactly the opposite of what you are supposed to do to stay relevant. Yet, here we are.

AC: So here's my theory. In your most successful films – all the rom-coms – you redefined masculinity with these characters. Sweet, sincere, bumbling boys becoming men. When you tried the old school masculinity in *Luck*, *Kidnap*, that didn't land. I think, you were woke before we knew the word? You were involved with gay rights. You filed a PIL when the drinking age was going to go to twenty-five. My thesis is that you are more of these times than those.
IK: I always felt like I was – it sounds egotistical to say ahead of the curve – I was trying to be the voice of a new, younger—

AC: Generation
IK: Yeah. The industry, our country, all of it. I was trying to say, 'Okay, we've all grown up watching cinema of the early 2000s, 1990s, 1980s, 1970s. How can I bring my thoughts and my sensibilities? And try to be part of the next wave.' That was always the idea. And by and large, there was not a lot of that being done. Films like *Kidnap* very much leaned into the classical style. And those were often the films where I had discomfort, I don't quite know how to engage with the scene because it doesn't make sense to me. But it's scripted that way. I guess you try your best. So there was always a dissonance I was trying to overcome. I was trying to find a way to fit into those worlds. I don't buy into it, but I'm trying. This guy's a big director. I guess he knows what he's talking about.

AC: But the guys that did work were all those non-toxic men?
IK: And those were all first-time filmmakers. *Jaane Tu... Ya Jaane Na* or *Break Ke Baad* or *I Hate Luv Storys* or *Delhi Belly*. All of these were guys making their first film, and were about my age. And who were trying to tell a story that came from themselves.

AC: And take the narrative forward in some small way.
IK: Yeah. The times that I tried to do legacy films – *Kidnap, Once Upon a Time in Mumbai Dobaara!* – these were filmmakers from another generation.

AC: Correct.
IK: I think we never quite got into sync.

AC: Yeah. I don't know if you'll remember this, but you were actually the first person who spoke to me about social media being toxic. I got onto Twitter, now X, like in 2010. The first few years were great. I remember you saying you were on Twitter, and you looked at your phone in between shots. And you said there was so much negativity. You said that it impacted on your performance in the next scene.
IK: There is an emotional residue that remains when you connect, when you engage in that way. And social media, it does this thing. I'm now very sensitised to it. I can perceive it like a physiological sense.

AC: Really?
IK: Yeah. So I was an early adopter of Twitter. I signed on in 2009. And I deleted my Twitter account in 2010. I remember the whole cycle. At this point, we have a better understanding. These are digital drugs. The addiction and the reward response, it does stimulate a physiological response in us. So I remember the feeling of, you know, I would think of a very witty, funny little thing to put onto Twitter. So then you open it up. And as you start to type, there is this excitement which you feel in the pit of the stomach.

AC: People are going to love it.
IK: They're all going to love it. It's going to get so many retweets and so many likes and so many comments. And then you post. You sit in, you wait. And the feeling of, ha ha ha. That entire physiological feeling, I started to become aware of it. And I was like, 'Oh, I'm feeling anxious.' And there is the high, this has landed and everyone finds it funny. Or nobody got this. They thought my spelling was wrong. So now it has bombed. I started to really become conscious of it and say, 'Oh, I'm not enjoying this. And I'm doing this in the middle of a day where I may be on set. And I'm trying to remain in a particular head-space for the scene. Or I'm supposed to meet with someone. And there's this entire residue that is now influencing the way that I'm interacting with this person. So I became very cautious and said, 'I don't want this experience.'

AC: You wrote a piece on why you're not on social media in 2013. You said, 'So all of us in the industry open up the papers and say, "Man, Shah Rukh Khan has built eight-pack abs. Oh, shit, he got paid 15 crore rupees for this film." Then I start to feel insecure. I tell my PR guys to put out a story saying I'm getting 35 crore for fifteen endorsements. But the rest of the world doesn't give a damn. It's actually actors taking shots at each other, directors and producers trying to one-up each other. You take a step out of the bubble and look around and you realise that nobody gives a damn. We lose perspective. Step back for a moment. We're making movies. You don't need to treat it like international espionage.' Amplified now, to the power of a hundred. With social media, pap culture.
IK: It's mind-boggling.

AC: How are you handling it?
IK: By disconnecting. I am not there. Instagram – I don't have the app. I post from my laptop.

AC: Correct. And long ones.
IK: Yeah. So I type it out on my laptop. I go to www.instagram.com. I log on from my laptop and I upload pictures from my desktop and I type the thing in and I post. I don't follow anyone. I don't consume Instagram. I don't use WhatsApp. All of these very fast digital media communications things, I simply cannot handle it. The pace and the emotional graph of the thing is simply too much for me.

AC: Now that you are engaging more, I saw some story on how you and your partner Lekha have perhaps rented Karan's house. How do you handle that?
IK: Again, it's one of those things that I have never fully been able to wrap my head around. Celebrity and fame and the people following you around literally to report and comment on you. I've had time to deconstruct the notion of fame. It's just weird that we have opinions on people far, far removed from us – the idea that I can sit over here and have an opinion about Timothée Chalamet, who I've never actually met. But I have very strong opinions about how he dresses and who he dates. Makes me very angry. It's weird.

AC: But you're zen-like about it?
IK: It doesn't fully make sense to me. I'm not trying to engage with that. Someone finds it interesting to report on me. Someone is interested in

reading it. But if a tree falls in the forest and no one is around to hear it . . . .
I was so disconnected, not aware if someone is saying something about me. I
travelled a lot. If I never hear about it, did it actually happen? Nobody comes
to me and says, 'Hey what about this?' It all happens among other people.
How do you engage?

AC: But here, now, are you disengaging?
IK: Since I'm not consuming any of this stuff, I kind of live my life on the
basis of what is actually happening. Who are the people actually in front
of me, reaching out and touching me and saying, 'Hi Imran, let's have a
conversation about a project?'

AC: But I'm also amazed at how honestly you are expressing yourself on
Instagram, which for most people is an instrument of projection. This is
the caption with a picture where you're pouring water on yourself.
IK: On the sets of *Ek Main Aur Ekk Tu*.

AC: You said, 'Sorry about the silence. When you've lived so long in
darkness, the sunshine can feel unbearably bright at first. I've been flooded
with so many messages of love, that it felt unnatural. I couldn't absorb that
much positivity. Instead I went looking for the ugly words, the hurtful
ones that sound more like the voice in my head, because that feels more
familiar to me. I checked Reddit, the comment sections of news articles,
wherever I could find words sharp enough. But some of the edges of the
words seem less sharp, the tips less pointy. They weren't drawing blood the
way they used to. They just didn't work anymore. And I think I know why.
We all have scars, old wounds that still ache, but love heals. It covers you
in a layer of protective armour. You make me feel 304.8 cm tall.' How do
you get this honest?
IK: It's easier. We have, most of us, developed the habit of wearing masks.
Different masks with different people in different scenarios. And my
journey has brought me to a place where the effort of wearing that mask
and saying the thing is more effort than I'm able to make. It's more difficult
for me to do that than it is to just say, 'Here's the truth.' You asked me
earlier – was it difficult to walk away? Is it difficult to be this exposed and
this honest? Funnily, these are some of the easiest things that I have done.
The hard thing is looking at the broken parts of yourself and trying to
fix them and engaging with that every day. I'm going to crawl forward a

quarter inch a day. Speaking my truth and acknowledging these parts of myself is the easy way out.

AC: You also walked away from this palatial house that you lived in. In Pali Hill. You don't live there anymore. You live in an apartment. And you said in *Vogue* that you have three forks and three plates.

IK: And so just around the time that I separated, I moved into this space where I have lived for the past five years. And I started by moving into what was basically an empty space. And then bit by bit, I started to bring in only things I actually need. I didn't have any live-in staff. I bought myself one of those Dyson vacuum cleaners, I will clean myself. If I have only three plates, one per meal, breakfast, lunch, dinner, there's only three plates to wash. If I go through the entire day and I don't wash anything, there's still only three plates. The mess can't get any bigger. Again, it was about separating from those external trappings, the things you're told you want. And it was about saying, what do I actually get value from? I wanted my space. I wanted to be able to manage and run it myself.

AC: And you cooked yourself?
IK: Breakfast. Lunch and dinner I got from my mom's place. So I can't lay claim to all of the cooking. I try eggs.

AC: Hey, not bad.
IK: And I can make a really good spaghetti carbonara.

AC: Pretty good.
IK: Proud of that one. So yeah, I can do some basic cooking. I make my bed. I vacuum the floor. I wash my three plates. I engage with all of this stuff in that way. And you possibly also read that I cut my own hair.

AC: I did. I did. How does that work?
IK: I use two mirrors. So there's the mirror in front and a little hand mirror that you hold behind the head.

AC: But kahi haath phisal gaya toh (If the hand slips or something)?
IK: It's always a little uneven, if I'm honest. Fortunately, the cameras are always slightly to one side.

AC: Thoda upar niche hai hi (It's just a bit uneven).
IK: But since I wasn't on camera, it didn't matter. If you're a professional actor, you'll have someone to do the thing. So I started to take more of those things onto myself and say, 'What do I need from the outside world?' It's possibly borderline pathological. Slightly overly self-reliant.

AC: There is such a thing.
IK: This might be a bit of a red flag with me. I'm not great at accepting external help.

AC: But now, Imran, you are in a relationship. Is she okay with three plates?
IK: It's an ongoing negotiation.

AC: I want five.
IK: Yeah. So that is the ongoing thing. Can we do five? Six? Okay. Three for you, three for me. So that is the ongoing negotiation that we're figuring out as we move into a new place.

AC: So Imran, Lekha is also an actor, an artist. Do you automatically become like professional bouncing boards for each other?
IK: Look, I mean, you're also married to a movie guy. It's hard to get us to shut up about movies.

AC: This is true.
IK: I don't stop. And she, being an artist, is always going on with the idea of, suppose there is a tree with a light and a…

AC: Right.
IK: Yeah. It's fun. It is entertaining. But if you spend too much time hanging out with movie people, it very quickly gets tiring.

AC: Amitabh Bachchan also famously took a break. For five years. And afterwards, he thought it was a mistake because everything had changed. Do you look back and think, 'What if it hadn't panned out like this?'
IK: Before I became an actor, I had already lived many lives. I didn't grow up in one place. I bounced around a lot of cities, countries, different schools. I've been to a number of very unorthodox, non-traditional schools. I spent some of my formative years from age eleven to fifteen in a gurukul, without

electricity. We lit kerosene lamps every night. We grew our own food. We got water from a stream. We chopped firewood. As such, I have always had the sense that life is kind of bigger. I cannot be a unidimensional person. I've acted in twelve films professionally. Now, Amitabh Bachchan has acted in a few more. Many, many other actors have acted in many more. A lot of people have acted in fewer than twelve films. I'm already ahead of half the population of the country in that way. But – what do you want from life? For me, there was always a sense of, if I really want to, I'll find a way back. Maybe I don't have to be an actor always. Maybe I can be a director. a cinematographer, a production designer. Maybe I'll make independent films. Unless following this one track, somehow you are not maximising – that's not a thing for me. What do I want to do in my life? And there is going to be a large number of things that have nothing to do with the film industry. And being able to separate those things is something that I've not encountered a lot. Most people have a sense of – you can't fall behind in the race. I'm feeling that this is symptomatic of us generally in the world. No one has a sense of enough. Wherever you are, whatever you are, whatever the thing is, the ability for someone to look into their bowl and say, I have enough – we have lost this thing. There is a greed for anything and everything, but no one ever is able to say, 'I have an abundance here.' I have been triply blessed. In my life in so many, many ways, I consider that I have more than most. Can that not be enough? So in ten years, I haven't made a film, but I've acted in twelve films, and at least a half dozen are films that we remember to this day. How many people get that? If I were to get another chance and make another film, that's yet another blessing. Every bit of it is a plus. Not a lot of people get to do this thing. There are many, many people in the world who love it just as much, maybe more, who never get half a shot.

AC: Imran, is there something you do daily for your mental health?
IK: It is kind of a conscious presence summed up in the mantra: be here now. We are more and more in multiple places at the same time. There is so much of that residue that we then take into all engagements. I feel that I am particularly prone to that. I have a narrow bandwidth, I'm not able to multitask at all. If I have some external residue I can very quickly become derailed. There will be perhaps a gut reaction from an anxiety-driven place and I have to step in with a kind of intellectual override and say, 'Okay, calm down. Look around for a second, where are you? What is your physical space? What are your actual circumstances? What is actually

happening? To what extent is it a residue that is just there?' That is what I do twenty, thirty times a day to de-escalate.

AC: Recognising your own responses. Okay, I have to ask, are you and Abbas Tyrewala working on a spy series?
IK: So that was the very first thing out of the gate that we started talking about, back in July of last year. Abbas called me out of the blue. I was on vacation in San Francisco. And he called me and said, 'I've written this amazing thing.' And it was a really cool story. 'Let's do this together.' And we started the conversation. And the project was in early development at Hotstar, before the acquisition. And then Hotstar got amalgamated into Jio. And that project fell by the wayside.

AC: And you were going to be a spy? I want to see this.
IK: Yeah. It doesn't look like it will be resurrected. All things said and done, I'm kind of glad that that ended up not coming together.

AC: Why?
IK: I don't want to play a character who solves problems with a gun. I have a sense about cinema these days, globally. There is a glamourisation and a fetishisation and a sexualisation of violence that makes me uncomfortable. I've grown up loving action cinema. When I was in my early twenties, my heroes were Sylvester Stallone, Arnold Schwarzenegger.

AC: Indiana Jones, right?
IK: Well, Indiana Jones a little bit earlier. But going to the 1990s, these were the stars. So I've grown up loving action cinema. I love Jackie Chan. I mean, there is a way to portray violence. This is not a morality thing. It is a language within cinema. There is a way to do it where you feel the weight of it.

AC: And the way we do it is like there are no consequences.
IK: Yeah. The *Joker* film, a couple years ago.

AC: Joaquin Phoenix.
IK: There's a scene in that where he attacks a guy suddenly with a knife and stabs him to death. It was shattering and brutal and horrifying. I was shaken. And we've started making films where heroes will just go in and

boom, boom, boom, boom, boom, shoot seven people in the head, and their heads will explode to music. And they make it cool and sexy.

AC: And you don't want to be that guy?
IK: There's enough of that.

AC: Well, I hope you find something that you like.
IK: Thank you. I'm looking.

19 April 2024

16

In Their Own Voice: Vicky Kaushal & Katrina Kaif

Audio: Katrina Kaif and Vicky Kaushal, welcome to *TapeCast*. You've both had a fascinating journey to stardom, and we look forward to discovering the truth to your drive and motivation. Vicky, will you pick the first question?
Vicky Kaushal: Sure! I will start with 'family'.

Audio: Your sister Isabelle is joining films. What advice would you give her?
Katrina Kaif: I was trying to make her do everything I had done. And advise her almost very similarly into all the things and all the routes that I had taken. I don't even think I did it consciously. And now I think the best thing I can do for her as a sister is to allow her to discover her own voice. Authenticity is always what works.

VK: She's shooting for a film right now?
KK: She's just completed a film.

VK: Best wishes to her.
KK: Thank you. Okay, I'm picking a question for you.

Audio: The general consensus is, what works in your favour is your boy-next-door vibe, you're approachable, attainable. As you become successful, how do you continue to be this?
VK: By not taking success to your head. To let that be a sinking feeling rather than a feeling that you get comfortable with. I still go to cafes and malls and restaurants and do the same things. All they want is just a couple of seconds, a selfie. I'll just lose myself if I lose that relatability, because that also is an asset to me as an actor. You need people who really keep bringing you back to your reality. Sometimes it's just my mom. Just be focused on your work, that's it. You know, I am the same Vicky Kaushal that I was. But I know I'm getting all that love and affection, I know that I can't take things for granted.

KK: That's the biggest mistake, to lose focus on what was was working.
VK: There's this beautiful poem, 'If' by Rudyard Kipling.

KK: 'Success and failure, just the same.'
VK: And he's called success and failure imposters. Which is so true. If you learn how to treat both of them the same, that's the trick. The times when I was knocking around doors and asking for work—

KK: But aren't those just such great times?
VK: No, it scares me. It makes me value my present even more. But it was fun, when I was doing that. You're just free, fearless.

KK: Because there's nothing to lose.
VK: And you're just doing it for the love of what you want to do.

KK: Your mom sounds like a very wise woman. And she checks you out and says, 'Got my eye on you.' That's important!
VK: Okay, I'll pick up a question for you.

Audio: Karan Johar recently declared that it's the age of the actor and not the star anymore.
KK: I think it's always been the age of the actor. I think there is no such thing as a generic star. I don't believe it's possible for any actor with a public persona to sustain the public's interest without the craft they are doing. Earlier, it was just you and your movies. The audience didn't see you on platforms. It's been that way for the majority of the films that I've done. Everyone values their time and wants to come to the cinema to be entertained. So, if what you're doing is holding their attention, then that means that they are connecting. Beyond a point, I don't really take it all too seriously.

VK: Right. It's what I see you as.
KK: It's your job to see me and decide what I do for you. You just can't all the credit, the pressure. I don't get too particular about who's this star and who's a superstar. I try and just keep coming back to my centre and what's true for me, however I find that centre. Recently I realised that I was not happy in a particular genre, and it was a space that I had worked for a long time. It was not exciting to me anymore. I'm trying to look for things that excite me, where I feel I'm learning something

new. Either the director is teaching me or even if the director is just capturing it . . . the people I'm trying to gather around me. Can they teach me something new? That's how I've made this chapter in my life exciting. Where can I change things up? Then the audience will continue with you on that journey.

VK: How was it for you to kind of gauge that shift from knocking doors to the superstar that you became?
KK: It was so gradual. A lot of people came in around the same time as me with one big grand launch. But for me, it was one small role in a film, then this, then that. I do remember the first time that I got a lot of acknowledgement – it was *Namastey London*. Before that it was 'Just Chill' – that song.

VK: Talking about your songs reminds me. I was in an acting institute in 2009 – and one of our exercises was to look into the camera and dance to 'Teri Ore'.
KK: Okay, so you're supposed to take the vibe of the song and the camera's the girl.

VK: Yeah, that's the POV of the girl and then you have to act it out.
KK: Okay, this is really funny. I'm just imagining all these poor students and that camera.

VK: It was your interpretation or whatever you feel like doing. It was also being . . . just free. A movement thing. Just like, *express*.
KK: So basically, one could say I've had a fairly large hand in helping you craft your skill.
VK: Very.

Audio: You've emerged as a mature and confident individual. What enabled you to reach this place?
KK: I think what life brings to you. Everything that I imagined could not happen, happened. The things you try and protect, disintegrated. And then you are faced with everything you feared and you realise that it's not so bad.

VK: You had it over-hyped in your own head.

KK: Fear is mostly just an illusion. Sometimes you don't realise it at all until later. You're in this structure and it's not purely just creative and it's kind of convoluted. And when that disintegrates, you come back to a place of feeling really fearless and not having so many rules for yourself. And with that came for me a new interest and excitement in what I was doing at work. I went through a phase of being on set when it consumes everything. So, I think it's about trying to find that place where you feel good.

VK: But did that happen while you were playing Babita or before?
KK: For that particular role, Aanand Rai was super. He came to me about two and a half years before. And when he came back to me later, I was like, 'You took away half my role.' So, we were at loggerheads in the nicest possible way. And he explained to me his vision. He's one of the best directors we have – so clear and precise. He was like, 'You're going to find it if you just submit yourself to this process.'

VK: Surrender completely.
KK: It was a really hard process, because you're supposed to be drunk, broken-hearted and distraught, vulnerable. And you can't really fake that. So, when we came on set, for an hour and a half, me and Aanand Sir would just sit and talk.

VK: Wow.
KK: Sometimes it was about the scene. Sometimes not. But he always knew which road to push me down gently, and then let it, let it play out. Because of the CG, there were long periods between each shot. Out of everything I've done recently, that was really fun.

VK: Do you think it became an outlet for you to express, through a character?
KK: I've understood it in a different way now. I personalise it – how is it sad to *me*? But I also like the freedom he wanted. That incorrectness of everything, because you're drunk, it allowed you to not have to do everything right.

VK: Be imperfect.
KK: That was the most liberating experience.

Audio: What have you learnt about things one shouldn't do from the artists around you?

VK: Firstly, it's taking yourself too seriously and creating this atmosphere – a serious actor needs this isolated space on set – which is a disruption to people around. It's not only you making this film, but also a team of two hundred people coming together. I've worked with amazing actors, Ranbir, Alia, Sanjay Mishra-ji, and they are so good with their lines. I've realised the magic that happens when you're just so prepared with your lines on set.

KK: Wasn't the question about things you learnt not to do?
VK: So, I shouldn't be ill-prepared with my lines on set.

KK: Oh, like that. I wouldn't think you've ever come on set without knowing your script backwards.
VK: But see, I don't really mug up my lines. Why is it that he's saying this and then that? So, if I know the thought process, I will never forget the line. That helps me improvise also. But sometimes that is not the requirement. Like for example, in *Raazi*, you had to say exactly the words in the script. Because anything outside that would just change the sur (note) of that character.

19 March 2019

17

Becoming, Not Performing: Vidya Balan & Shefali Shah

Anupama Chopra: I want to congratulate you both on *Jalsa*. It's a very unsettling and very gripping film. And it's such a treat to see the two of you work together. There are many things I want to get into without giving anything away.

Shefali Shah: Tell! We'll do the interview later. I want to know everything!

Vidya Balan: It's the first time that someone used the word 'unsettling' and I actually laughed, I was happy.

AC: And especially if you're a mom like me. It's not just about morality, it's also about motherhood, it's also about being a working mother and all these layers are in there. I have many questions. But first of all, Vidya, I was very intrigued to read that you had said no because you said, 'I didn't have the guts to do it.'

VB: Yes.

AC: When did you become an actor who doesn't have guts to do scripts?

VB: No, it's also about one's state of mind, right? I just felt that Maya Menon could be . . . maybe I was judging her. I was like, 'Do I want to play someone who makes certain questionable choices?' But then, the pandemic happened and I happened to chat with Suresh – he told me he had made changes. So, I said, 'Oh, I'd like to read it.' I knew I was ready to do it now. Something had changed. I now knew that I didn't want to judge her anymore. Even though I think of myself as someone with a great amount of empathy and all that, I was surprised that I had the reaction when I read the script. So, I think the pandemic made me realise you can't ever judge anyone unless you're in that situation yourself. I think I have a problem with not owning up to what one has done as a person. That was my challenge with Maya Menon.

AC: Do you two have very different processes as actors?

SS: I really want to know Vidya's process.

AC: You still don't?

SS: No.

VB: Because we hardly had any scenes together!

AC: There is that one stellar one in the kitchen, which I want to talk about. But so, you didn't observe her enough?

SS: I've seen her work. I admire Vidya. She transcends being Vidya Balan into being the character, and there is unpredictability. Unpredictability in the small things. What I admire the most is, what comes through the screen is real. When somebody is real, it just straight comes out. I want to know how she works.

VB: Similarly, I've forever been a fan of her work. I wanted to know how is it that she always affects you. I want to know how she does it but I don't think we had enough time. The kind of scenes we had didn't allow for that, but I was part of that scene. We were interacting as actors

SS: And also, Ruksana and Maya, they have a divide. There is that uncomfortable space in between.

AC: Yeah.

SS: I'm so glad we're doing promotions together because I've gotten to know her better.

VB: And we shot it right after the second wave. So on set, we used to keep a distance from everyone.

AC: We'll talk about it without giving anything away. There's this scene in the kitchen, very intense and it's the two of you. Maya is in a position of power and speaking from anger, but also she's fearful, vulnerable. Morally, Ruksana has the upper hand. Tell me about the rhythms of that pivotal scene.

VB: I remember, we landed up on set. Suresh wanted us to just do a reading before we went into makeup. We got the mechanics of it. And I did the first take and told Suresh, 'This is . . . off.'

SS: I was totally off.

VB: Yeah, I think it was because it was difficult to grapple with. See, because as Maya, there's fear. I think the anger is always an expression of fear. that scene is so beautifully written because I think Maya somewhere resents the fact that her son loves Rukhsana.

AC: There's this layer moms have with the help.

VB: Exactly. It's that working mother's insecurity.

AC: Yeah.

VB: I've seen women around me behave like that, and feel like, 'It's ridiculous. It's your child.' All of that came to mind when I was playing out this scene, because she's actually not saying what she wants to be saying. There's anger, there's frustration, there's doubt, there's insecurity. And the fact that she wishes that she'd say something nasty to her and get it over with, just not carry this burden. But she can't. Secrets are very claustrophobic and they leave you suffocated and stifled, and that's what that scene is about. On set that day, there was a tension. Suresh screamed at the unit, walked out of set, you know, smoked and came back. So, I think it was one of those days.

SS: Also, they're both hiding.

AC: Yeah.

SS: Ruksana's hoping she doesn't find out and Maya's hoping Ruksana doesn't find out. Ruksana's overcompensating. That whole friction of this guilt—

VB: And how much does the other one know?

SS: How much does the other one know, you know? And also, a quality of Ruksana, she gets stuck on something. Maya is in a much higher position than Ruksana but when she believes in something, she sticks to it. Without arrogance, but she's almost stubborn. When she's leaving and she says what she says, she wants to make her point. And like Vidya very correctly said, her relationship with Ayush is so strong. For Maya, it's like a displaced anger.

AC: Conversation toh gas khuli rakhi ki nahi (the conversation was about leaving the gas on or not)—

SS: But it's not about that! I think she doesn't want to see Ruksana anymore. Because Ruksana is a reminder.

VB: And her self-image has been one of being always correct. The purveyor of truth. And now…

AC: It's all gone. This layer of the mother aspect. Both the characters are moms. And there is guilt, resentment. Was that always part of the script?

SS: Yeah.

VB: That's Suresh's writing. It's very layered. We have to show up and internalise that. But it's all on paper. And forget the paper, when he narrates to you, you get it. He's one of the best narrators.

SS: And he's a very good actor.

AC: So, does he enact scenes?

VB: And every character!

SS: And he's very good. Terrific.

AC: But the two of you are such amazing actors. Do you not get mad with that?

VB: No, no. In a narration, not on set.

Top L to R: Anupama Chopra with Vicky Kaushal, Konkona Sen Sharma; *Middle:* Anupama Chopra in conversation with Shah Rukh Khan; *Bottom L to R:* Pankaj Tripathi, Ranveer Singh

Top L to R: Anupama Chopra with Kareena Kapoor Khan, Hrithik Roshan; *Middle:* Anupama Chopra with Karan Johar; *Bottom L to R:* Deepika Padukone, Anupama Chopra with Madhuri Dixit Nene

Top: Sneha Menon Desai with Shabana Azmi and Zeenat Aman;
Bottom: Anupama Chopra with Sanjay Leela Bhansali

Top L to R: Sushant Singh Rajput, Alia Bhatt; *Middle L to R:* Nandamuri Taraka Rama Rao Jr., S.S. Rajamouli, Ram Charan; *Bottom:* Payal Kapadia and Ranabir Das

Top: Nawazuddin Siddiqui with Anupama Chopra;
Bottom L to R: Ram Madhvani, Sneha Menon Desai and Sushmita Sen

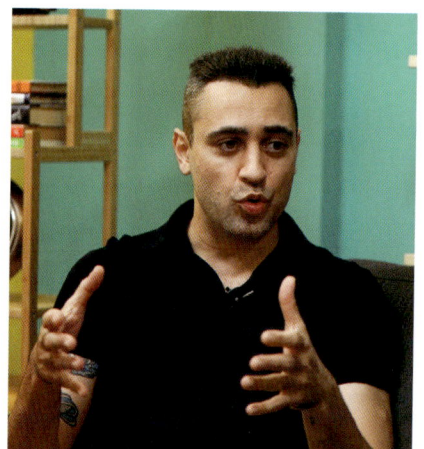

Top L to R: Imran Khan, Priyanka Chopra Jonas;
Middle: Anupama Chopra in conversation with Fahadh Faasil;
Bottom L to R: Irrfan Khan, Diljit Dosanjh

Top: Anupama Chopra in conversation with Sandeep Reddy Vanga;
Bottom: Vijay Sethupathi, Manoj Bajpayee, Vijay Deverakonda, Ranveer Singh, Ayushmann Khurrana, Parvathy Thiruvothu, Anupama Chopra, Alia Bhatt and Deepika Padukone

Top L to R: Anupama Chopra with Saif Ali Khan, Shefali Shah and Vidya Balan;
Middle: Sneha Menon Desai in conversation with Ratna Pathak Shah and Ayesha Jhulka;
Bottom: Anupama Chopra in conversation with Ranbir Kapoor

AC: So, he's enacting the part as he narrates.

VB: Every part!

SS: And he told me, 'What audacity I have! I'm sitting here in front of you and acting.'

VB: He's so insightful. And he really goes deep inside the layers. He's inquisitive. Secondly, he loves his actors. He's gotten us on board because we're going to bring something, add and create these characters along with him. We had extensive sessions individually with him, where we bifurcated the character and the script.

AC: Both of you married very successful producers. You ever just say, 'Make this film for me?'

VB: Never. Siddharth and I decided we won't work together.

SS: Really?

VB: Yeah, after *Ghanchakkar*.

AC: She told me once, 'How will I talk money with him?'

VB: Yeah, I'll start comparing how much he's paying another actor versus how much he's paying me. I want to be the most-valued in his eyes. But importantly, when *Ghanchakkar* released and didn't do well, both of us were feeling low. And that's when I said, 'If one of us is going through the low, the other one should be able to say, 'I'm here for you.' It's too much to go through together.

AC: But Shefali, you work with Vipul.

SS: I've worked with Vipul in *Waqt*.

AC: And *Human*, which you just did.

SS: I'm an actor. But Vipul's films alter the lives of the entire family. His cinema is very different from what I've done. He will never offer me something if he doesn't think it's not worth it. And I have never asked him to do anything for me.

AC: In any case, now you don't have time. So, he can just get in line!

SS: I have lots of time this year! I'm thinking, 'Shit, I don't have work.' Can I assist you, Anupama, please? I don't want to stay at home. (To VB) I'm going to just follow you around.

VB: Come with me to London.

SS: Can I please?

VB: Yeah, please.

SS: I'll just be your actor's AD. I'll just hang around.

VB: Anyway. No, I also don't want anyone to reduce my achievements, 'This happened for you because of your husband.' Because one has worked very hard to get here. As much as I love him, I don't want that to happen for either of us. People say, 'Arre, aapka toh production house hai (You have a production house).' I say, 'Mere pati ka hai, mera nahi hai (It's my husband's, not mine).'

AC: Yeah. They don't see the difference.

SS: In fact, a lot of people come to me with a role only because they want Vipul to produce it.

AC: That must be annoying.

SS: No, I'm just like, 'Fine, I'll give.' He has to deal with it, I don't.

AC: I've had conversations with both of you about what a great time it is for female actors of all ages. But what is it that we're still not doing? What are the gaps?

VB: I think we've come a long way, Anupama. I don't have the foresight to say what more could be done. When we did the MAMI panel in 2015,

I remember talking about wanting to change the glorification of the mother. And that's actually happened for me with *Shakuntala*. I've been seeing other work that delves into that for the first time, it's a better time to be a female actor than a male actor. The variety of roles we're being offered is far more exciting. The male actor space, it's all still a certain type.

AC: It's still in service to the hero.

VB: Whereas we are playing the ordinary, and it can't be said enough that the extraordinary emerges from the ordinary.

AC: And how exciting it is for all of us. Vidya, this is the third release on streaming. After *Shakuntala Devi* and *Sherni*, there is the reach of the platform, but there's also a school of thought that says streaming will never have the same cultural impact as theatres. What do you guys think about that?

VB: I don't know about that. Because it's a collective experience when you watch in a theatre, maybe the cultural impact can be sensed more. But streaming is taking the content to people all over the globe. It's really opening up markets and audiences. For a film like *Jalsa*, where the theme is universal, an OTT platform is the best possible thing to happen.

SS: I like that you use this word because I say going to a theatre is a culture, a religion. It's 'Go with the family and have your samosa and watch a film.' I don't think that is ever going to go away. But we have an alternative, which is sometimes even more powerful because it's not burdened by what happens on the box office on a Friday. It's for posterity. A global audience. And content does not have to stick to the box of what is required in a commercial Bollywood film, you know. So, I believe that OTT has given us a chance to explore, express and experiment.

AC: There's no downside to it. Okay, last question. Is there an essential tool of acting? Vidya, you once told me about perfumes that you change.

SS: Nothing.

VB: Just to know the person you're playing, I think. I normally sit with my director and figure that out. The backstory – you don't see it, but it helps you make the person. Whatever zodiac sign, for example, or perfume, where the person lives. I'm not a trained actor, I have my own process.

AC: Shefali?

SS: I don't have any tools. What works for me may not work for somebody else. So, it's their growth, it's their process and whatever ticks. I chew my director's brains off.

AC: Suresh just lost all his hair!

SS: He had three. But I really dissect everything. I just want to know. And then I start becoming that person. Because I don't want to act like Ruksana, My pursuit is to become Ruksana. When the camera goes on, I have no control over what I do.

AC: It just comes?

SS: It just comes. And touch wood, my instinct hasn't failed me yet. And I don't see the monitor. But when I'm doing it, I'll know it.

AC: Your gut tells you.

VB: Feeling.

16 March 2022

18

'A Love Affair with the Camera': Madhuri Dixit

Anupama Chopra: Madhuri, it's so, so lovely to have you back on the big screen again. You look gorgeous. Tell me, what exactly happened? We didn't see you for four years and now it's *Bucket List, Kalank, Total Dhamaal*.
Madhuri Dixit: There are times when you just want to pause. You have kids, other responsibilities. There's so many things other than acting and being in films. And when I thought it was the right time, I decided, 'Okay, now let's start working again.'

AC: I always felt like, maybe Bollywood just doesn't know what to do with you. Is that true?
MD: You said that to me the last time we met. The decision to take a pause was completely mine. There were many scripts I read, things I was doing during that time. I even did my album, which will release sometime this year. I was busy in a different way. But this script came to me – *Bucket List* – and inspired me.

AC: Just grabbed you.
MD: It's a very relatable story about a housewife who's so involved with her kids, her husband, her in-laws. She's looking after everyone. She loses herself, her own identity. And she finds this bucket list and feels it's her responsibility to complete it now. And finds herself again. I think every housewife goes through that. I loved her journey and the humour in the film.

AC: And once you signed that, did you feel excited about movies and then sign the others?
MD: It so happened, when I was doing *Bucket List*, Indu-ji approached me for *Total Dhamaal*. I heard the script – it's a mad caper – and I haven't done comedy in a long time. There's Anil in the movie and the whole star cast. And then *Kalank* happened, and it just grew after that.

AC: And now the pause is done?
MD: Yes.

AC: Are you still scared before going in and giving a shot?
MD: No, I feel very comfortable in front of the camera. My only challenge is, am I doing it differently? Or how has the director envisioned this role? And I'm in front of the camera, and I'm trying to think of all the things discussed. Those are the challenges.

AC: And it's still exciting?
MD: Absolutely.

AC: Alia told me that it's like a marriage. Some good days, some bad, but you never fall out of love.
MD: She's bang on. This is a love affair going on with the camera and for a very long time. And you're trying different ways to capture the camera, capture its attention, and trying different roles. You also have to feel challenged.

AC: The demands of stardom today are very different. Do you find it easy to adjust?
MD: I think it's easier now than it was.

AC: In what way?
MD: In the sense of personal comfort. When we used to shoot outdoors, we never had vans, we had to go with whatever weather. There were physical hardships. And today it's much easier. Your scripts are ready, you know every dialogue you're going to say, everything is worked out. From your look to your makeup in a particular scene, everything is very organised. We still made good films spontaneously then. And today hopefully we are still making good films.

AC: But the demands . . . actors now talk about themselves as brands and stardom is bigger than what you do on screen. There's also social media, appearances and events.
MD: To a certain extent, I do enjoy it. I enjoy social media because you hear what people are thinking. It's a gateway to address your fans directly. If there's something you want to clear, you just put it out there. The only difficult thing is when you're promoting your movies. It's very intense. But, whatever needs to be done, you do it.

AC: Do you ever struggle to balance the artist in you with these demands?
MD: No, I don't think so.

AC: You can keep the sanctity of that.
MD: It's up to you how much you want to do. There are no rules, right?

AC: But you don't feel the pressure?
MD: I personally have never felt the pressure. People around me feel it. And I understand that. But some days you can't tweet and that's fine.

AC: All your male contemporaries you started out with have these blazing careers. There's just not many great roles for women of any age, right? So, what do you think might be a solution? Is producing an option?
MD: I think today roles are being written for women. You see *Tumhari Sulu*, *Raazi*, so many films which are very woman-centric without stereotypes. I mean, women are women. And they're treated as such in the movies. Their characters are written as such. These are ordinary women, everyday women being portrayed on screen. I think it's a great time for women to be in cinema. Even Hollywood has its own issues with women-orientated scripts. Have you seen *Ocean's 8*?

AC: It looks crackling. So, you don't ever feel frustrated as an actor about the quality of scripts that you're being offered?
MD: I've been offered quite varied scripts and not been disappointed.

AC: Enough meat there?
MD: Yes, yes.

AC: I was talking to Rani about *Hichki*. She said it's important to know whether the audience still wants to see you on screen. And my counter was, 'But you're beyond the box office now.' How do you feel?
MD: Yeah, I feel you should do any role that excites you, because there's nothing left to prove. What is left is whether you can handle different kinds of role and that's what I'm trying to do now.

AC: You're completely zen-like about the box office?
MD: It's wonderful when, you know, women-centric movies do well, because then more get made. It makes them very secure in the knowledge –

if we make this film, make it right and it can still run and people will still watch it. That's the only thing about the box office.

AC: Do you care, Madhuri, about your image?
MD: No, I'm never worried about that.

AC: Not even earlier?
MD: Never. I did so many roles. 'Oh, you're a commercial actress, you should not be . . . it's an art film,' – that's what everybody told me. And I said, 'It doesn't matter. It's a role and I want to play that role. And it's such a good film and the maker is so good. The director is so good and I would like to do it.' I don't regret it because Ketki was a beautiful role.

AC: You've always taken those risks and you're open to doing pretty much anything now?
MD: Yeah. I did *Gulaab Gang* in harness, I was fighting.

AC: You were a don!
MD: And there was *Dedh Ishqiya* which had its little intonations and its little con. I thought it was very cleverly written.

AC: And very edgy in what it suggested.
MD: Very edgy, yes. I want to do every kind of role that is out there.

AC: Would you be open to playing something negative and dark?
MD: Why not? If it's challenging, I'll do it.

AC: Shah Rukh called you 'the most solid man in the industry'. He said, 'She's solid emotionally, she's the only person I feel I'm not as good as.'
MD: I think that he's being very modest, generous.

AC: I think he meant well.
MD: Yeah, I love Shah Rukh, we are on very good terms. But what I'm trying to say is, women are women. They're always strong, always stoic. She's the thread that binds everyone together.

AC: But what was it like to read these things?
MD: It was very nice. Maybe he was just trying to say, 'If she believes in something, she's going to do it.' I don't second-guess myself.

AC: So, despite the fame and glory you've enjoyed for so many decades, you're fairly detached.
MD: Because I'm attached to something else, I'm thinking of something else at that point.

AC: But it's not easy.... You walked away.
MD: Yeah, because life is much larger than being insecure and being in the movies. And these experiences teach you to be a better actress.

AC: When you look back, which films make you say to yourself, 'I really got that right'?
MD: There are a lot of movies like that.

AC: The ones where you have impressed yourself?
MD: I don't know. It's never like, 'Oh, I'm so impressed with myself.' I just felt, 'Yeah, I got the character or scene right.' And in that sense, I did *Mrityudand* when everybody was like, 'You're a commercial actress.' And it was freeing. I could just play a character without having any rigid rules. I really enjoyed doing that.

AC: That stands the test of time for you?
MD: Yeah, where performance is concerned.

AC: And do you miss dancing? Now everybody's like, 'Nahi, lip-sync gaane nahi hone chahiye.'
MD: Well, Bollywood is about song and dance. And we are making films which are otherwise too, especially in Marathi. They're taking different subjects and making them with so much conviction. I think song-and-dance movies will always be made.

AC: I would miss it if it's not there.
MD: See, when a musical is made in Hollywood, look at the kind of response it gets.

AC: Are you a very different person from the person who started?
MD: I think I'm different in only one way; I was very young. I had not experienced life, it was one studio to another.

AC: We used to discuss pimple remedies.

MD: Yes! Those worries were very different. After I got married is when I actually experienced life, I went out there and I did things I'd never done before – experienced the outdoors-y life, met people in very different circumstances. And it expands you, your experiences just make you. In that sense, I have changed a lot.

AC: It's such an amazing story. Is that happening with Priyanka?
MD: TV is a different medium. There are a lot of loops you have to jump through. So, it's churning.

AC: What do you want people to take away from *Bucket List*?
MD: Well, it's the journey of this woman who has completely lost herself. People around you take you for granted. 'She doesn't want anything.' But you are an individual. And she discovers herself. It's not that she's unhappy in her life, it's just that extra something that you need in your life to make it sparkle again. And the people around her change their perspective. I would want every woman to feel that way, that they should have some time for themselves.

23 May 2018

19

Sanjay Leela Bhansali on Silence, Scars, Cinema

Anupama Chopra: Sanjay, welcome to FC Director's Cut. You took ten months to say yes to this interview.
Sanjay Leela Bhansali: Yes, I'm quite amazed by your relentless pursuit. And a little upset because I find that there's no need for me do interviews. You've mostly not liked my films and have given harsh reviews. But I really love you as a person.

AC: Not harsh, Sanjay.
SB: We will sit back after the interview and revisit those reviews and discuss them. But I'm happy that I'm finally sitting here and talking to you. It's my first interview in two years.

AC: Really? Thank you for saying yes.
SB: Anything for you.

AC: Sanjay, why are you so elusive? *Padmaavat* became a blockbuster. What have you been doing since then?
SB: Getting over the trauma . . . . I think no filmmaker in the world should ever go through it. What I went through was not acceptable, not civil. For a filmmaker to invest in something so ambitious and do a film that is as difficult as *Padmaavat*. And to make it through morchas outside the studio or when leaving the house. Or in the evening, when you're editing in the office, there are women-led morchas; relentless assault on your mind, your nervous system. But I was very relentless myself. I did not allow any of these problems to ever show on the screen. It takes a lot out of you. And how will my unit go home? To shoot a film with fifty-two cops surrounding you through Film City, through the three months – or to be physically attacked. I didn't know if the film would release. Then how are people going to react to it? So all that took its toll. I wanted to recover. You have to eventually get over it. I've gone through problems all through my career, but this one I couldn't even imagine.

AC: Do you feel healed?

SB: Absolutely. People responded and said, there was nothing to protest about. That kind of box office numbers – ₹550 crore worldwide – it was the biggest overseas. That kind of love for the film, you feel humbled. I've lived with *Padmaavat* since 2008. So something that I've lived for and nurtured in my mind eventually manifested. Healed, yes. Still, there is a slight reservation. Let my work speak. Let me not give explanations. Silence and quiet became a part of me this last year. I was thinking and writing and creating the next film. But yes, it changed my perspective, scarred me.

AC: In what way?

SB: How much to trust people, how much to believe in the freedom of expression; to believe in whether you have to take approval from 20,000 people. I was short of being lynched. These scars won't just vanish. But I'm not letting them bog me down. I'm in a calm, meditative, humbled space. It was also a lesson to keep you on the ground. If a film like that had done very well without problems, it would have gone to my mind. This year has been introspective, I'm assessing my flaws, looking into what I want to say after twenty-five years of making films. From *1942: A Love Story* to now. And through failures in *Khamoshi, Saawariya* . . . . I've seen failure, success, love, hate. I've felt jealous of filmmakers. I've experienced anger, jealousy – everything. So it's to understand all emotions which help you as a filmmaker.

AC: I don't think any of us can even imagine. Let's get the rumours out of the way. Are you making a film with Shah Rukh and Salman?

SB: I don't need to answer rumours and justify them.

AC: You don't lie very well. See, you're smiling also…

SB: I don't have to accept all your feelings. I have not yet completely zeroed in on the film I want to make from the three subjects dear to me right now.

AC: So there are three?

SB: That I'm choosing from.

AC: And can you tell us anything about any of them?

SB: Next interview.

AC: Sanjay, even when the films are based in contemporary times, like *Khamoshi: The Musical* or *Ram-Leela*, they're set in a Sanjay Leela Bhansali world. The way they speak, dress – they're not connected with reality outside this office. So I have to ask, Sanjay, do you have a God complex?
SB: Not at all. Every filmmaker has his own world. Raj Kapoor, Satyajit Ray, V. Shantaram. It's a filmmaker's state of mind and personality and perspective of life and characters. But I feel that my characters, even if you may not relate to them in today's time, are still very lovable.

AC: It's an emotional reality. Absolutely.
SB: My style – it's texturing, frame, textile, art and colours. For me, a film is bringing together five, six art forms – music, architecture, paintings or textiles or dance – in a way that I don't think other filmmakers do.

AC: It's what it evokes.
SB: Say the horse that you've painted doesn't look like a real horse. The proportions are different, but that's a painter's perspective of the horse. It is my way of interpreting real life through my own warped senses.

AC: Around the time of *Padmaavat*, you said 'I'm dying to get back into the studio, the cinematic part of my brain is peaking.' What does it mean?
SB: I express myself more effortlessly, with more control, through a visual now. I don't find the need for words. The studio is my temple. It's goosebumps for me.

AC: Even now?
SB: Even now. Even from the whole joy of suffering – for this one year, not being able to start a film because I wanted to calm down and get my energies right. Writing relentlessly every day, so that I can go to the floor and then transform it into my world. It's bare walls. It's a catwalk. My gods live on the catwalk. I feel very inspired. As a four-year-old I was taken to a shoot by my father. And I was fascinated by the world he put me in, a cabaret was being shot. I knew this was my world. And his words were, 'Don't move from here.' I still feel the power of those words. And from there to imagine sounds, art.

AC: It comes easier?

SB: I am enjoying filmmaking far more than I did ten years ago. I feel I can go in and start doing what was in my mind. There was a time when I could not convert it for my lack of ability to communicate. Since *Ram-Leela*, I have far more control. I don't live any other thing. I don't go for dinners, movies.

AC: You don't watch?

SB: I don't go to the theatre. I'm consumed by the thought of the film that I want to make. Even now, if I want to go for a drive, I go up to Film City, to my *Ram-Leela* set, *Bajirao* set. Nostalgia inspires me. People say, 'You don't go out.' But I enjoy the world that I live in.

AC: And you savour your own company?

SB: Completely – because you're constantly thinking, I cannot connect it to people around me. When they talk to me, I'm like, 'Yeah, are you done?', because something has come to my mind. It's not normal or healthy. But I enjoy every minute of pursuing to the point of madness. I give it all. And then outside the filmmaking, I give nothing.

AC: That doesn't mean that you're not interested in people?

SB: Of course, I'm interested. I love people. I connect. Once I meet people, I'm charmed by them. And I'm charming enough to charm them. And we all have a great time. I'm very accessible in that sense. You can tell me anything. I'm a great listener. I will listen to your criticism. I'll say, 'You know, Anupama has gone mad. But she has a right to say what she wants to say. And I appreciate that.' So I'm a good listener. But I get consumed by what I want to do. I listen to music in my car. Or watch a great painting or a film. Life is beautiful. It's just cinema all the time in my mind. Though I make few films, those two years that I invest show on the screen. A lot of people don't agree with my films. But I've found a large audience. Even on the road people are saying, 'Wonderful, we like it.' And I say, 'But how do they know me?' I hardly come on television. That connect for the work is so immense that I feel it's worth staying in that meditative state and realising that it pays off.

AC: Alternate reality. And where does this hunger for beauty come from?

SB: From the lack of beauty in my growing years. We lived in a very poor house. We had no paint on the walls. Mom was a wonderful dancer.

So she would dance in that small hundred-by-hundred-foot space. We didn't have good clothes. There was a lot of things that I felt deprived of as a child. And my mind was always a filmmaker's mind. I would sit and do homework and wonder what colour the wall should be. My mind was preoccupied with finding beauty in that lack. Therefore, my sets are very humongous. We were all crammed into . . . almost breathing onto each other. So all these things . . . . You keep finding it all the time as you grow. And today, I have the luxury to arrange the kind of funds to make the film I want to. I feel deprivation is a very important part for any artist to find expression. It's only when you crave it inside your soul. I want to find beauty, not in the sense of plastic and snow-capped mountains and flowers. Beauty in that little thread that comes out of a shawl – that minutest level. Take one little Santoor piece in the orchestration, I would want to use it when shooting the song. It's hours of working with the costume designer, art director. Then forget about all that and concentrate on the narrative and the scene. I keep saying I give it all. Sometimes I wear torn pyjamas and go; let's just concentrate on the work, nothing matters. What matters is – how do I create that one moment of beauty within which I also tell my story? Half the job is done with the actors because they immediately respond to the colour, the weave, the texture, the music that I play on the set for them to emote. It's not just beauty. It's a frame. Frame is sacrosanct. I feel very guilty if a shot is not right. I can't live with something that is not done to the bestest of my ability.

AC: You always had this eye for beauty? Did you cultivate it?
SB: It was there. I was constantly told to watch V. Shantaram, Raj Kapoor, Satyajit Ray. My father was a film producer in his own way. He didn't fulfil his dreams. So all these unfulfilled dreams became my angst. What was he trying to pursue? But I think that comes naturally. You cannot cultivate, you cannot say, 'Gaitonde sahib, aap aise paint karo (Paint like this).'

AC: It's in your DNA.
SB: You're born with it. Then you are born to a place deprived of all beauty. Then you pursue it, find your mission. People say I'm 300 years old as a soul. So maybe all the things of the past subconsciously remain . . . . Sometimes people see a song and say – goose flesh. What is it that creates the goose flesh? So many years culminate into that frame or moment. Many years of living it, craving for it.

AC: You said the frame is sacrosanct. You don't want to be on your deathbed and see a mistake in a frame. When you're constructing down to the last detail, does it leave enough room for spontaneity or imperfection?
SB: Everything is spontaneous. All my homework that I do, everything changes on the set.

AC: Meaning you have one idea and then you get there and you change it?
SB: I've rehearsed it one night with the actors; then I come in the morning and I change everything. So the actors, Ranveer, Deepika, Priyanka, after a point, stop rehearsing the scenes. Improvising and spontaneously reacting to the space is what makes a deep impression on the people watching. That mix of perfection with spontaneity, that's the challenge which I've overcome over the years – and found my way to be spontaneous through perfection. By the time I take my first shot, the actors have a nice nap, they come back . . . . So it's constantly writing with the camera on the set. Living that moment. This bathtub song in *Padmaavat*, 'Binte Dil' with Jim Sarbh and Ranveer – I didn't know what to do. I went over there and said, Jim Morrison and Zeenat Aman, mix the two. He says, 'Give me one hour, I need to first debrief myself.' And then he came and I said, 'I don't want a rehearsal, we'll go for a take straight away.' When he performed, I was so moved because it's about constantly discovering the moment on the set. Even after the rehearsal, after we've changed everything, I still change when they come back.

AC: And you say, there is yet another.
SB: They say, 'Can we do it tomorrow?' And I am graceful enough to understand that it derails them. If it means a little extra money, time, it doesn't matter. I took 260 days to shoot *Padmaavat*.

AC: And the producers?
SB: They don't ask questions, and—

AC: That's a great privilege position. You let them come on set?
SB: Yes, sometimes. I'm not very comfortable, but I'm not uncomfortable either. It's their money. They're very kind to me, what more respect can I ask for from a studio head who says, 'I'm with you. Let's just go and do what you want to do.' I am blessed. I feel that all that I was deprived of as a child, God has blessed me with as much paint as I want to.

AC: In abundance. Ranveer told me that of all the three films he's done with you, *Padmaavat* was the most enjoyable. How much of these characters come from you and how much residue do they leave behind?
SB: Oh, completely. I dived into the evil side of me, the demons. I was tripping while making Khilji. Ranveer would walk in and I'd say, 'Take the crown and push it onto her face.' And he said, 'But Sir, are you all right?' I said, do it. Then I said, 'You push her on the bed and let all your hair fall onto her and like a snake move over her.' He said, 'Sir, are you really a good human being or an evil human being?' I said, 'I'm enjoying the dark side of it.' All my bitterness, anger, jealousy, love, laughter, humour, has to be brought in as a filmmaker.

AC: Sab ras (All flavors).
SB: So if you've not experienced all this and you don't express it. . . . I enjoy doing mad characters. I am a very happy person. Yes, I'm intense. I can slip into the dark side in seconds. But when I'm enjoying life, I'm enjoying it to the fullest through my characters, not through my own personal living.

AC: But you don't want to actually live some of this?
SB: Of course, I'm living the life I've chosen. I'm enjoying everything. I've always waited to do this. I want to live only this. I just hope that I have more energy because my mind is exploding with so many ideas.

AC: You know, one of my favourite moments in *Padmaavat* was when he puts the perfume on the girl and then rubs her against himself.
SB: That was my subconscious. It was on the set. I said, 'You know, just splash it on her. And rub her onto you so you get the fragrance.' He said 'Are you mad?' I said, 'Just do it.'

AC: It was amazing because it captured who he is so completely.
SB: But it also captures who I am completely, the anger, the arrogance – I'm letting it all out.

AC: Catharsis.
SB: Just purge, purge all the . . . Because you need to evolve as a human being. I've become far nicer; the plan is to become even nicer. And even better as a human being. Another ten films I'll take, to cleanse myself. And finally find that God is somewhere waiting for you there to say, 'Well done.' When I say God, it could be Raj Kapoor, Shantaram and—

AC: They'll be waiting.

SB: They're waiting and saying, 'You did well. You did well.' Sometimes I feel they come and hover around. You invoke energies. It's a world of illusion you create. Even a simple scene of two people arguing over a mundane, stupid thing, you still give it a certain dignity. K. Asif and Kamal Amrohi and all these great filmmakers. We don't make films like that anymore – we're too much into edgy, raw. And then they get great reviews. When you come to *Navrang*, or *Pinjara*, where he's tripping as a filmmaker...

AC: There are no boundaries.

SB: We write off today these kind of films, and say, 'Oh, but that's legacy.' The West went mad watching *Padmaavat*. They said, 'Ah, finally we see the exotic, old, lyrical India.' It's important to also talk about those things and everything doesn't have to be raw, edgy and social and solve an issue. They are very important films. But this kind is normally looked at with great scepticism now – 'Oh, he spent so much money. Look at the luxuries.' Do you also look into the angst and the pain that I go through to make it? No. So you look at this side of what I'm afforded; God has allowed me to afford today and you're not looking at the other side. Kamal Amrohi, making ten years of *Pakeezah* or *Mughal-e-Azam* – they're cult films. I'm still very jealous of K. Asif saab and say, 'When will I ever be able to make a film of that calibre and that nuance and that lyricism?' Kamal Amrohi was connected to another energy. Ten years, twelve years, nothing changes. Where are these great films being made? I feel I'm the only one left. There are eighteen historical films being made, but this kind of invoking creative angels . . . . Somewhere I'm invoking those energies all the time, praying to them, talking to them, looking at their work, worshipping them. Still so much to explore. So I'd better get down to making things fast, rather than getting out of the trauma of *Padmaavat*.

AC: That's done and it was a huge success . . . . You have a very long-standing relationship with your writer Prakash. What is the process?

SB: Very random . . . . When the moment comes, it comes. It could come while having coffee here, talking or improvising suddenly. We meet, we talk. I'll say *Devdas* – I don't want those lines but I think there is something in between, discover that idea of Paro and Chandramukhi meeting. He says, 'Blasphemy.'

AC: They crossed in the train, right?
SB: In the palkhi (palanquin). That was not in the book. So if he's improvised, ten more *Devdas* are being made in the next fifteen years. Suddenly he'll write a scene and come – and he writes random scenes. He'll start with scene number forty-eight. And I say, 'It's fabulous.' Then suddenly, scene number five will come—

AC: How do you connect the dots?
SB: But I'm so used to it. I send him five ideas—

AC: Do you write as well?
SB: Yeah. Not the dialogue . . . . I can't type. I write with my pencil or a pen or have somebody sitting next to me and typing.

AC: You're dictating?
SB: Yeah. I can't message also. Wrong things happen. I don't answer messages and all that.

AC: I've noticed.
SB: But I'll send him two ideas. So it's a lot of give and take and I really respect that man's writing. He's a genius.

AC: He's in Mumbai?
SB: In Mumbai. We lived in the old chawl which I keep talking about – where I spent my childhood. He was five buildings away. He's also a Bhansali. But we didn't meet in the twenty-eight years that I lived over there. I was an intense, introverted child. We met for *Devdas* and . . . . Can you imagine? I enjoyed working with Bhavani also for *Black* and *Guzaarish*.

AC: So it's just a back and forth?
SB: Yeah, he can put together abstract ideas. Then I take his writing and say, 'You wrote a great scene, I'm going to shoot a better scene.' So we challenge ourselves. But I never go to an outside location or a great place to write a screenplay. I want it to be in my office – as chaotic as my office is, with 5,000 things.

AC: You're housekeeping and writing.
SB: And office also. So it's like, I create chaos also around me to be able to find that one thought that says, 'Ah, I solved it.' Eight years of my life I was

with Vinod Chopra – and I learnt so much from his eccentricities. I took everything. And then I realised I wish I had not stayed that long. Because I have picked up—

AC: Kuch cheezein nahi learn karni chahiye thi (Some things you shouldn't have learned.) Vikram Motwani who assisted you says what a great education that was for him.
SB: You have to express fully. A flower blossoms completely, with thorns. Some things will have fragrance. And then you perish at the end of it. So while it is blossoming and growing, you must do it fully. Otherwise you are leaving so much unsaid. 'No no propriety. What will people say?' What will people say? When I've evolved into a better human being people still say things about me. They still call me arrogant, inaccessible. I'm nothing of the sort. I'm simple. My favourite city is Film City. Favourite food, dal chawal. Favourite pastime, watching news. When I made *Devdas* I had a one-bedroom house. Mom used to be in the bedroom. I used to live in the hall.

AC: On Yari Road.
SB: And Rekha-ji came home one day after *Devdas* and was a little surprised. 'You live in this house?' It didn't strike me that I didn't have a bedroom. Nothing mattered. *Devdas* was a humongous film at that time.

AC: I remember. That set was unbelievable.
SB: But the director doesn't have his own bedroom. The maid is wiping, sweeping in the morning right next to your face by 9:30 a.m. I'm a very grounded person.

AC: How do you create music? You have no formal training.
SB: In the bathroom.

AC: You're standing in the bathroom and 'Lal Ishq' comes to you?
SB: I shower and sing the song. Simple as that—

AC: You just sang 'Lal Ishq'?
SB: Yeah. I'm having a bath one day. Suddenly I start singing. A song doesn't have to come with, 'I took my instrument. And then we said let us create a song.' I listen to so much music. Non-stop, twenty-four-seven, till I sleep and I switch off the light. As a child – and I wasn't too interactive

with people – and sitting on a terrace, I would sing a song. My escape . . . .
I used to go and buy film books.

AC: Booklet types?
SB: For 25 paisa or whatever it is and I would remake that song. As a child, I was a little demented. My father and mother were sometimes worried when they heard me sing. After *Saawariya* I said let me look into areas that I've still not tapped into. So I take a song and I sing it. Then I record it on my phone with great difficulty. Many of them were lost because I pressed the wrong button.

AC: They don't stay in your head?
SB: They stay if I sing them again and again. So then they stay. Then I come here and I have a music team; I say, 'Here is a song.' Sometimes they add to it, sometimes they correct it. So everybody together makes a film. It's not like writing a poem where you sit alone in a room and write. It's a great collaboration.

AC: But it just comes?
SB: If I don't let it simmer and live long, it goes. I'm very fond of Jaidevji and R.D. Burman, Laxmikant Pyarelal . . . . So I keep doing music…

AC: What a gift.
SB: It's getting better. 'Ghoomar' was difficult, 'Binte Dil' was so difficult. And now there are versions being made in the Middle East. It's a great moment of pride for me.

AC: Amazing.
SB: Sa re ga ma pa. It's spontaneous expression. Are we done?

AC: No. With the benefit of a year away from *Padmaavat*, you have the benefit of hindsight. That sea of red and those women and those flames – when you sit down to create that beauty, do you think at all about the messaging?
SB: Chittor bled in that moment. That was a sea of red. It looked beautiful because it was lit beautifully. But the well – I said it can't work unless they go down the steps. So while we shot at Sunil Maidan, they were making the set. The power of running into fire – it's against human logic. These women had decided: the war is lost, we run into fire. You don't even see a shadow.

AC: But do you see—
SB: Is it gruesome?

AC: No. Is it a glorification?
SB: There was no other end for the women in Chittorgarh at that point of time and there is no other alternative end today, if I were to tell the story again. Everything was over. The war was about surrendering. They didn't surrender – they ran into fire. It is not glorification of, 'Oh the women were helpless.' It is an act of war, of courage. Harakiri – the women had to do it, because if you surrendered, you were put into the harem – or you died a death of dignity. That's why I made the film. Courage to find your power at that point. Today, a woman may fight back. But sometimes you realise – there's no fight left. Either I give up, or I take this stance and there's no glorification. I've not designed it to make it look beautiful, I didn't want to make it look gruesome. I would not have been able to see it. I made this film to salute those women's power. Chittor bled and that red flowed over the steps.

AC: It was a stunning sequence.
SB: Fifteen minutes of silence, just music and people finding their way to fight.

AC: But do you think at all about messaging when you're creating?
SB: No, what messaging? I'm telling the story that happened – the message was courage and strength. I'm not a documentary filmmaker. I love documentaries, their great revelations. But my cinema is a work of art that makes you think, 'Do we subject women to this? Was it right? Was it wrong?' That is an achievement for me. When Hussain paints something, what social message does he give you? When the Taj Mahal was made, what social message did it give? When a great poet talks of personal angst, of romance, what social message does it give you? Pure art, it sets your emotions, it makes you cry, smile, think, makes you want to live.

14 January 2019

20

Shabana Azmi on the Golden Era

Anupama Chopra: Shabana, thank you so much for making time for this special project on the golden age of Hindi cinema. I'm hoping you have some memories. I've read the amazing things about your home Janki Kutir, and you said it was a cultural hub, with Guru Dutt and Chetan Anand and Faiz Ahmad Faiz coming in and out.

Shabana Azmi: Remember that I was born in 1950. I was about seven or eight years old. Guru Dutt – my father was working with him in *Kaagaz Ke Phool* and then there was Chetan Anand, Faiz Ahmad Faiz, Begum Akhtar, Firaq Gorakhpuri. All these people were house guests; Josh Malihabadi, the biggest names in the business at that time. We were also close friends with Sardar Jafri, with Majrooh Sultanpuri, Sahir Ludhianvi. It was an open house. There were artists that believed art should be used as an instrument for social change and that reflected in their work and the choices that they made.

AC: I heard this lovely story. Your mom had this expensive kadha (bracelet) pawned to host guests like Faiz.

SA: You have it true up to a point. It was just one golden kadha, the only jewellery my mother had. But she was a huge supporter of her husband. Food on the table was a big thing. We've always had dastarkhaan (dining space). Anybody who came at any time, there was always good Muslim food. My brother and I, we would know that some guests are coming when that kadha would disappear from my mother's hand. Then we would have guests like Josh Malihabadi and Firaq Gorakhpuri living with us. Abba would write and then the kadha would come back. They could very easily stay in five-star hotels, but there was something here. We had no attached bathrooms. When these guests came, I would move into my brother's room and they would live in my room.

AC: Did it bug you?
SA: It didn't. I didn't quite understand what was happening, but I used to find it very fascinating. Smoke-filled rooms, glasses tinkling, laughter and

Urdu being spoken. I would hide behind the curtain and my father would say, 'Come and sit with us. You can sit here for as long as you want, as long as you get up and go to school in the morning.' So, I felt very grown up and responsible. I think there is just something magical about having artists around you.

AC: What were these people like? What was Guru Dutt like?
SA: Shy. Very shy, spoke very little. I found him extremely attractive. My father would say something really *mazedaar* (interesting). You would imagine when a song as beautiful as 'Waqt Ne Kiya Kya Haseen Sitam', or 'Bichhade Sabhi Baari Baari', being written, that the words came first and were then set to tune, but first, the tune would be made and then the words written to the tune. My father Kaifi Azmi always says, 'It was like as if you first dig a grave and then find a corpse that can fit into that grave. I was able to fit corpses into the right grave.' There's a lovely story about 'Waqt Ne Kiya Kya Haseen Sitam'. Sirf uska jo mukhda hai, woh unhone likha. Aur S.D. Burman ne uski tune di aur Kaifi Saab ne likha 'Waqt Ne Kiya Kya Haseen Sitam' (He just wrote the rhythm of the song. And S.D. Burman gave the tune and Kaifi Saab wrote 'Waqt Ne Kiya Kya Haseen Sitam'). Guru Dutt fell in love with the song. 'Poora gaana bana dijiye, situation mai create kar dunga (Make the whole song, I will create a situation).' Chetan Anand would come to the house. He would come every single day.

AC: They were very good friends?
SA: Very good friends. *Kaagaz Ke Phool*, these films flopped. Although the music became extremely popular. My father stopped getting any work as a lyricist, he was considered bad luck. One day, Chetan Anand walked in. 'Kaifi Saab, I'm making a film and I'd like you to write the songs. My stars are also not good. So, maybe two minuses will get together and make a plus.' And that's how *Haqeeqat* was born.

AC: Unbelievable!
SA: There was a veranda that still exists. My father would sit here, Chetan Saab at some distance. And not a word would be spoken. And I would say, 'Surely this is not how songs are made.' But somehow, they communicated with each other. I would just see them sitting in silence, but in complete harmony, as if understanding each other by osmosis.

AC: That's amazing.
SA: But Abba says that Guru Dutt had a very keen ear for music. He didn't know the language very well, neither did S.D. Burman. But then look at the wonderful thing that came out. Hindi film songs to me, particularly those written in the early era, are not just songs. They're little philosophies of life. They help you negotiate your way around life. You get strength from these songs. These songs were written from the heart, from a heart that had a strong connection with the mind. This was the work of people who had been actively involved in the freedom movement. Their resource-base was life itself.

AC: They weren't watching other movies.
SA: It's from life itself. And the observation of life was influenced by their philosophy, which was for a better world. So, they actually studied human beings. Bimal Roy, Mehboob Khan, any of the greats; they were really rooted in their culture, in Indianness, trying to free themselves from the shackles of feudalism.

AC: Where did Kaifi Saab write? Was there a place in the house?
SA: He had a desk. He would only write with a fountain pen. He had a little writing pad, which was lined, and he would write with blue-black ink or with black ink. His Mont Blanc pens were the only worldly possession he had. He had... many people had gifted him Mont Blanc pens. Interestingly, when he had a deadline, the most unnecessary work would start happening. He would start cleaning his drawers. Letters would suddenly need to be replied to.

AC: So, a procrastinator?
SA: We realised much later that actually the creative process was happening as he was doing this. But he was never precious about writing. In his study, his door would always be open. Life would be touching him. We would be shouting, screaming, radio on, children laughing. None of that ever disturbed the work. He'd say, 'Ek nazm ho gayi hai, sunogi (A poem has happened, will you listen)?' It would just be something that happens.

AC: Who were the bouncing boards? You also?
SA: I'm surprised, but I would be the first person to whom he would recite.

AC: How lovely! How old were you?

SA: Nine. Happened right up till the very end. And if I took objection to a word, he always changed it. So I said, 'But how can you take me so seriously?' I didn't even know the language. But he said, 'For precisely that reason, because see, you were reacting to the phonetics of it.'

AC: So, you were the first audience.

SA: Yes. My father did it as a way of just being charming, I think. But I took myself very seriously.

AC: I read that your favourite actors from the time are Dilip Kumar and Balraj Sahni.

SA: Not from the time. Forever and ever. If people have not seen the work of Dilip Kumar, they shouldn't say they know anything about any cinema. Dilip Kumar and the method acting, the intensity, the passion, whether it was his voice, his body language. Dilip Kumar in a romantic song in *Tarana*, where he's only lying down and Madhubala has her face turned towards him. If he had looked at me like that, main toh bas bichhke, marke tabah ho jaati na (I would have been destroyed). When he looked at a woman with love, you felt that nobody else existed. And look at his versatility! *Devdas* and . . . . Just watch *Mitwa*, just watch; it is an ocean of sadness on his face. He doesn't have to do anything, you just look at the face and that face is just speaking. To the really crazy kind of comedy that he was capable of doing.

AC: *Ram aur Shyam*, my God!

SA: *Ram aur Shyam*. And how he enjoyed taking the mickey out of the characters around him. Then he could be so dignified. He has influenced generations of actors. His command on the language. He was also an extremely dignified person in real life. Very charming. When he's with people, he can just hold forth and they will just die at his feet. He inhabits both those worlds like the world is a stage.

AC: Did you ever study his performances?

SA: I've not been a great film-goer as such. But my mother was a huge fan. Dilip Saab also used to come to the house. He was friends with my father. But also, he's a chatora (foodie) of the first order and he likes pakoras and all kinds of rubbish food. He said, 'Saira put me on a diet and give me some soup and boiled chicken. At two o'clock in the morning, I got up feeling so sad for myself that I ate everything in the fridge.'

AC: What did you like about Balraj Sahni?
SA: He had this amazing ability to speak the most inane dialogue in a believable way. Look at him in *Haqeeqat*, he's unbelievable. But his most definitive performance is in *Garm Hava*, the most flawless performance ever in Hindi cinema. Abba wrote the script, and he said, 'But I don't know this world. Will I be able to do it?' So, Mummy, who had worked with him in theatre said, 'You're the only person who could do it.' So, he went and lived with my father's friends for ten days. He slept on a charpai (cot). *Garm Hava* remains the most definitive film on partition. My mother, who's in the film, says that she never felt she's speaking dialogue. A lot of the scenes between Balraj Sahni and Geeta, who played his daughter, were dialogue exchange taken straight out of his life with me.

AC: Really?!
SA: Yeah. It was so closely observed and so realistic. Most of the actors were from theatre also, and they had to make the film on a shoestring budget. They say ke Muslims ko mainstream join karna chahiye. Toh kya hota hai mainstream? Agar woh shoe factory ka owner hai, toh mainstream hi toh hua (That Muslims should join the mainstream. What is mainstream? If he is the owner of a shoe factory, he is mainstream). It's just a stunning film and Balraj Sahni's performance is incredible.

AC: That scene where the grandmother hides under that sink.
SA: Taken from my mother's life! Her grandmother refused to leave the house and she went and hid.

AC: Oof, goosebumps.
SA: And they didn't have a Nagra (portable audio recorder). They couldn't afford it. They just recorded the dialogue on a very small cassette player. When Balraj Sahni was dubbing the film, he said, 'My God, this is truly a very important film.' And then he did the last bit of dubbing and the next morning he died. It was as if he was born to play that part and to complete it. It's unfortunate that he never got to see *Garm Hava* on the big screen.

AC: At a mushaira a couple of years ago, you talked about how during the 1950s and 1960s, Hindi cinema actually protected the Urdu language. And now we're just shunning it.

SA: See, first we must remember that poetry was revered. People liked poetry. Mushairas were big things. Poets at that time, my father and Majrooh and Sahir, they used to be like major stars.

AC: They were rock stars.
SA: There were girls falling all over them. And they were really major rock stars. These people were from the progressive writers. The Hindi film song became the natural repository of the Urdu language. And I think the Hindi film song, with its language and its music as it used to be, is something that we need to reclaim rather than the noise that is happening at the moment.

AC: Do you think actors today should know about these movies?
SA: It's like saying that I want to be a writer, but I don't know the alphabet. How can you write a story in India if you've not read Premchand? It's that kind of thing.

AC: Foundation hai na?
SA: In order to take flight, you have to first be rooted. And how can you be rooted if you do not know about the greats in your own field?

AC: If you had to recommend a film to all the millennials out there who don't know this time, what would it be?
SA: There are so many. *Mother India*. It's melodramatic, of course, but if you see the character that Nargis played, she is rooted very strongly in our mythology. Indian cinema borrows very heavily from mythology. The hero and the heroine are created from Ram, Sita, our mythology. And so, who the mother was, who for the sake of good would sacrifice even the son that she loved, as the epitome of what motherhood meant – you see it in *Deewaar*, and a hundred films after: the Hindi film-mother. But it was amazing for its structure, script, it had everything. We must remember that Hindi cinema actually emanated from Parsi theatre, which borrowed from various art forms. *Mother India*, to me, is an epitome of that form.

29 November 2023

21

Alia Bhatt: The Bhansali Heroine

Anupama Chopra: I want to start with a conversation I had with Sanjay five years ago. We think about the Yash Chopra heroine, but there's also a Sanjay Leela Bhansali heroine. And he immediately said, 'Yes, if Guru Dutt and Meena Kumari had a daughter, that would be the Sanjay Leela Bhansali heroine.' This idea of intensity, lyricism, self-destruction and the strength to endure real pain. Does *Gangubai* fit this mould?

Alia Bhatt: Yeah, absolutely. I can't tell you the number of times he's spoken about Meena Kumari, even while prepping. The adjectives he used to describe would never be without the opposite – strong, but vulnerable; humorous, but has anger in her eyes. This but that. And that's literally life, right? He always wanted two layers to come out. She's saying something, but her eyes are saying something else. Extremely challenging, but what I also enjoyed the most.

AC: This woman's circumstances are so extreme. How did you actually get into her head?

AB: What I enjoy about a biopic like this – not everybody knows Gangubai's story. Even I didn't know. I read the one chapter of Hussain Zaidi's book and then the script. She came to Bombay, she was sold by her lover at the time. She became a prostitute. You know that she then became a madam. You know then this happened and that happened. You know that she gave this speech and met Nehru. But how did she reach those places? Now you start carving the personality – was there like a filminess? Was she dramatic? Dreamy? She became mafia queen, became Karim Lala's sister – that means she had a strength to her; an ability to hold a conversation. So, these things are very enjoyable because you're creating. It's factual in terms of plot points but the in-betweens are the imagination you have fun with. Getting into the character's skin was, of course – the world, dialect, how she's responding to things. But I don't think anything would have prepared me for the character that actually happened on set. I was shooting for two years and we shot at night. I don't think I left that character.

AC: That's amazing.
AB: While making it, it was all I knew at the time.

AC: Sanjay is the last of the great traditionalists, the only director working with the legacy of V. Shantaram, Guru Dutt, K. Asif. What's it like to be directed by a person like that?
AB: Oh, it's totally different. I've also have had a very protected upbringing. I had different kinds of friends. But actually, when you're in your Juhu-Bandra gang, you don't really get out and you're not really communicating. My connect with India was through movies. But I used to watch the entertaining masala movies, there was a certain grace, an old-world charm, a certain understanding of the basic issues. Sitting and talking to Sir, the way he deals with people, the way he converses, his energy, his openness . . . he's very connected to India's roots. He would say, 'Watch *Mandi*.' Once he said, 'Watch *Memoirs of A Geisha*.'

AC: Did you see *Pakeezah* since Meena Kumari . . .?
AB: I saw *Pakeezah*. I saw a lot of films, I'm forgetting because my memory doesn't stick anymore. He made me watch YouTube videos of old women, random women walking, the ways to walk with a saree on. He's like, 'I want that style.'

AC: Flamboyance.
AB: Very flamboyant and there's no superficiality. No restraint. You talk openly, feel openly. I really enjoyed that. And that's how he is on set. He knows every secondary artist, junior artist, dancers, background, everyone's name, where they are standing. He doesn't go for parties or do interviews. But he's very connected.

AC: Yeah.
AB: And very, very proud of India. I picked up a lot from that. He believes in connecting with the whole country.

AC: A couple of years ago, Ranbir had done an interview on *No Filter Neha*, where he talked about Bhansali's dark madness. And he said he couldn't cope but there's no better acting coach than Bhansali.
AB: I don't think he's a coach. He doesn't tell you what to do. He pushes you to find it. It's very easy for somebody to say, 'Touch this, look up,' etc. He doesn't. He gives you adjectives, makes you think. He wants your body to start feeling it. It's like a completely different language. He likes the

unpredictability of performing. He approaches the scene from different angles. There are no rules, no one way of doing anything.

AC: Yeah.
AB: He's looking for magic, always, and he wants it to hit here (points to heart). Sometimes he would say, 'No rehearsal for Alia. We need to just straight-away shoot.' I would not call him a coach, but I don't think there's anybody who's more interested in your ability and your potential.

AC: The stories about him are urban legend. Ranveer told me, that for *Bajirao*, he did this massive scene, and thought he had done really well. Sanjay said, 'You're boring the shit out of me.' It's a whole other way of creating.
AB: I was not thrown off by it. I got very into it. I went prepared that it's going to be totally unpredictable. Also, I'm a little bored with routine. I really connected with his frequency. It's also, 'Oh, every day is a new experience.' It was exhausting, but in a great way.

AC: This year is your tenth year in the movies. After this, you've got *RRR*, *Brahmāstra*. What are you really hungering for now?
AB: I don't really know. We've been in pause mode for two years. I'm first waiting for the unpause to actually happen, which will happen now with *Gangubai* and then *RRR* and *Brahmāstra*. I also have my first production, *Darlings*. I'm just sort of sussing and seeing what keeps me happy. It's about whatever is exciting and fun.

AC: Is that a stage of evolution where you become zen-like and it's not so much about being number one or any of those things?
AB: Zen-like I'll never be because I just don't have that.

AC: I don't have a zen bone in my body!
AB: I don't. As much as I try and hope for it. In some situations I can be. I want to do well because I'm a competitive person, but I'm competitive with myself. I've always said this: 'I'm competing with myself.' If a film doesn't meet my expectations, I get disappointed with my mind. I'm dying to do a comedy. I feel like I'm a very funny person. But I'm not like feeling like, 'Oh, some bone in me as an actor is not satisfied.'

AC: You're in a happy place.
AB: I'm in a chill place.

AC: You're in a place where you can get any film you want made. So, why production?

AB: It's not really a burden if you are recognising the potential of a script and I'm getting a percentage on the profit. It's a great thing for me. But for me, it's actually about [the fact that] I've reached a certain point where I think I'm in a good position to support new work and talent. At the end of the day, we are all contributing to cinema. So, why can't I be part of the creative production process? Putting a project together creatively, holding the director or the writer's hand, that's something that I want to do. My next ten-year plan – it's building my production house.

AC: What's the larger ambition for it?

AB: Funding new voices, telling beautiful stories – heart-touching, emotional, sometimes strange, psychological, thriller. I want to tell stories that are unpredictable. I don't think I can do the big tentpole films. But the films on OTT, those are the films I want to produce, start a conversation.

AC: You want creative control. You want to nurture new talent.

AB: I would like to do that. It's not going to happen overnight. I have to build it. People who maybe watch this in these interviews, if they're young writers, directors, reach out to me.

AC: How do they find you? Is there an email?

AB: Good question. There is an email ID which I think I should put out. I have an Instagram page called 'Eternal Sunshine Productions.' They can DM on that.

AC: And somebody's minding those DMs?

AB: Yes.

AC: In December, we did a 'Producers Adda'. I was talking to Zoya about *Jee Le Zara*. She said the reason you can now make this film with three massive female A-listers is because of intent. She said that Priyanka talked to you and Katrina. They reached out to her. Farhan independently already had this idea about three women in a movie and it all came together. Do you feel like women are a little more evolved now?

AB: It's taken even the women a lot of time to get here.

AC: But ho toh raha hai (it's happening at least).

AB: It's about time! *Gangubai*, for example. They've been saying words like 'female-led film' and the conversation has always been there but for some reason the action has not happened. With *Jee Le Zara*, the action of us coming together is basically saying that, 'We're all very comfortable in where we are at in life.' Also, we're working with makers who are very well known for writing every character so beautifully – Zoya, Reema, Farhan, Ritesh. There's no fighting, 'Yours is bigger, mine is smaller, whose dress is nicer.' We're past that.

AC: Way past, I'm sure.
AB: But I think even with male actors, now it's different. It's happening and I feel like the less we give attention to ke ho raha hai, nahi ho raha hai (whether it's happening or not), the cooler it'll be.

AC: Yeah, and also the less attention perhaps we give on your marriage. How do you deal with this?
AB: You know, it's actually caused some fights between me and my friends.

AC: Do they think they're not invited?
AB: No, because the thing is I'm so busy and I forget a lot, so they sometimes think, 'Has she forgotten to tell us or something?' It's become like the boy who cried wolf. They're crying wolf so often that actually when I am supposedly getting married, people will think it's a rumour and it'll be great for me because no one will know.

AC: Okay, last question. *Gangubai* is going to the Berlin Film Festival.
AB: Yes.

AC: Carlo Chatrian, the artistic director said that they were just taken by this story of an exceptional woman in exceptional circumstances. What does the festival do for you as an actor?
AB: Well, I don't know. It's my third time there. *Highway*, I was so new and so unaware. *Gully Boy* also was a great experience. But every time you go to this festival, it's just about like taking your film outside the country. Even when my father saw that film, he was like, 'This international crowd will be very impressed with this film.' And also, when we do premiere the film, they're watching the film with the audience.

AC: It's a massive hall.

AB: Massive hall, walking a red carpet – it's fun to get to dress up. How do I measure whether it's a success or not?

AC: But do you see it in any way as a step to international movies?
AB: I am. And I'm not doing it because of, 'Oh, I want to do an "international film".' I want to do challenging roles, I want new experiences. And it's about trying to create that experience for yourself.

AC: So, good luck. And I cannot wait to see it.
AB: Thank you so much.

12 February 2022

22

Karan Johar Unfiltered: Love, Legacy, Rocky Randhawa

Anupama Chopra: Karan, welcome to FC Postmortem. We have so much to unpack with *Rocky Aur Rani Kii Prem Kahaani*. But first, congratulations.
Karan Johar: Thank you, Anu.

AC: It really put a smile on my face and a spring in my step.
KJ: Yeah, well, I'm breathing finally. I've never been this stressed before a release. I had close friends, who would hug me and say, 'Hey, your body's shaking.' My friend Kajal said, 'Come with me, what has happened to you?' It's been a seven-year gap. Also, anxiety that built over the last three years with a lot that happened on social media. I suppressed and it all just came out. I found myself vulnerable and just tears rolled down right before the release. My mom held my hand and said, 'You okay?' and I just teared up. I have two grown-up, I mean two twin children, in the next room and I'm the one behaving like a baby. There was a lot of fear, anxiety, stress at the time of the release. I'm glad it all just came out. When the film released I just said it's out there now I just have to hope for the best.

AC: How are you feeling right now with the box office, the rave reviews?
KJ: The box office is lovely and it's gratifying. I have never received these kinds of reviews. I'm not used to them. There's always a certain level of polarisation where my films come – two stars, some three, or you get bashed completely. *My Name is Khan* got some good reviews, 60 to 70 per cent positive. This time there was like good reviews everywhere and I was like. 'What is happening?' When you liked the film I got worried. I was like, 'Oh I'm not used to Anu liking my film.' Everyone at *Film Companion* liked it. I asked you for Rahul Desai's number, because I was like, 'Rahul Desai liked my film?' Mayank Shekhar liked it. People are writing columns on it. Apoorva was trying to track the box office collections, I was so happy to revel in this critical love. Anurag Kashyap

called me and said I've seen your film twice. In the same breath, I got a call from 'Guddu Uncle' Mr Rakesh Roshan. I was absorbing it. I was like this is not what I signed up for. I thought they're going to talk about the same song and dance, there are designer clothes. But I'm hoping they see . . . . I always feel like I try to do stuff but it never gets acknowledged. I was feeling surprised shocked and elated.

AC: I want to start with what I love most in the movie, Rocky Randhawa.
KJ: Yeah.

AC: He is just fabulous. I want to understand where he came from. What was your brief to your writers, Ishika, Shashank, Sumit?
KJ: In the pandemic when I put *Takht* on hold and I wanted to write a love story, I used to be on the gram a lot. There was a lot of these 'West Delhi' influencers, content creators, and I was very amused – they were so full of life and joyous, saying the funniest things. Rocky came from there. People kept thinking it was like two states – two different communities – mine was never about that, it was about patriarchy and matriarchy. Punjabi families are essentially patriarchal in nature.

AC: Even though they're led by a woman.
KJ: Yes. I brought the irony. Bengali families – how matriarchal they are and how beautiful that is, that is the core thought. Then I went back into a personal story which I don't want to speak about – which formed the crux of the Dharam-ji and Shabana-ji love story. When all that came together Rocky needed to be lovable, he had to be 'Poo', but updated.

AC: I think he's the most charismatic character you created after 'Poo'.
KJ: He was the male 'Poo'. He was like Ken to Barbie, but borrowing from 'Poo' who is Barbie also. It's ironic that Barbie is out. But he was like the perfect kind of Ken who had rough edges. I'm always amused and impressed by gym culture, I feel like boys who go to gym—

AC: Protein-shake drinking.
KJ: I feel like they only talk about that. I wanted him to be a gym boy, but also golden-hearted. He's into his BFF and into the family, he's everywhere but the type who will go to Emporio mall and shop.

AC: And buy everything!

KJ: Branded, because that's what he thinks is cool. That's how Shashank and Ishita and Sumit collectively brought Rocky Randhawa to life. But the important thing was – never should he come across as annoying, grating. It's a fine line.

AC: Yeah, it is.

KJ: Ranveer is a genius!

AC: It's such a match of actor and character, haina (right)?

KJ: Yeah.

AC: What was your brief to him?

KJ: I have no credit to take for that, Ishita wrote some great dialogue – she's half Punjabi, half Bengali – she grew up in Delhi. Shashank grew up in Kolkata, Sumit is Bengali. It was a clear writers' room of people who have seen these people. Rocky is lovable and vulnerable and obviously clueless, he really doesn't know his politics and he doesn't care. His aim is to run the family business and be himself, ride his Ferrari. When we gave it to Ranveer, and he heard the dialogue when we were on a recce for three weeks in Delhi, he would meet those Instagrammers. We had a long list including Yuvraj, who was with us on set right through. He would pick up lingo. Raat ko (in the night) he would be driving around Delhi, just getting the flavour. He never came on the locations but he was in the hotel working with the team, meeting Instagrammers, content creators, influencers. He created the Rocky Randhawa.

AC: Did he improvise lines?

KJ: Yes. He never veered away from the script but the lines were intrinsically very funny, so he had a lot to play with. He brought some Delhi lingo that he had picked up. In many ways Rocky is an OTT extension of Ranveer, but he is not like this all the time. He'll own the room but otherwise he'll vanish into his thoughts. He used to sit for hours with the character. The first day we shot with him – he thought we were shooting another scene. So he was like, 'Oh, I'm not prepped.' So I said, 'Okay take your time.' He went and, I don't know what he did, he came back and nailed the scene: boom! His best friend played by Abhinav, Vicky, was just as hilarious. Alia's sheer genius – she was organically reacting to them. Rani's reactions make Rocky even more intriguing. I said to her, 'You're turned on at this point but you don't want to admit it.'

AC: The dance that Ranveer and Tota Roy Chowdhury do – 'Dola Re Dola' – was spectacular. What was it like to create that?
KJ: Two homages – Yash Chopra with 'Tum Kya Mile'. I copied a Sanjay Bhansali set, with a lot of love and respect. But the sequence was beyond the set; I wanted to subvert 'Dola Re Dola'. As a child, I was very effeminate, and I used to dance to Lata-ji's songs. My dad used to watch and clap. Every time his friends came he would say, 'Karan, woh dance dikhao sabko (Karan, show the dance to everyone).' No one told me there was anything wrong with that at that time. Much later in college people look at you and laugh. Tota's character is borrowed from my childhood. He says, 'Hunar ka koi gender nahi hota (Talent has no gender).' I believe that. Rocky's coming around had to happen. The most macho man doing Kathak – everybody at the Sangeet laugh. That's what 90 per cent would do. They find feminism funny instead of appreciating it as an art form. Full marks to Vaibhavi who worked tirelessly on Tota and Ranveer. At one point, Ranveer had a meltdown, 'Man, I don't have this kathak in my body.' Tota was rehearsing for six months, in Kolkata. Ranveer rehearsed for over a month and a half just for that one-and-a-half-minute clip. He said, 'This is possibly the most challenging thing I've ever done.'

AC: Just like the joy, the high of the dance.
KJ: A lot of it came from my own . . . I wouldn't even call it traumatic, my dad was okay with me dancing – then why isn't the world?

AC: My all-time favourite moment. And the kiss . . . between Dharam-ji and Shabana...
KJ: Shabana-ji is a trooper . . . a master actor. Dharam-ji was like haa karna hai (Let's do it). I needed it to be a peck. One of my all-time favourites is 'Abhi Na Jao Chhod Kar'.

AC: No greater love song.
KJ: It had to be their song. That became the thematic connection of Rocky and Rani as well. It was just glorious. At one point I said, 'Let's go Manmohan Desai on this' – he stands up and sings. He's on a wheelchair but he only walks up for Shabana-ji twice. Love makes him walk. There is no logic and maybe we get away with it, go with the romance.

AC: And the lines. We have fallen off our chairs laughing.

KJ: A lot of the characterisations are born within me or from observation. I've met Ranis, I've seen Rockys. Full credit to the writers because we needed a commercial lens, we also needed a 'woke' lens. Shashank brought commerciality, Sumit and Ishita brought so much sensibility and political correctness. In stereotypical territory, let's not go wrong. Even Golu – as in Gayatri's character – I've been fat-shamed.

AC: A lot of critics have said that the film is like that line Rani thinks for Dhan Lakshmi.

KJ: 'Soch nayi, swaad vahi (New thinking, same taste).'

AC: Your soch (thinking) has always been nayi (new), your influences are maharatis (legends) of commercial mainstream but you push the envelope.

KJ: Because if you are messaging, if you don't do it in the packaging of a mainstream entertainer then, how are you going to reach many millions of people? An anthology like *Lust Stories*, *Bombay Talkies* – we talk about repressed sexuality or a woman's right to pleasure. How many people will see that? You have to walk that tightrope, and you can fall off. But it's all coming with conviction. When Shruti Jog completes 'Aaj Phir Jeene Ki Tamanna Hai', you can laugh at it or you clap with her. But it's coming from my space of Subhash-Ghai-conviction. Like Pyaar karne wale kabhi darte nahi, jo darte hain wo pyaar karte nahin – I've grown up clapping to those sequences. Even the song 'Dhindora' is from that, just updated. So I walk that tightrope.

AC: Do you struggle as a storyteller? When you sit down to create, do you think about – I can say this but not that?

KJ: Not in this film. I quite enjoyed the characters. Their backstories. The struggle was where Alia and I had to sit down and say how do we make this character lovable. It's credit to Alia's genius that her character is strong but also vulnerable. We struggled internally with projections of performances – but Anu, what did I not do? I went to the mountains for a love song. I did a Bhansali ode, a lip-sync song with all the girls in the industry. Big sets and dancers – everything I love about mainstream Indian cinema. But within that there was a story to tell that would hopefully resonate with a large section of society.

AC: The great propelling force in your cinema is love. You said to me that the one regret that you have is, you weren't very mindful of your own personal life. Is there a connection between that and the love in your films?

KJ: I think you live vicariously through cinema. Filmmakers can live their incomplete dreams. I'm only living vicariously. I'm not being able to translate that into finding my own big love story. You never know, though, but I enjoy creating those magical looks between two characters. It satiates that void within me. My love story with cinema is perhaps the biggest love story.

AC: Okay let's go back to the movie. The other scene that really moved me was when Rocky is telling Rani's family you can't cancel everybody. What was the challenge of writing that scene?

KJ: Oh, Ranveer really worked on that scene. Full credit to the writers. To flip the clichéd scene on its head. Of course he's gonna say sorry but what about the times they offended him? I saw Rocky saying, 'I screwed up I messed up, but what about you guys?' He says you know, mooh kholne se dar lagta hai (It's scary to open my mouth), which is relatable to a gazillion people. I keep lecturing my mother, because all the wrong words come out—

AC: I do it with my husband—

KJ: Your husband, more than my mother. Now today we'll say 'plus size', 'vertically challenged' . . . . We never said any of this. That scene resonated with people. He says, 'I don't speak language right – English language, and you laugh – that's also shaming right?' For the people who understand, it's a cancel culture scene. But the people who may not will still look at it and say, 'Yaar yeh sahi bol raha hai (He's right).' I've also had to be corrected, sometimes I think 300 times before speaking.

AC: But Karan, I felt that in the second half, the narrative did wobble under the messaging.

KJ: The edit was challenging. Nitin Baid is a genius editor. We tried very hard. There were ten principal characters and each needed closure. It was tough to pack in humour and say what you need to. The film was three hours and ten minutes long originally. We cut twenty-two minutes. I was ruthless, as was Nitin.

AC: Why did you truncate the songs?

KJ: Because I know people want to get on with it. Watch it on YouTube, our Amazon version will have the songs. The most beautiful song is

'Kudmayi' which ended in a dabba (box). I'm like it has to be 2.48 mins. The producer and the director fight. I care about how the film performs at the box office. Some decisions were taken to tighten it.

AC: When the music first dropped it was not appreciated. What have you taken away from that?
KJ: You can't compare *Ae Dil* to *Rocky Aur Rani*. *Ae Dil* has heartbreaking songs. This is a celebration film. This music will start picking up now with context. Pritam and Amitabh Bhattacharya are genius. 'Ve Kamleya', 'Tum Kya Mile', 'Kudmayi', 'Ro Lain De' – they will have a long shelf life. I never bought into the criticism.

AC: There was criticism of the chemistry. Ki chemistry nahi hai (There's no chemistry).
KJ: Ye toh kaha se, mujhe samaj hi nahi aata, unki itni chemistry hai (I don't understand where this came from, they have so much chemistry).

AC: And there was direct comparison with Shah Rukh...
KJ: How can you live up to that legacy? But I wanted to go to Kashmir and shoot a love song. Abi hoga comparison, of course. Maine hi woh gaaane banaye hai (Now there will be comparison, of course. I have made those songs). Kajol and Shah Rukh are an iconic pair. How can you even compare? Chemistry ke upar problem hai, gaano ke upar issue hai (There is a problem with the chemistry, there is an issue with the songs). They're feeling ki ye thoda serious film toh nahi, hai stupid toh nahi hai (This is not a serious film, it's not stupid). I just felt I'm not able to communicate. I had many concerned people messaging me.

AC: Did you lose heart?
KJ: No, experience and an onslaught of being hated gives you resilience. What got to me was, 'The film is gonna be out!' And I needed the validation, I was feeling very vulnerable. It's like your body needs sugar sometimes. It's been a weird couple of years. I wasn't sleeping. I reached out to people and said 'Can you be with me for these four or five days?' I found myself just weeping. I can't show this side to my mom – she feeds off my mood. Apoorva was a pillar, I had so much love.

AC: When did you breathe?

KJ: This morning . . . Eka Lakhani walked in and she said, 'Karan! How do you feel?' I said, 'I feel happy today.' But I don't go by statistics. It's my own feeling—

AC: Can I just hold your hands? It's so lovely—

KJ: I don't know how to react to this love? I feel like 'Wowww aisa bhi hota hai (Wow, something like this can also happen)!'

AC: I have one more question. Where do they live after marriage? Pratyush, my colleague, needs to know.

KJ: Absolutely valid question to ask. Rani would not move into Randhava Paradise. I think they would move into a separate home because now they get along with each other's families well enough for them to create a world of their own. I'm not so sure she would depend on Rocky's aesthetics, but well, you see – Rocky would not stop being Rocky . . . . So somewhere in Delhi.

AC: And what are you doing next? Holiday?

KJ: I am going to sleep . . . for many days and when I wake up . . . . I have films releasing, I have shows on, I have to do *Koffee with Karan*. I took a four-month sabbatical, I don't know if anyone noticed.

AC: This was your down time?

KJ: Yes . . . . I was keeping it low. My orange shoes just came out today—

AC: I missed it?

KJ: I'm very upset that no one noticed my low-key, strategic marketing vibe that just went down the drain.

AC: Please do consider my idea of the fashion line of Rocky and Rani—

KJ: Rocky and Rani need a fashion line, Manish Malhotra tells me that he has never received so many messages.

AC: The car and the coat . . . . It was fab.

KJ: The car and the coat was a happy accident.

AC: And in terms of films, are you thinking of anything else?

KJ: I'm writing, ideating . . . I don't want to take a long gap again.

AC: Dude, what is this seven years and all?
KJ: See, two and a half years went into *Takht,* and then two years with the pandemic.

AC: Which will get made?
KJ: Yes, it's a passion project, but I'm writing and developing.

AC: Congratulations again.
KJ: Thank you, Anu.

31 July 2023

23

'I'm Sexy and I Know It': Diljit Dosanjh

Anupama Chopra: First of all, congratulations on *Soorma*.
Diljit Dosanjh: Thank you, ji.

AC: You did a great job. I watched it just yesterday in the hall. It was packed.
DD: Oh, Waheguru!

AC: At the end, there was applause too. Really great work. We met in this very room two years ago. I've been following you for two years. And these two years have seen your career rise to new heights. But you said, 'I think I haven't achieved anything yet. So when I achieve that, I'll do another interview.' Was this an excuse to avoid me or do you *really* think you haven't achieved anything?
DD: Abhi film aayi hai ji toh maine kaha ki chalo yahaan aake thoda faayeda ho jayega film ko. Lekin banda interviews mein zyadatar gappe maarta hai aur apni badhai karta hai. Aur jo saamne baitha hai, who khud accha hai toh woh obviously unko accha-accha hi bolega. Toh uss se na baatein zyada dimaag mein bhi chad jaati hain, aur woh mujhe accha nahi lagta. Tabhi mujhe interviews dena achha nahi lagta. (Well, now there is a film that has just come out, so I thought that coming here would benefit it. But you know, people usually just chat and praise themselves during interviews. And the person sitting opposite them is also kind, so they too say only favourable things. This starts getting to your head too much, and I don't like that. And so I don't really enjoy giving interviews.)

AC: Do you accept now that you are an actor?
DD: Nahi, actor nahi. Actually, bande ko na koi prediction nahi karni chahiye. Kyunki apne haath mein kuch nahi hota, basically. Kayi baar banda sochta hai ki 'main aise kar sakta hoon'. Par yeh har roz ka process hai, learning ka. Aur jo aap kar rahe ho, kya aapki utni ehemiyat ya aukaat hai apne aap karne ki? Woh bhi Bhagwaan hi karwa raha hai aapse.

Waise toh hum sab part hi hain Bhagwaan ka. (No, I am not an actor. Actually, one shouldn't make predictions because, basically, nothing is in our hands. We may think, 'I can do this', but it is an everyday process of learning. Besides, can you really do something on your own? All of it is God's work. Actually, we, too, are a part of God.)

AC: But Diljit, when you watch your performance, especially in the second half of a film like *Soorma*, where there are such tough scenes, don't you think to yourself, 'Well done, I did a great job'?
DD: Aap kabhi sochte ho, main achha karunga, lekin kayi baar aisa hota hai ki jab aap shoot karne jaate ho, tab aas-paas ka mahaul aisa hota hai ki jo aap karna chahte ho, kayi baar nahi kar paate. Aur kayi baar koi itni achhi cheez nikal aati hai jitna aapne socha bhi nahi hoga. Usmein bhi aas-paas ki cheezein aapki help karti hain. Toh mujhe lagta hai nature hi help karta hai aapki. (Sometimes, you think, 'I'll do well', but it so happens that when you go for the shoot, the atmosphere around you affects you and you're not able to achieve what you want to do. And sometimes, your performance ends up being better than what you had expected. To achieve that, too, your surroundings help you. So I think nature itself helps you.)

AC: Do you never pat yourself on the back?
DD: Nahi ji. Abhi time nahi aaya woh. (No. It isn't time yet to do so.)

AC: In these two years, you've become a style icon.
DD: Oh my god!

AC: *GQ* magazine is writing so many articles about your style. When did this happen, and how did it happen?
DD: Yeh hi nahi pata chala ki yeh kab ho gaya, actually. (Actually, I didn't even realise when all of this happened.)

AC: Really?
DD: Haan ji, *GQ* main khareedta thha. Main khud uska grahak hoon. Hum waise hi sochte thhe ki, yaar, ismein kabhi humaari bhi photo aa gayi . . . . Aur woh sach mein aa gayi! Toh bande ko sahi-sahi sochna chahiye, apne liye bhi, doosron ke liye bhi. Fir sahi-sahi hi hoga. (Yes, I used to buy *GQ* magazine. I myself am its consumer. I used to think, maybe one day my photo would appear in it, too . . . and it actually did!

So a person should think positively, for themselves and for others. Then, only good things will happen.)

AC: But where did this fashion sense come from?
DD: Thhi, but paise nahi thhe. Abhi bhi Karan Johar jitne nahi hain mere paas. Unke paas bahut fashion hai. Paise ke saath hi aata hai fashion. Par, of course, soch bhi hoti hai. (It was always there, I just didn't have the money. I still don't have as much as Karan Johar does. He's got fashion sense, and that comes with money. But of course, there's also good taste.)

AC: There's a platform called Arré. And on that platform, there's a great writer, Karanjeet. I'll read out from an article she has written about you. She says, 'When has a Sikh man in mainstream Hindi cinema been considered an object of desire? When has his body been sexualized?'
DD: Nahin . . . sahi keh rahe hain . . . main samajh raha hoon, unke jazbaat sahi hain. (No . . . she's right . . . I understand, her emotions are correct.)

AC: The emotion is that you are sexy.
DD: Haan ji. I am sexy and I know it.

AC: How does it feel when you are seen as someone taking it forward singularly as the only mainstream Sikh hero?
DD: Mujhe lagta hai ki aa jayenge aur. Bahut saare aa jayenge. (I think more will come. In fact, many more will come.)

AC: You think?
DD: Haan ji. Aa jayenge, aur aane chahiye. Mujhe bahut saare ladke milte hain. Naye ladke bhi milte hain, jo turban baandhte hain, aur bolte hain ki 'yaar paaji humein bahut khushi hai, aap grow kar rahe ho … hum bhi aage badhna chahte hain.' Mujhe bahut saare mails aate hain, bahut saare ladkon ke portfolios aur photos aati hain jo sardar hain aur actor banna chahte hain. (Yes, many more will come, as they should. I meet a lot of young boys who wear turbans, and tell me how happy they are to see me represent them and how they wish to get ahead too. I get many emails as well as portfolios and photos of Sikh boys who want to become actors.)

AC: You had said in an interview that, 'I am hungry for good work.' Now good work isn't just Bollywood. Good work can also be Punjabi cinema, it

can also be your music. But are you not seduced and blinded by the power of Hindi cinema - its reach, the way it dazzles? Don't you get drawn to it?
DD: Bollywood mein abhi itna paisa kamaya nahi ji. Maine jo thoda bahut kamaya hai, woh apne shows se kamaya hai, apne music career se kamaya hai, Punjabi filmon se kamaya hai. Bollywood mein maine itna paisa nahi banaya hai kyunki maine itni koi badi hit di nahi hai, toh itna bada artist main hoon hi nahi. Paise deke aap kisi ko le lo aur uska mann hi na lage wahan par, wo mujhe nahi karna. Uss cheez se main darta hoon. Main jitna karna chahta hoon, apna karna chahta hoon, chaahe who thoda hi ho. Aisa baadu-buddu type nahi karna chahta ji. (In Bollywood, I haven't made much money yet. The little I've made, I've made from my shows, my music career, and Punjabi films. I haven't really delivered a massive Bollywood hit, and so I'm not such a big artist yet. You can pay someone to be a part of a project, but if their heart isn't in it, it doesn't work. And I don't want to do that; I'm afraid of that. I want to do what I *truly* want to do. And I don't want to be a sidekick to anyone.)

AC: But has your mind settled in Bollywood?
DD: Hindi film industry mein jo bhi kaam mil raha hai, main woh kar raha hoon. (In the Hindi film industry, whatever work is coming my way, I am doing that.)

AC: And is there happiness in that work?
DD: Haan ji bilkul, khushi hai. Main kaam hi woh karta hoon jis se khushi mile. Lekin kayi baar aisa kaam bhi karta hoon, jismein khushi nahi hoti. (Yes, definitely, there is happiness. I only do work that brings me happiness. But sometimes I also take up work that doesn't bring me joy.)

AC: Do you have any advisors for Hindi cinema who guide you about which script is good and which is bad? Do you ask anyone?
DD: No.

AC: So how do you choose?
DD: Bas jo dil ko theek lage. Waise hona chahiye koi? Main aap se poochna chahta hoon. (I just choose whatever feels right. But should I have an advisor? I want to ask you.)

AC: People usually have advisors. Like I just interviewed Janhvi and Ishaan . . . maybe their advisor is Karan, because they're working in Dharma.

DD: Karan-ji toh bahut intelligent hain. Woh toh bata sakte hain. Humare paas toh Karan-ji nahi hain. Toh hum toh apne aap hi karte hai. Hum apne hi Karan-ji hain. (Karan Johar is very intelligent. He can guide you well, but I don't have him in my life. So I do it myself. I am my own Karan.)

AC: So you pick what pleases your mind?
DD: Bilkul. Agar kisike paas ho toh bahut achhi baat hai. Lekin jiske paas nahi hai, chalte chalo aise hi. Bante jaayega raasta. (Exactly. If you have advisors and things are sorted, then it's great. But for those who don't have any such support, create your own path and keep moving. Things will naturally fall into place with time.)

AC: So what's next? What would you do in Hindi cinema now?
DD: Kuch bhi. Jo theek lage aur jo pyaar mohabbat se karwa lein, wo hum kar sakte hain. (Anything. Whatever feels right and is asked of me with love, I'll do it.)

AC: What do you mean if they ask 'with love'?
DD: Maine kayi baar dekha hai set pe na logon ko ainvayi kisi aur par chillate huye. Kayi baar log mic par chilla rahe hote hain. Chillane ki zarurat nahi hoti hai. Mic toh hota hi issliye hai ki aap slow bolo aur aapki awaaz idhar-udhar phail jaye. Toh artist bechaare ka mann aisa ho jata hai. Mera mann bhi dukhi ho jaata hai phir. Main bhi toot jata hoon fir udhar ke udhar set se. (Many a time, I've seen people shout at others for no reason on set. Sometimes people shout into the mic, even though it is there in the first place to ensure your voice reaches a large audience even if you speak softly. So the poor artists feel bad. I, too, feel upset and end up feeling disconnected from the set.)

AC: Now, as an actor, are you willing to take more risks? Because after *Soorma*, your range is visible to people, showing that you can do this too. So are you willing to do other things?
DD: Haan ji, haan ji. (Yes, yes.)

AC: Okay Diljit, tell me this. The Spanish song that you did was totally gangster, mafia-style, with high-end cars, private jets and long luxury vehicles. In these music videos, are the kind of stories that play out your own fantasies?

DD: Haan ji, woh meri fantasies hain. Wo jo Spanish waala gaana aapne bola, uske music video ne mere paise kharaab kiye. *Peaky Blinders* dekhi hai aapne? (Yes, those are my fantasies. That Spanish song you mentioned, its music video made me pointlessly splurge a lot of money. Have you seen the series *Peaky Blinders*?

AC: No.
DD: Wo Netflix pe hai aur mujhe bahut achhi lagti hai. Toh main waisi video banana chahta thha. Wahin mere paise kharaab hue. (It's on Netflix, and I really like it. So I wanted to make a video inspired from it. And I ended up unnecessarily splurging a lot because of that.)

AC: Yes, the production value was quite high.
DD: Bahut high thha. Wahan mere paise kharaab ho gaye. (Yes. Indeed. A lot of money was wasted.)

AC: Why do you say it was wasted?
DD: Punjabi gaane ko itni badi video ki zaroorat nahi thhi, kyunki itni income nahi hai. Na toh koi buy karta hai, na CD bikti hai, na koi royalty aati hai. Sirf YouTube pe hits hain. Punjabi gaane ki itni mehengi video worth nahi hai. Business point of view se sahi nahi hai. (There was no need for such an expensive video for a Punjabi song, because the income isn't that much. Nobody buys it, CDs don't sell, and royalties don't come in either. These are only hits on YouTube. From a business point of view, it's not right.)

AC: Did you get a sense of satisfaction though?
DD: Satisfaction toh baad mein pata chala. But uss samay music video plan karte karte budget badhta hi gaya. Maine kaha, 'Oh my god, yeh maine kya kar liya?!' Bande bula liye thhe yahaan wahaan se. Toh jab saare set pe aa gaye, tab pata chala ki budget bahut badh gaya hai. Phir baad mein pata chala ki bahut badi galti kar di. (Well, the satisfaction came later, after the music video came out. But when I was planning it, the budget kept increasing manifold! I was like, 'What have I done?!' I had hired people from all sorts of places. So when everyone gathered on set, I realised the budget had gone way up. Later, I realised I had made a huge mistake.)

AC: All right, now tell me about another hobby of yours. Last time I met Badshah, he was telling me that sneakers, like the ones you're wearing, all cost lakhs. Even branded jackets and watches have become so expensive.

You have to lie to your family by lowering the price when you tell them how much these cost.

DD: Tag toh kabhi jaa hi nahi sakta. Aaj jo yeh meri chamakti shirt hai, yeh meri mummy mujhe pehnne bhi na dein. Aur jo maine Gucci pehna hai . . . yeh sochne waali baat hai ki ismein aisa kya laga hai, hai na? (You just can't remove the tag. This shiny shirt that I'm wearing today, my mom wouldn't even let me wear it. And the Gucci I'm wearing . . . it really makes you think what all goes into this to make it so expensive, right?)

AC: What's with Punjabi stars and their addiction to shopping?
DD: Matlab agar aap humaara bank balance dekho toh zero hai. (I mean, if you look at our bank balance, it's zero.)

AC: How is that even possible?
DD: Sachi, kapdon-kupdon mein hi hai sab. Bas kapde le lo, ghadiyan le lo . . . dikhaava hi hai bas. (Honestly, it's all about buying clothes, watches, and other expensive stuff . . . it's all just show-off.)

AC: Really?
DD: Haan ji, bank balance nahi hai apna. Utna bada banda nahi hoon jitna log kehte hain. Ek kapde ka, ek khane ka, do hi shauk hain mujhe. Baaki mere mein aisa koi bura shauk nahi hai, toh phir main apne aap ko rokta nahi hoon. Pata hai mujhe yeh galat baat hai, par aapko pata hota hai na yaar, ki yeh khaake main mota ho jaaunga, yeh meri sehat ke liye theek nahi, fir bhi khaate ho, peete ho. Wohi cheez mere liye fashion hai. (Yes, I don't really have a big bank balance. I'm not as big a guy as people think. I only have two indulgences: clothes and food. But since I don't have any other bad habits, I don't stop myself from indulging, even though I know it's wrong. It's like you know you'll gain weight if you eat something, or that drinking is bad for your health, but you still do it. Fashion is the same for me.)

AC: How lovely! Your Instagram and Snapchat tell me everything about your life, like when you're making smoothies with almond or coconut milk. By the way, I bought a smoothie blender because of your Snap but made the smoothie only once.
DD: Maine bhi do ya teen baar hi banayi. (I too only made it only two or three times.)

AC: So Diljit, though you're so open, we don't know anything about your family. You have a sister, but you never show her face. In your last interview, you mentioned that you only listen to your mother, but I've never seen her either. Why is that?

DD: Ji maine life mein bahut criticism sahaa hai pehle. Main ek aisa Punjabi artist hoon jiske ghar ke bahar protest hua hai . . . kisi gaane ko leke, jo do saal tak hit raha, bahut log uspe naachte thhe, aur uske baad ekdum se protest ho gaya. Uske baad logon ne meri life aur career mein kaafi interfere karne ki koshish ki. Shayad kayiyon ko lagta thha ki main unka business kha raha thha. (I've faced a lot of criticism in my life. I am a Punjabi artist who has experienced protests outside his very own house . . . for a song which was a hit for two years, with many people dancing to it, after which, suddenly, there was a protest over it. And after that, many people tried to interfere in my life and career. Maybe some thought that I was taking their business away.)

AC: Were they meaning to sabotage you?

DD: Kaafi kuch hua. Meri cheezein tab sabke saamne aa gayi thhin kyunki social media aa gaya thha. Mujhe yaad hai ki jab ghar ke bahar protest shuru hua, maine apni mummy ko bola ki, 'Aap Mama-ji ke ghar chale jao. Kal maine suna hai kuch hone waala hai yahan.' Jo bhi thha, galti toh meri hi thhi. Lekin meri mummy ka mere mama-ji ke ghar jaana mujhe itna dukhaa. Meri pehli album aayi thhi, mai atthhra saal ka thha. Aaj main taintees saal ka hoon. Toh obviously banda uss age main galti karta hai. Kayi baar aap right subject nahi choose karte ho kisi gaane ka, main usko bhi maanta hoon, lekin usme parivar ki galti nahi hai. Woh mera decision hai. Aap mujhe gaali do, achha-bura bolo, lekin mere parivar ko nahi. Jitna koi kisi ko peeche kheechta hai, banda utna hi aage nikal ke aata hai. Toh tab maine decide kiya thha ki parivar par kabhi aanch nahi aane dunga. Issliye family ke baare mein kabhi discuss nahi kiya. Na kisi ko batata hoon, na kabhi photo daalta hoon. (A lot happened. My issues became public because social media was around. When the protest was happening outside my house, I remember telling my mom to go to my uncle's house because I'd heard that some demonstrations had been planned for the next day too. Whatever happened, the mistake was mine. But my mom having to leave the house really hurt me. My first album came out when I was eighteen. Today, I'm thirty-three years old. Obviously, a person makes mistakes at that age. Sometimes, you don't choose the right subject for a song, and I accept that. But that wasn't my family's mistake, it was my decision. You can call me names, say good or bad things about me, but not about my family. The more someone tries to pull you down, the further you rise up and move forward. So I decided back then that I wouldn't let anything happen to my family. That's why I've never publicly discussed them. I never tell anyone about them, never post pictures of them.)

AC: Really?
DD: Hundred per cent! Main kyun bataun kisi ko ki main kahan hoon? Main yeh sabh sirf issliye karta hoon taaki main logon mein bana rahoon. Aur koi maadhyam hai nahi, na hi koi godfather hai. Koi bataane wala nahi, koi salaah dene wala nahi. Aur aisa koi bank balance bhi nahi. Yahin se shuru hua hai, yahin pe uda rahe hain. Toh issliye main family ko nahi involve karta. Mujhe bura bolein, main seh sakta hoon . . . lekin parivar ko koi bura bole, main jaan le loon uss bande ki, kyunki mere parivar ki koi galti nahi. (A hundred per cent! Why should I tell anyone where I am? I only do it so I can remain relevant and popular among people. There is no other medium, no godfather, no one to tell me what to do, no one to give me advice. And there's no big bank balance either. It all started from here, and so I spend it here. That's why I don't involve my family. If someone says something bad about me, I can handle it. But if anyone says anything bad about my family, I won't leave them, because it's not my family's mistake.)

AC: You note every fan comment, retweet fan tweets and respond to them, too. And it's not just during film promotions; you're constantly active on social media. Does this ever feel like a burden, now that you have millions of fans, or do you still enjoy doing it?
DD: Abhi toh main sabko jaanta hoon, personally bhi. Bahut log milte hain, mere itne fans hain. (Now, I feel like I personally know them. I meet a lot of people, I have so many fans.)

AC: Social media is almost like a beast. You have to keep feeding it every single day. Does this come naturally to you?
DD: Haan. Kayi baar main apne aap ko rok doon, toh rok doon. Otherwise toh overflow hi chalta hai kaam. (Yes. Sometimes, if I'm able to stop myself, I do so. Otherwise, the work keeps overflowing naturally.)

AC: Now you've even made it to Madame Tussauds!
DD: Oh my God! Yes, wo pata nahi kaise ho gaya. (Oh my God! Yes, I don't know how that happened.)

AC: What was that experience like? I heard that they were even measuring your eyeballs! What exactly was the Madame Tussauds team doing?

DD: Woh kal aaye thhe. Main soch raha thha, jab gaon mein hum darzi se kapde silwaate thhe, toh woh pant nahi deta thha mahinon-mahinon tak. Uske peechhe pade rehte thhe: 'Yaar meri pant toh dede, byaah nikal jayega, byaah ke baad maine pant ka kya karna hai?!' Kal mujhe wohi baat yaad aa rahi thhi. Pehle darzi measurement leta thha, aaj Madame Tussauds waale measurement le rahe hain! Bhagwaan pata nahi kya karna chaahta hai life mein. (The Madame Tussauds team came yesterday. It made me think of times when we used to get clothes stitched from the village tailor. He wouldn't give me my pants for months. I used to keep on chasing him: 'Man, give me my tailored pants. Otherwise, the wedding will be over. What good would the pants be then?!' Earlier, it was the village tailor taking my measurements, and now it's people from Madame Tussauds! Who knows what plans God has for me and my life.)

AC: How exciting! So Diljit, now that you've reached this point, what else do you wish to do? I remember you once said that you want to learn English and star in a Hollywood film.

DD: Ji yahi karna hai . . . Angreji seekhni hai aur Hollywood mein film bhi karni hai. (Yes, that's it. I want to learn English and star in a Hollywood film.)

AC: And are you 'urban' or still 'rural'?

DD: Bahar se chaahe Gucci–Balenciaga ho rakha ho saara samaan, main andar se bilkul pendu hoon. Urban-urban baahar hai, pendu-pendu andar hai! (Everything I'm externally wearing is Gucci or Balenciaga, but I'm still a total villager internally. Urban on the outside, rural on the inside!)

AC: Diljit, thank you so much and many congratulations once again!

DD: Thank you so much ji mujhe itni khushi ke samay bulaane ke liye. Bahut achhe reviews aa rahein hain film ke. Aur ab *Udta Punjab* bhi release hogi. (Thank you so much for calling me on such a joyous occasion. The film is receiving very good reviews. And now *Udta Punjab* should be out in the theatres soon.)

18 July 2018

24

In Conversation with Decade-Defining Actors

Ranveer Singh, Ayushmann Khurrana, Deepika Padukone, Alia Bhatt, Vijay Devarakonda, Vijay Sethupathi, Manoj Bajpayee and Parvathy Thiruvothu

Anupama Chopra: *Film Companion* has done a list of the hundred greatest performances of the last decade. And we managed to get some of the actors on that list into a room. Ranveer, let me start with you. You started in 2010 with *Band Baja Baraat, Gully Boy, Simmba*. You are that adbhut mishran (wonderful or amazing mixture) of outside stardom and acting chops. How has it been for you to find that balance between box office and quality?

Ranveer Singh: It's something my mentor Adi Chopra encourages me to achieve. Ideally, you want a credible film that does really good numbers. The appeal of every film is different. A film like *Simmba*, it came out around the same time as *Padmaavat* and *Gully Boy*. People talk about my performances specifically in *Padmaavat* and *Gully Boy*, but I can never figure out why! Because for me, the performance is *Simmba*. He's goofing around in one scene, dead serious the next. That was a task. A real winner film is one that people love over decades.

Ayushmann Khurrana: When he made his debut in 2010, I was prepping for *Vicky Donor*. I wanted to be that Delhi guy. And after watching it, I was like, 'Isne toh kar diya! Main kya kargunga? (He did it, now what do I do?)'

Deepika Padukone: Actually, when I met him afterwards, I always thought—

Alia Bhatt: That he was from Delhi?!

RS: Exactly!

AK: For two years, I was thinking he's a Punjabi!

DP: I would have been very happy with a South Indian boy.

RS: Just wait for two days, I'm going to Tirupati in a dhoti.

AC: It's the choices all of you have made. You've pushed the boundaries. Alia, you picked *Highway* as your second film. Deepika picked *Piku*, Vijay [Sethupathi] begged to play a transgender character in *Super Deluxe*. How do you find that sur? Is there fear?

DP: I think there's always that fleeting moment of fear or doubt. But you remind yourself of that moment when you said yes to the script. And you kind of sail through. And you've got to go through those experiences otherwise there's no excitement. It's the risks, that's what makes you want to go to work every day.

AC: Vijay, did you have that moment of fear with *Super Deluxe*?

Vijay Sethupathi: Yeah, but the script was so awesome. In one scene my kid asks me, 'Why you weren't born as a female?' That scene was written so well that I decided that I don't want to miss this film. I begged him actually, you don't need to pay me I just want to do this film. So the first scene took about fifty or sixty takes. Finally, I realised that female-self inside me. I never ever wanted to copy from anybody. Just I want to feel it inside, I never go and watch the monitor also. If it touches me, then I feel it's working. It takes n number of takes, but that doesn't matter.

RS: May I just add, Sir? Manish Sharma called me and told me to watch *Super Deluxe*. That there's a ten-year-old kid in there who'll make you rethink your whole craft. Raj Kutty is a phenomenon. Must watch for the chemistry between you and the child.

VS: Whenever he forgets the dialogue he says, 'OK, I'll go for one more'. Kumar Raja as a director never says, ok. He always asks for one more. One day that kid was directing other kids himself. So the two kids are acting and he says, action. Cut. One more.

AC: Shoojit Sircar said the women are far braver than the men. Is this true?

RS: Well, I just think you're dead if you're not taking a risk.

AC: Are female actors more willing to take risks?

RS: Not necessarily. Ayushmann delivered seven hits in a row. Can you imagine these films being considered mainstream even five years ago?

AK: He sent me this amazing video message. So beautiful. It touched me. Thank you so much for that, Ranveer.

RS: Please, Sir, answer the question.

AK: I think life is about risk-taking.

DP: Yes, I think women are [braver], yes. Not to interject.

AC: Vijay, you're saying no?

Vijay Devarakonda: How can you say that? Poor man went bald.

DP: I don't mean from the current generation of actors who are taking risks. Take female actors before us, Tabu, for instance. They were okay to play older women, transgender, bisexual. They attempted that much earlier than the guys.

VD: It was much harder for them.

DP: You wouldn't see a mainstream hero be like that . . . . He's still trying to be the hero when he's fifty and sixty. Women had no option but to break into different kinds of roles.

AC: Vijay, what were you saying?

VD: It's been much harder for them. The actresses get judged—

AB: I think what DP is also trying to say is that mainstream heroes feel that they owe it to their audience and their fan base to do a certain kind of film more. Which I don't think is a bad thing. If you take all the actresses together and you compare them to . . . actors, the actresses would have probably done more versatile parts. But it's not like that makes the actor lesser actors.

DP: I rest my case.

AB: But I wanted to say, about *Simmba*, it is very difficult to make a film like that. To reach out pan-India, for everybody to dance in the theatre along with you. It's harder to make a hit film. It's easier to make a good one.

DP: That's also a function of it being comedy. People will think Khilji is far more difficult because of the intensity. But comedy seems casual, when, it's one of the most difficult genres to do.

AK: Formula commercial film is the most difficult to make.

RS: What is the formula, Mr ROI.

AK: *Simmba* is the most difficult film.

AB: Let's put it this way. Every actor's performance, versatile or not, it's still very inspiring because it's hard to do both.

AC: Absolutely!

AB: It's not easy to do either.

AC: But, Ayushmann, can that brand become a trap? Because you are now the poster boy for woke, socially responsible cinema.

AK: I would love to do an *Article 15* or *Andhadhun* in between, but this is my staple. It's like asking Tiger Shroff not to do action. The messaging should be correct in the end. I would love to do a grey character. For a while and then come back to it again. But it depends on the kind of scripts I get. I would love to break away every two or three films. But this is my zone. I love it.

AC: So when an actor is making a choice, is there a moral responsibility? Parvathy, you've been clear that you will not do films that have item songs. Even if you like the film, you're not going to break that?

Parvathy Thiruvothu: Well, if I have to like the film, then it won't have that. I mean it's a very fine line between reflecting misogyny and glorifying it. When a man is being misogynistic and is shown in a way that incites applause, that's glorification. If you make the audience think, then you are collaborating with them. The other one is almost like spoon-feeding you [and telling you] that this is okay. I remember sitting in the theatre watching such films as a teenager and squirming, but everyone's clapping. So I was very confused. And then it reflected in my personal life. I thought passive-aggressive and abusive relationships were all right. When you're sitting for two and a half hours in a dark room and you have this collective expression subconsciously something remains within you. I can feel lustful towards a character and not make that make you vulgar and dispensable. You can always show bad characters, but that's where the visual grammar in a director comes out. You can reflect.

Manoj Bajpayee: I personally don't care about the messaging. I do it for myself. I'm in this business because I wanted to be here. When you're facing the camera you're not thinking about the audience. So I disagree with Alia when she says that it's easy to make a good film. Everybody wants to make one, but a hit film *happens*. You know you put your heart and soul and belief into it to first make it a good film and then you start praying for it to be a hit.

DP: Sir, you'll be surprised the number of people who work backwards.

RS: Matlab (meaning)?

DP: Who start counting the numbers and say now let's write this script and cast these people.

MB: But, you know, this trend I have been seeing for many years.

DP: It's dishonest.

MB: But all those people failed. Post *Satya* things were changing. Ram Gopal Varma was ruling, they started trying to find some kind of formula in his films. He became the victim of his own formula. But a good film . . . Whether it's Ayushmann's films or Alia's or you know Ranveer's or

Deepika's. I loved *Arjun Reddy*. There was so much talk about misogyny, but primarily it engaged, and this is what matters.

AB: I'm a selfish actor, I want to play a character for the heck of it – serial killer, an abusive lady, demure chick who suddenly goes mad. It may be totally off, but I want to do it to satisfy that thing within me that says you can't be that in real life so might as well play it. A film like *Joker*. It's gotten into so much controversy. 'Oh, are you glorifying this?' It's an adult film, the director is very clearly proving that he is mentally unstable. So if you give that padding to prove this is not okay.

PT: I agree with Alia. I want to play a sadistic character, someone who manipulates everyone. Because I want to understand how they get there. There's an anthropological pattern to acting. That's what excites me. But how it affects the audience, I came to see that only later. *Arjun Reddy* or *Kabir Singh* – both had the visual grammar of glorification, *Joker* did not. We can watch a tragedy and leave it without feeling inspired to follow it. Whereas if you're telling there is no passion in a relationship without slapping, I see the comments on YouTube where people are resonating with that. That is murky space. I think we have to be a little responsible.

AC: Sure. But, it's amazing that this character has connected in so many languages. Vijay, I need you to come in here.

DP: He looks like he's done.

RS: He came here to chill. He's here in shorts.

AK: He's such a hot guy. Man crush.

AC: So, I bought into the love story completely. Right? But I get your point. For an actor is it really interesting?

VD: I don't have any answers, I have questions. I feel like the world is fucked. By making a better film, can I save it? Pollution, water, behaviour, policies. . . . When it comes to films, I'm in between, I'm not like Manoj Sir. Like, this is a role I want to do, so I will do it. Neither am I like, social responsibility. I think it's too much – a film does not decide your behaviour. Family, parenting, schooling do. I've seen films where actors smoke, I don't smoke. I've seen murders. So, multiple reasons that decide how we become and behave. If I really like a role, I'll justify it to myself. Sometimes I use morality. I don't want to justify this, but it is completely possible that a couple is completely in love, and they give each other little hits, and they're still in love. I saw my father abusing my mother . . . when I come from that background – *Arjun Reddy*, it's scary. I can't make a film for everybody's values.

AK: The primary goal of films is entertainment.

MB: Please say engagement, not entertainment!

AK: Message will never carry entertainment, but entertainment will always carry message. So I've not seen *Arjun Reddy* or *Kabir Singh*. Fame makes you an opinion leader. Why don't sportspersons smoke openly? When I was fifteen, I saw *Mohabbatein*, and I thought I should break the gates of my school, start dating this chick and run.

AB: I went and cut my hair after watching *Kuch Kuch Hota Hai*!

AK: So, you get influenced!

MB: I completely disagree with you, because films can only change the way you dress, your hairstyle. Not your moral values. It starts with family. I have seen so many films, but someone cannot molest a girl in front of me, I'll thrash his skull. This is the way I have been brought up!

DP: In our country, cinema influences. It may not be the only influence – upbringing, schooling, peers, are important. But cinema and cricket are the two most influential things. You want to do films because you just want to tell stories, then so be it. You want to be an actor that feels responsible – I want to be responsible, that's a choice.

AK: Very well said.

AC: This is an eternal debate.

VD: And there is no solution.

AC: Vijay, when I interviewed you last time, I said you're a star, isn't it your job to be liked? And you said, no, it's my job to tell stories. But so much of much of the fame that you all have now is dependent on social media. So, how do you handle that?

AB: Apart from getting trolled and stuff.

MB: She deleted her social media

AB: Yeah, I deleted it.

DP: But then she came back on it!

RS: If you're doing well then you should be back on it!

AB: Be yourself. I want to dress up, take pictures of myself, post them. That's genuine to my core. But yes, this trolling culture. People who are not celebrities also get stuck, checking how many likes they have, checking positive comments on their pictures.

DP: That's very toxic.

AK: It's become a profession.

AB: So people keep telling me, 'Oh, did you read the comments?' I've been not reading comments since my first film, because from my first film I've been getting hate. Nepo, this, that . . . so that affected me.

MB: I feel that you promote your film and disappear .

AC: (To Vijay Sethupathi) I hear you're very big on Facebook.

VS: No, I don't use Facebook or Twitter.

AC: Use it to promote and get out.

VS: And I don't watch any comments or anything. I get so much anger, so...

MB: Same here

VS: I stopped reading comments. So my admin, I just ask him to post.

AB: Sometimes sitting with your friends and reading the mean comments is a very fun exercise. Also to just kind of address the other side.

AK: It's like a reality check in a way. I'm the social media baby. I'm the relatable guy, I was a VJ, an RJ, I am that person.

RS: Haan haan, nangi wali selfie bhi toh daali hai (Yes yes, you've even posted naked selfies)!

AK: Yaar, mujhe apni filmon mein mauka nahi milta body dikhane ka (I dont get the opportunity to show my body in my films).

AC: Vijay [Devarakonda], what about you? Are you very active?

VD: Right now I need it so I'm there.

AC: You don't enjoy it?

VD: I don't know a quicker way to reach as many people.

DP: Go door to door.

VD: So I'm not particularly fond of it.

DP: The positivity or the negativity cannot be your only metric. If people are trolling you, it doesn't mean the whole nation feels that way.

PT: But that's what – it can affect you like that. For the last two years, I've taken an annual digital detox. By October, I'll fall off social media. Too much of me out there, too much noise in my head, and then, I want to be invisible. But as an actor, I feel like I have to be thin-skinned enough to be a sponge every time I perform, so I can't be indifferent. In order to save my 'sponginess' I have to go away for a while. How do you come back to the limelight? I don't know, but I want my sanity,

AC: So, let's talk about craft a little bit. Ranveer, apparently while shooting *Lootera*, when your character gets shot, you put staples into the side of your stomach, and then you hit yourself.

AB: You stapled yourself?

RS: So, at that time I was very raw as an actor. I didn't know how to do it. When you're not comfortable with your craft, you operate from a place of insecurity, nervousness . . . and tend to do a lot more to achieve a certain effect. But I don't do that anymore. Now I know there is a more efficient way.

AC: You still go very deep into the character, and at the other end, Vijay [Sethupathi], there is you. I read an interview, you said that this whole thing about internalising is a myth. So how does an actor find his or her process?

DP: I've always been very averse to this question.

RS: Revealing things about your process?

DP: An actor's process. You never ask Roger Federer what he did to win the Wimbledon.

AK: But he sleeps for twelve hours.

DP: My point is, he's on the court and you see the performance. But you don't see athletes discussing their process.

RS: Yeah they're very protective. They feel like okay these are inside tips.

AK Everybody has their own trick. I used to be a method actor during theatre days, but then I realised it's good to be natural, go with the flow so that you are in sync with the director.

MB: You are never blank if you're reading the script. But I agree, don't over-prepare.

AK: Leave some blank canvas for the director also.

MB: So in the beginning, you have to go through the process, go through the grind to learn your own method, to acquire your own skill. As he [Vijay Sethupathi] said, I come out of it. But in the beginning of his career, he must have given his heart and soul.

AK: Was it like that, Sir [Vijay Sethupathi]? In the beginning also you used to be switching on and off? Or you were—

VS: I just understand the character through the dialogues and the way it is narrated. I'm a very spontaneous actor, so I go to sets and teach my co-actors. I believe in rhythm. then I make myself and everybody very comfortable. Nobody should fear that hero has come, then we should be like this . . . I always believe that my movies should give some hope to somebody. I always tell my co-actors, just go with the flow, I will do anything.

AB: Yeah, because you don't know what's going to happen when you're on camera. What I enjoy the most is, if I don't remember what I'm doing in a shot. Switching on and switching off, I agree, comes with certain kind of experience. I don't think I've had one particular process—

VS: Keep on changing.

AB: Some days I listen to music, some films, I'm chatting on the side.

MB: Shekhar Kapoor in *Bandit Queen* said, 'I don't care a fuck about your process. You deliver it in front of the camera.'

DP: Sanjay Bhansali's tactic is the same.

AB: Zoya came and said, 'Just act. Just do your job.' So I was like, don't take it seriously.

AK: What if your co-actor becomes too chatty with you before you close?

AB: Oh that's happened to me once.

AC: Vijay, you are taking your shorts very seriously and not saying anything and just chilling.

VD: No. I'm here to listen about process, so if anything works—

PT: He can take it!

AC: No, you have to comment.

VD: I have no clue what I am, but I hate these making videos and CG videos being put out.

RS: I've put this in my contract, no BTS.

AC: Post *Baahubali*, I think it's fair to say that regional is the new national. What are your biggest concerns about Hindi cinema? What is your fear?

VS: My fear is language. And then I don't know much about this culture and I don't watch Hindi films, so...

MB: Same. And he's working with Aamir – *Laal Singh Chaddha*!

VS: No, but I believe language anybody can learn. But the culture is very important.

AB: By culture, what do you mean, Sir?

AK: The nuances—

VS: Not the body language. You guys may think in a different way and we may think different. Maybe family-wise, friendship, financial status – anything. Every city and state has an energy I can connect with. South India – Tamil, Telugu, or Malayalam, I was working in Dubai for three years, I used to speak Hindi fluently. Now it's been sixteen years, so I have not kept in touch with it. We should know the culture, then only we can connect with the audience. If you have that pure love for the people, that innocence and purity, you can connect.

AK: Innocence for the craft is very important for sure.

AC: Vijay, what are you concerns?

VD: I think he said it perfectly. But coming from Hyderabad, there's a lot more Hindi, but you speak a different dialect called Dakhni. If I do Hindi, it will be restricted to some kind of neutral cinema that is not very rooted culturally.

PT: When I did the movie with Tanuja, I still had the South Indian accent, the nasal twang. But I do have a habit of mimicking.

AB: Same thing!! I always start talking like the person I was spending time with. Sponge!

PT: That's great for the job, but in real life you come across as fake because . . . I love learning languages, but I've done Kannada, Tamil films. It's like a little baby learning to walk, you'll keep emulating what the other person is doing, but you make mistakes. I make the effort to learn the language – bare minimum. And I do beg to dub. And if I do a bad job, please find the right person for it.

AC: If you could take advice on process, craft, acting, fame from one actor in Indian cinema, alive or dead, who would it be?

AB: It's a tough question.

AK: Let me just think about it.

MB: Marlon Brando.

AC: Nahi, Indian cinema!

MB: India mein Naseer, the God of cinema. I've never worked with him, I keep praying. Him and Om Puri Saab, who is no more. Single-handedly changed the definition of acting and Indian cinema. At this age, he's so passionate, he's so obsessed with the craft. I would like to spend some time with him, and learn a few of the things that he has done . . . somebody told me that Al Paccino watched *Sparsh* before doing *Scent of a Woman*.

VS: Sivaji Ganesan, he could do any kind of role. And then Kamal Sir. Brilliant. And then I like Mohanlal Sir. He is just doing it very easily.

MB: I would also like to spend some time with him [VIjay Sethupathi].

VS: Thank you so much Sir. M.G.R Sir.

VD: A lot of people on this table, I've had massive crushes, like been in love with some.

AC: Tell us!

VD: Like these two [Deepika Padukone and Alia Bhatt]. She [Deepika Padukone] got married—

DP: She [Alia Bhatt] is getting married—

AB: Excuse me, why have you made this declaration?!

DP: Guys, I made that up!

VD: And I've loved some of Manoj Sir's performances. Ranveer's work, when I watched *Gully Boy*, I couldn't sleep. I've really liked Ranbir, I also really like Meryl Streep, but these two, I don't want to talk to them and ask them their process because actors bullshit a lot. I don't think actors are even aware of what all they do.

DP: I'll always watch a movie and take away bits. But it's never been like one person or one kind of thing. Just keeping your eyes and ears open and learning everyday.

RS: Amitabh Bachchan is like my all-time hero. I started out wanting to be a Hindi film hero. But what I do love to do – and I do this like a fiend – whenever I get the opportunity to sit with the mainstream heroes, I love to learn about the movie business. Just to hear them out, their perspective, their history, their experiences. And most of them are very generous in sharing it.

AB: I should have thought about my answer this whole time, but I do have a fantasy like – get all the heroines together . . . yesteryear, living, dead, alive – in a room and for us to just have a conversation about experience to learn.

PT: Wow, what a beautiful dream. But we have that, because of the Collective. We kind of came together, and I realised how cool it is to have really veteran actors, female actors, talking about their experiences. I would love to work with Vijay [Sethupathi]. I think his process is very different. And so I hope it'll be a challenge and I'll be undone. Geetu Mohandas. She's a dear, dear friend, I just watched *Moothon*, about four days ago, and I wake up to scenes from it. It is so visceral.

AC: And Nivin Pauly is so amazing.

PT: Nivin and Roshan and all of them. But Geetu is very cut-throat with giving you feedback. Like, she's told me, you try too much, you're performing. Like everybody is just raving about it and she'll actually tell you. I want her to do that to me so that I'll be like, I can rearrange myself. Geetu is so brave, she just figured her own new technique. This business aspect Ranveer was saying, I would love to co-create a project with Zoya to understand how beautifully commercial she is and bang on with characterisation. She doesn't—

AC: She doesn't compromise.

AK: To begin with, while I was doing *Article 15*, the reference point was Manoj Sir's character in *Shool*. I think he was brilliant in that film. It's so internalised.

RS: I used to dress up as Bhiku Mhatre, I'm just saying.

AK: And taking a cue from him, I came to Mumbai in 2007. Ranveer is also one of the most versatile superstars we've ever had.

AC: Tell me, what do you all want to use your power for? Vijay, you said that, you know, anybody can walk in for an audition, and everybody will be heard. Because you were treated badly.

VD: I think stories are really important. If a lady is trying to take a picture, I get annoyed first. And then I start feeling guilty, then I'm like let me make a moment for her. I can go to set, make my movies, make my money, but I think it's about giving people and myself . . . some stories to tell. So it's about just trying to create as many stories as possible. And I love him [Ranveer] for just doing whatever the hell he wants. Even your MakeMyTrip ads are like . . . who makes the rules? Like I will dress how I want to, do what I want, be happy, how does it bother anyone?

RS: I'd just like to submit a broader perspective. I believe that we live in the Ghor Kalayug, it's the worst it's ever been. I believe I was born extra sensitive to the agonies of existence. So, I just want to make it bearable. Make people smile, make them feel light, make people happy, make them laugh . . . . And that's it.

VD: But, on our terms. I'm not like a puppet. I want to set the expectations.

AC: Let's just manage expectations here.

RS: Self-preservation is very important. But I find that I'm ever so willing for people to have a piece of me.

MB: What I'm finding so beautiful when I entered here is, this is the time we all have been fighting for. The coexistence of all kind of actors and all kind of cinema. All of them are doing well. It's so amazing.

AC: I'm so happy!

AK: In this era, it's so beautiful to be an artist.

DP: It's the most exciting time.

25 November 2019

25

Of Masks and Monsters: Nawazuddin Siddiqui

Anupama Chopra: Today we are going to talk about five amazing characters you have played, and *how* you planned and played them. And now when you see them, do you feel like you could have done something differently? First, Faizal Khan from *Gangs of Wasseypur 2*. How did you approach the character?

Nawazuddin Siddiqui: Jab mujhe Anurag ne script bheji thhi, maine socha nahi thha ki mujhe itna powerful character dega Anurag. Mujhe nahi pata thha ke usne kis tarah ke glimpses dekhe hon meri performance main. Toh main khud shocked ho gaya thha. Main seedha apne gaon chala gaya. (When Anurag sent me the script, I hadn't thought he would give me such a powerful role. I didn't know what glimpses he had seen in my performances. So I was shocked. I went straight to my village.)

AC: Just after reading the scripts?

NS: Mera dimaag seedha apne gaon chala gaya . . . via *Godfather*, via *Scarface*. Achha, mujhe laga ki haan theek hai, *Scarface* ka Al Pacino ya *Godfather* ka Brando, woh toh main kar dunga, but woh mere par shayad jaayega nahi. Lekin uss tarah ke attitude ke log mere gaon mein rehte thhe. Jo zamindar log thhe, jo baithte thhe, aur poori politics wahin shuru aur wahin khatam ho jaati thhi. Unko gaon se baahar ki knowledge nahi thhi. But woh jis tareekey se baithte thhe, baatein karte thhe . . . lagta thha poora sach wahi hota thha, jabki saari jhooth baatein hoti thhi. Woh America ki baat karte the, bolte the, 'America mein toh ye hai...' Kyunki bahut bade log the gaon mein. (Yeah, I read the script. And instantly, my mind just went straight to my village. I thought, 'All right, I can do this', whether it's Al Pacino from *Scarface* or Brando from *The Godfather*, but maybe it wouldn't quite suit me. However, there were people with that kind of attitude living in my village. I had to leave those film references behind and focus directly on them, the landlords. The kind who, just by sitting down, could start and end all village politics right then and there. They had no knowledge of the world outside the village, but the way they sat, the way they spoke, it felt like everything they said was the absolute truth, even if it was all lies. They'd talk about America, saying things like, 'In America, this is how it is...' Because they held such power in the village.)

AC: Like a king...
NS: Bilkul raja waala attitude thha. Desi. Wahan se bahut saari cheezein mujhe milin. Plus usko adapt karna . . . . Bahut saari cheezein hui hain. Incident hue, jaise yeh meri life ka bilkul real incident hai . . . mere saath hua hai yeh. (It was a completely royal kind of attitude. Desi. So I got a lot of knowledge and exposure from there. And then adapting all of that. A lot of things have happened. Incidents, like the ones in the film, are like completely real ones from my own life . . . these have actually happened to me.)

AC: Are you serious? So this is your life?
NS: Ji, meri life ka part hai yeh. Toh actually woh attitude meri hi life se inspired thha. Aur Anurag ka jo brief thha, woh sabh milaake, Faizal Khan bana. (Yes, this is a part of my life. So actually, that attitude was inspired by my real life. And along with Anurag's brief, all of it came together to create Faizal Khan's character.)

AC: Superb. Okay, next is Aslam Shaikh from *The Lunchbox*. Where does this innocence in your eyes come from?
NS: Yeh actually mere ek dost thha. Actor hai, aur mera roommate bhi raha hai wo kaafi saalon tak. Toh uski life mein iss tarah ke bahut saare disappointments hue thhe, jo who mujhse share karta thha. Maine usko copy kiya thha, actually. Jab yeh release hui thhi film, toh usne bhi dekhi. Tab tak main uske saath nahi rehta thha. Main kahin aur shift ho gaya thha. Toh usne mujhe message kiya: 'I saw Lunchbox. Thank you.' Sirf itna. Aur uske baad usko kaam milna band ho gaya thha. Kyunki jahan bhi jaata thha aur audition deta thha, log bolte thhe: 'Yaar yeh character mat kar, yeh Nawaz ne kar liya.' (This was actually a friend of mine, an actor, who was my roommate for many years. He had faced a lot of disappointments in life, which he used to share with me. I actually copied him. When *The Lunchbox* was released, he watched it too. By then, we weren't living together. I had shifted elsewhere. He messaged me: 'I saw Lunchbox. Thank you.' Just that. And after that, he stopped getting work. Because wherever he went for auditions, people would say, 'Don't do this kind of character, Nawaz has already done it.')

AC: My God.
NS: Toh wo bolta thha ki 'Hum toh origin[al] mein hi aise hain. Unhone humaara copy kiya hai.' (So he used to say, 'This is how I originally am. Nawaz has copied me.')

AC: Somewhere, deep inside, he was sad.
NS: Wo kahin na kahin andar rehti thhi. Lekin bahar se wo bahut normal rehta thha. Maine yeh scene karte waqt try kiya ke Nawaz *andar se* jitna bhi ro sakta hai, main usko capture karoon. Mukesh . . . uski jo tragedy thhi, wo main bilkul aise, truthfully capture karoon. Trust me, woh time pe meri shart khud se yeh thhi ki na toh main isko eyes mein leke aaunga, na face pe leke aaunga. Koi expression nahi hona chahiye, nahi toh defeat ho jaayega woh character. Toh maine kaha, *dekhte hain kya result aata hai.* (That stayed somewhere deep inside him. On the outside, he always appeared normal. While doing that particular scene [in *The Lunchbox*], I tried to capture all of that – how much Nawaz could cry on the inside. I tried to portray Mukesh's life's tragedy truthfully, exactly the way he used to speak and behave. But I had made a deal with myself: I wouldn't let it show in my eyes or on my face. No expression. If I did, the character would lose. So I said to myself, *let's see what happens.*)

AC: Moving on to the next one. Ye hai Shiv Gajra in *Kick*. Where did this laugh come from?
NS: Actually, yeh jo theatre mein nuances add karte thhe, uss dauran ka recall ho gaya thha mujhe. Hasi jo thhi, maine *Aks* ke Manoj Bajpayee ki li thhi. (Actually, I was reminded of the nuances we used to add in back in theatre. I took the laughter from Manoj Bajpayee in *Aks*.)

AC: I remember we had an interview where you mentioned that your mother is very happy when you're wearing expensive clothes and playing a rich man. But when you do a film like *The Lunchbox*, you said you tried to approach it differently, that the need for that was absent. You're working on a completely different pitch here. So is it like a different acting muscle? How does it work as an actor?
NS: Jo iss tarah ke discussions hote hain, ke yeh iss tarah ki film hai aur woh uss tarah ki film hai, actor ke liye nahi hote woh. Actor toh sirf craft se kaam karta hai. (Discussions like these, about one film being a certain kind and the other being a different kind, are not meant for the actor. The actor works solely with the craft.)

AC: But is there no difference in the rhythm?
NS: See, maine Shakespeare ke bhi plays kiye hain, aur Bharat Muni, Stanislavski bhi padha hai. Form badalta hai, par actor ke craft mein badlaav nahi hota. Parsi theatre bhi hum log karte thhe, jisme last seat tak aawaz sunai deni chahiye. Baaki usme bhi jo kharaab actor hote thhe, pata chal jaate thha, aur jo achhe hote thhe, wo bhi pata chal jaata thha. Parsi theatre hazaaron log ek saath dekhtein hain. Toh I think jaisi ek actor ki sensibility hai, woh ussi ke according kaam karta hai. Yeh jo bahar se tag laga diya jata hai, categorise kar diya jaata hai, woh actor ke liye nahi hota. Actor ke liye sirf character hai. Usko jitni bhi honesty, character ka jo knowledge hai, aur director ka jo reference hai, uske according kaam karna hai. (See, I've done Shakespearean plays. I've also studied Bharat Muni and Stanislavski. The form changes, but the actor's craft doesn't. We also used to perform in Parsi theatres, where the only task was that the voice should reach the last seat. Even there, both bad and good actors were easily identifiable. In Parsi theatre, thousands of people are watching at once. So I think the actor works according to their own sensibility. The labels and categories that are imposed by people outside – they aren't for the actor. For the actor, it's about the character. They have to work with as much honesty as possible, based on their knowledge of the character and the reference from the director.)

AC: Generally, in your mind, is there a perception that 'this film will be easier than *Lunchbox*'?
NS: Nahi, bilkul nahi. Har character utna hi mushkil hota hai, jitna *Lunchbox* ka thha, jitna *Gangs* ka thha, jitna *Sarfarosh* ka thha, ya *Munna Bhai* ka thha. Actor ke liye koi farak nahi hai. Actor apni poori koshish karta hai, chahe form koi bhi ho, ya kisi bhi genre ki film ho. (No, not at all. Every character is as difficult as the ones I played in *The Lunchbox*, *Gangs of Wasseypur*, *Sarfarosh* or *Munna Bhai M.B.B.S.* For an actor, there is no difference. An actor gives their best effort, whether it's in any form or any genre of film.)

AC: So whatever you feel is naturally right...
NS: Character khud bata deta hai ki 'Mujhe iss tareeke se prepare karo. Main yeh hoon.' Economy, matlab jitna kam karke zyada impact de sakte hain, bas woh hi director ka reference hota hai. (The character itself tells you how to prepare for it. It tells you who it is. The economy, meaning how to create a bigger impact with minimal effort, is the director's brief.)

AC: But at least the costumes are fancy now.

NS: Sab filmon mein, sab tuxedo pehente hain, toh dekh ke meri mother thodi woh ho gayi thhin ki, 'Sab pehente hain toh tu kyun nahi pehenta?' Ek film maa ke liye karenge. (In all the films today, everyone wears tuxedos, so seeing that, my mother was a bit like, 'Everyone wears it, so why don't you?' I will definitely do one film for her.)

AC: Then, Raman from *Raman Raghav 2.0* is still so disturbing for me. Where did he come from?

NS: Main iski script leke Lonavala gaya thha teen din ke liye, film ki shooting shuru hone se pehle. Dialogues sab yaad kar liye thhe, aur main baar-baar unhe repeat kar raha thha. Ek waqt aaya shaam ke time, main baitha hua thha aur dialogues ko recite kar raha thha. Tabh mujhe khud se hi lagne laga ki yeh aadmi [Raman] sach mein main hi hoon. Iss aadmi ki philosophy hai ki: 'Main toh aaram se maarta hoon, mujhe pain bhi nahi hota. Khate, peete, hagte, mootte hue, kisi ko bhi maar deta hoon. Main aap logon ki tarah nahi hoon. Koi insaniyat ki aadh mein maarta hai, koi dharm ke naam pe maarta hai. Par main vaisa hoon hi nahi. Mujhe maarna achha lagta hai. Jaise daily routine mein hota hai, waise maarta hoon.' Iss cheez pe believe karna mere liye bahut mushkil thha, actually. Issliye main teen din tak harr waqt, harr second apne aap ko yeh convince karta raha, ki haan, main maar sakta hoon kisi ko. (I took the script with me and went to Lonavala for three days, before the film shoot started. I had memorised all the dialogues. One evening, I was sitting and reciting the dialogues, and at one point, I started feeling like this person [Raman] is really me. This man's philosophy is: 'I kill with ease and feel no pain. I can kill at will, whether it is while eating, drinking or whatever. I'm not like you people. Some kill in the name of humanity, some in the name of religion. But I just enjoy killing – it's just part of my routine.' Believing in this kind of honesty was actually very difficult for me. For three days, I kept convincing myself, every moment, that yes, I can, indeed, kill someone.)

AC: So that there was terror in your eyes…

NS: Nahi, maine yeh koshish nahi ki main aisa dikhoon. Mere mind mein maine bas yeh soch rakha thha ki aaj koi bhi mil jaayega, main thhok dunga. Doosra, yeh jo apne andar hota hai na, weirdness aur violence, hum society ki wajah se chhupa ke rakhte hain . . . ki 'nahi yeh dekh na le koi, jaan na le ki main kya hoon'. Hum humesha achha dikhaana chahte hain logon ke saamne. Anurag na humesha uss cheez ko todta hai. (No, I didn't try to *look* a certain way. I just had it fixed in my mind that I'd kill whoever crossed my path. Secondly, things that don't come to the surface, that we bury deep inside — our weirdness, violence — because of society. We hide these, thinking, 'No one should know what I *really* am.' We all try to show the good side of ourselves to the world. Anurag, however, always tries to rupture that attempt.)

AC: But are we really *that* bad? Is all that really inside us?
NS: Of course hota hai. Main guarantee de sakta hoon ki agar kisi insaan ke andar na ho itna bura insaan, toh main acting karna chhod dunga. (Of course it exists within us. I can guarantee you that there is a monster inside all of us, potentially speaking. I'd quit my career if there wasn't one.)

AC: Hum sab mein? (In all of us?)
NS: Itna jakad ke rakhte hain apne aap ko, because of society. Hazaaron log aapke andar hote hain. Bahut saare log hain jinko lagta hai aap aisi nahi hain, waisi hain. Insaan toh ek hi hai lekin attitude alag-alag hai sabke saamne. Toh ek hi aadmi satra jagah pe alag-alag hai. Meri maa boltin hain main bahut seedha hoon, meri biwi bolti hai main bahut tez hoon . . . par main toh wahi hoon. (We're all bound by what society expects of us. But inside us, there exist thousands of different people. Many people think you're a *certain* kind of person, others think you're the opposite. But the truth is, you're still the very same person. It's just that the way you behave changes depending on who's in front of you. To my mother, I may be simple man, but to my wife, I'm cunning. But I'm the same man.)

AC: When you're playing — or after you've played — a character like that, the kind who terrifies people just by walking down the street, once you've brought him out of yourself, do you ever fear him? How do you rinse off a character like that?
NS: Of course, waqt toh lagta hai. Aisa toh hai nahi ki shooting khatam hui aur character bhi khatam ho gaya. Aap character se kuch lete ho, par wo bhi aapki life se bahut kuch leke jaata hai. Toh ultimately actor keval dry ho jaata hai, empty ho jaata hai. Usko kheech ke laana padta hai apne andar se emotion. Matlab nikalne ke liye wohi reality check karna padhta hai. (Of course, it takes time. It's not like the shoot wraps up, and the character suddenly disappears with it. They say you borrow some aspects from a character, but the truth is, the character also takes away a lot from your life. In the end, the actor becomes dry, empty. You have to drag

emotions out from within yourself. To come out of something like that, you need a reality check, something to remind you who you are.)

AC: Do you have any rituals? Shah Rukh once told me that he takes a shower – like physically stands under running water – to rinse off a character. Do you do something like that?
NS: Main mostly gaon chala jaata hoon apne. Unn logon ke saath jaata hoon jo mujhe iss field mein aane se pehle se jaante the, jo mujhe ussi tareeke se lete hain. Ya biwi ki daant sunn leta hoon reality check ke liye. Do minute mein who hosh thhikaane laga deti hai! (I mostly go back to my village with the people who have known me since before I entered this field, people who treat me as I really am. Or I end up getting scolded by my wife – a reality check. In just two minutes, she brings me back to my senses!)

AC: Okay, the fifth and final character, Nawaz. In *Haraamkhor*, Shyam was just a terrible person and yet I felt sympathy for him. Somewhere inside, I felt that he's just very sad . . . and brutal. How did you create so many things in one person?
NS: Ek toh ye thha ki maine apne gaon mein iss tarah ke teachers dekhe hain. Dusra, maine apni life mein bahut saare aise log dekhe hain jo apni tragedy ko ya apni sadness ko kabhi bhi glorify nahi karte. Jaise hum log maan ke chalte hain na humesha ki agar ek film main gora sa insaan hai, ye bahut achha hoga, aur agar ek ugly sa insaan hai, woh bahut kharaab hi hoga . . . . Yeh itna bhayankar tareeke se filmon mein dikhaya jaata hai, ki mujhe toh bahut gussa aata hai. Itna generalise kar rakha hai na filmon mein logon ko, personalities ko, looks ko. Main maan ke chalta thha, jo bade log hote hain— (One reason was that I had seen such teachers in my village. Another reason is that I've seen a lot of people in my life who never glorify their tragedy or sadness. It's like how we always assume in movies, if someone is fair-skinned, they'll be good-natured, and if someone is ugly, they'll be ill-natured. In our films, this prejudice is conformed to in such a horrific way that it really angers me. They generalise people, personalities and looks in our movies. I used to believe that the older, more accomplished people—)

AC: Are good people, too?
NS: Nahin. Mujhe lagta thha ki wo peshaab bhi karte honge toh white colour ka karte honge. (No, I used to think that even their urine must be white in colour.)

AC: Good in every way, you mean...
NS: Jab kareeb jaake dekha toh pata laga woh kitne ghhinaune hain. Jisko main sochta thha itna ganda hoga yeh insaan, woh itna khoobsurat nikla mere liye. Jab aap gradually bade hote chale jaate hain, toh bahut shock milte hain aapko. Unhi logon mein se ek ye [Shyam] bhi thha. Bechaara jiske kaam karne ke tareeke galat hain, lekin kahin na kahin society se daba kuchla insaan hai. Society se darta bhi hai. Pyaar bhi karna chahta hai, wild bhi hai, fantasy bhi hai uski. (When I got closer to some of these accomplished people, I realised how disgusting they were. And on the other hand, the person I thought would be ill-natured [based on external appearances] turned out to be so beautiful from within. So as you grow up, you experience these kinds of shocks. You expect one thing from someone, but when you get closer, you realise they're someone else altogether. Shyam was one of those people. A poor guy whose ways of doing things are wrong, but deep down, he's a person crushed by society. He's also afraid of it. He also desires love; he's wild and has his fantasies.)

AC: But when you take on characters like Shyam or Raman, is it important that you understand these characters? Or like these characters? What do you have to do?
NS: Mujhe iss tarah ke weird aur layered waale characters bahut pasand hain. Mujhe jo typecast hero hai Bollywood ka, jo ek sarvgun sampann waala aadmi hai, bilkul nahi pasand. (I really like these weird and layered characters. I especially don't like the typecast hero in Bollywood, who is this all-perfect man.)

AC: The ideal, virtuous man...
NS: Main uss se bachna chaahta hoon. Yeh character main nahin karna chahta hoon, na main kar paaunga. Theek hai, kyunki market mein hai, to main bhi shaayad kar loon. But mera andar se nahin aata. Kyunki main itna chatt chuka hoon na, ek hi type ki filmein dekh dekh ke. Yeh bahut saalon se dekhte aa rahe hain hum log. Bas yeh waala character chhod ke sab mazza aata hai karne mein. (I want to avoid that kind of role. I neither want to play this character, nor will I be able to do it. Because it's popular in the market, I might end up doing it, but it doesn't come from within me. I'm so tired of watching the same kind of films, this same type of stuff, over and over. Apart from this ideal-man character, everything else feels fun to do.)

AC: As dark as it can get…

NS: Hum toh compromise karte hain. Main toh aur dark karna chahta hoon. (I end up compromising – in reality, I want to take up even darker roles.)

AC: Really?

NS: Haan. Yeh censor se hi pass nahi hoga. (Yes. Our censor board, however, won't allow such characters or clear such films.)

AC: Okay, Nawaz, I hope you keep doing such characters. It's been such a pleasure to listen to you.

30 August 2017

26

Saif Ali Khan on Privilege, Parenting, Passion

Anupama Chopra: Saif, it's been such an eventful year for you – three movies, *Rangoon, Chef, Kalakandi*.
Saif Ali Khan: Yes.

AC: *Baazaar*, too?
SAK: Probably not.

AC: It's a Saif year.
SAK: Well, let's see if it's a Saif (Safe) year. I hear that joke quite often.

AC: Oh, man. And you've started shooting for the Netflix original, *Sacred Games*.
SAK: Ji, yes.

AC: You've hogged your share of the media headlines about nepotism. What's your headspace right now? And what's your learning?
SAK: There's a constant learning. Sometimes I think I live, not in isolation, but in an ivory tower in terms of what I'm reading and who I'm speaking to. It's nice to have a balanced point of view, I'm quite accepting of what people say, criticism or compliments. I've been reading. I've been working on trying to be a better actor. I've really enjoyed Taimur. I'm watching Sara acting and Ibrahim being a teenager in school.

AC: It's a happy place?
SAK: It feels wonderful.

AC: You said it's been a year of getting better perspective on work and life – not a midlife crisis, a midlife resolution. What does that mean?
SAK: A lot of what I've done till now has been as a young actor. When I joined the industry, Salman Khan was number one, there was Aamir

Khan and Akshay and Ajay. They're still there – when people start calling them old and say they should retire, then I'll start worrying. So it's not an age thing. I feel very comfortable at the age and stage I'm at, the kind of work I'm being offered. I'm clear for once as to why I'm doing everything I'm doing. I think it's really important. Sometimes at two in the morning, I'm sitting at home with the script and I'm happy. With my family and friends and holidays, lifestyle, everything. I realised the glue is having a creative job. And I would just like to continue to have that for as long as possible.

AC: Nepotism is the elephant in the room. I want to get it out of the way. Earlier you had put forth this very elaborate sort of argument about why stars get cast, star kids get cast.

SAK: That joke when we made it on stage was not particularly funny. I thought I was making a joke at Varun and didn't realise the deeper implications. So I wanted to apologise. It became a bit of a mess because I proceeded to try and clarify the difference in my mind between nepotism, star kids, advantage, privilege. Possibly one of the most tone-deaf things I've done. It was very foolish of me. I must have been reading something on Greek philosophy or having a very balanced and open-mind, without really being in touch with how offensive that can be. So again, I apologise for that. And I've never been pro-nepotism. It leads to mediocrity – you're giving somebody undeserving a job over someone who is more deserving. I'm one of those people who shouldn't say the word privilege often, especially while trying to argue about how it's a good thing in a country like ours. That was insensitive. I mean, if I could just set it right . . . . I think too much talking is not good.

AC: There's no justification.
SAK: I've had an incredibly privileged life. I'd love to give back in whatever way I can. We work hard and are balanced in that way, but there's no two ways about it. There's so many people in this country that have no chance. It's so unfair. I apologise for sounding insensitive about that.

AC: When you do stuff like this, does Kareena come? I do this, my husband is always doing stuff like this.
SAK: But he thinks, and he's got a strong take on things.

AC: Too strong. I'm like, 'Be quiet.' But does she have this look on her face?
SAK: Most of the time she agrees. But this, I sneaked it out without running it by anybody. So I am on my own. I think it's a learning experience. My mom always said, 'When you don't know what you're talking about, be conservative. And when you do know, try and be liberal because that's what we've taught you.'

AC: For the last four or five years, your films haven't really landed with an audience.
SAK: Right.

AC: Do you think about why that is? And how does *Chef* fit in?
SAK: I'm the first to blame myself and say, maybe it's just me. Actors tend to do that when something doesn't run, you start blaming all kinds of things. But I think there's more to it. There's been a change in the kind of movies being accepted, and I haven't timed that well. Like *Bullett Raja* – people were kind of done with that kind of movie. I was a very modern, multiplex kind of actor, and suddenly chose something outdated. Same with *Phantom* – there was fatigue from films like *Baby* that had already covered similar ground. How *Chef* fits in – one thing I've learnt is, I want to work with good directors. People ask if the script, co-stars, or producers are important – I want to work with directors I look up to. They create an atmosphere and give you a feeling of being an artist on set, which is wonderful. With *Rangoon, Chef, Kaalakaandi* – I wanted to redefine myself as an actor and a deserving member of the industry. After the previous year's choices, I felt that was questionable. *Rangoon* didn't work at the box office but got good reviews – it was a step in the right direction, an artistic experience. People applaud brave, cinematic choices. *Chef* came after Raja Menon made *Airlift*. When Vikram Malhotra offered it to me, it was a no-brainer. What resonated was that it's an urban story about priorities and not spending enough time with your kids. What is success if you're paying for your son's education but have no relationship with him? You could say it's like the *Rocky III* of food – a guy who's had everything, loses it, then goes back to basics.

AC: Find the love again.
SAK: And find his passion for cooking again from an unlikely source. It's kind of home turf, because it's urban. The same character I played in

Dil Chahta Hai, if he's grown up and run into a few midlife problems, this is what he would be like. That's what drew me to it.

AC: Absolutely. You said that this lot of films you're doing now, they've reignited your passion for acting.
SAK: So I've been watching Al Pacino. He's an acting guru and God, and it's perfect for Hindi film. He's perfectly calm and then explodes.

AC: So you're studying acting again.
SAK: Studying, reading about it, and trying to apply it and doing things I was never taught, I never went to acting school. There's some wonderful books out there. There is a danger – too much analysis really leads to paralysis. If you're thinking about it, you can't do it. But sometimes when you run into trouble in a scene, it's good to have some technique to fall back on. I know what I am trying to say here, and break it down in that sense, rather than shooting in the dark. The first take, you're basically playing yourself, not making any choices. As an actor, you're not saying, okay, you know, I'm going to do this. Half the job is to know which shot to give. Say, okay, I'm going to say this accusingly. But there's nothing like obviously accusing – and therein is the art. And that's the fun.

AC: That's exciting to rediscover acting.
SAK: I think so, after twenty-five years or something—

AC: Twenty-five years next year!
SAK: Yeah. But also because times change. And some of us have been lucky enough to have relevance. Maybe because you haven't got a particularly fixed image or style.

AC: Sara's making her debut as you're rediscovering yourself as an actor. You said, I don't know why she would want to do it to herself. Does the fear become less?
SAK: No, it doesn't. I've realised recently that there's energy driving everything we do. So that energy is box office success now. About Sara, I don't know if I'm going to answer this question correctly . . . you ask me about my daughter, I want to be protective about her, but that comes across wrong. What I actually mean is, I think she's really talented and hardworking. She works hard on another level. I remember when she came to our wedding – never thought I'd say that about my daughter – she had such

a good time. We were all up till five in the morning. Then she took an auto rickshaw from the Taj to Ambani to take a history exam. And she got an A plus. And I think she'll bring that same focus to her work.

AC: How do you deal with the immense attention that the kids are getting? I wonder about the pressure this puts on Sara to be photographed every day. I look at Taimur and I think, how will you ever teach him work ethic when he's a star at ten months old?

SAK: Taimur is beyond a star. You work hard to reach a certain stage in life. But I see people like this, really rich people, but the guy, the patriarch has made it on his own. So he's got a look of contentment, but it's also humility. And he knows the world. But the kids, sometimes, the most important thing is manicure first and then a massage. They have an annoying vibe. Not just entitlement, an aura of slow luxury. It's like a TV programme about the rich and the luxurious. But you want to look after your kids. So when we worked hard, Kareena, she's earned that holiday, because she works very hard. So I'm concerned. Taimur's roaming the corridors of the imperial. So I don't know.

AC: And stardom.
SAK: I was going to say he's the biggest star in the family. But there are all these things.

AC: Does that worry you?
SAK: I hope there's an innocence to him because he doesn't know anything else. But it does worry me slightly. It's important to be grounded and well brought up. But I'm confident. All of us in the family are actually fairly straight and strictly brought up. Nothing a boarding school won't solve eventually.

AC: You're a big believer in boarding schools.
SAK: I am. Especially in this kind of environment. Kareena and I have already discussed a nice boarding school in England. It's done the trick for everybody else in the family. But I don't know. It's something he's going to . . . . As long as he grows up with good values, we'll do our best. He's certainly grown up privileged. I honestly can't tell you what's going to happen. It's easy to spoil our kids. And none of us are spoilt. But you love them. But I think Kareena will be a wonderful mother. She's not going to be very impressed if he's spoilt.

AC: She's a toughie?

SAK: She's also . . . . Both of them, mom – Babita-ji, Auntie – has also brought them up with really strong values. Handling fame is also something that you get taught by your parents. My parents taught me. You say Namaste Dada to him or go get it yourself, make your own bed. Tiger Pataudi is also quite a grounding influence in our lives. He was such a big star but wore it very lightly. And be polite to everybody. So it's got nothing to do with fame. I was shooting with a kid recently, not in *Chef*. And I said, 'Namaste karo beta and he didn't do it.' So after the cut, I said, 'How do you greet adults?' So he said, 'I say hi.' I said, 'Oh, you would have got one behind the ear in my house.' We do our best. I think he'll be brought up by the media also.

AC: He will be!

SAK: If he does anything wrong, he'll be policed. He'll have to behave himself. Like Prince Harry. I imagine. Taimur in the nightclub. Cigarette in his hand. . . . No, no, not in public, young man.

AC: Saif, this whole nepotism thing really took a life of its own at the IIFA Awards. You said, sometimes I ask, why do we participate in this charade?

SAK: Which charade?

AC: This awards charade.

SAK: Oh God.

AC: Is it just the paycheck?

SAK: I guess so, or somewhere. I don't know. But honestly, if we're taking an ethical stance it's the biggest joke in the world. Every channel has their own award show. They give these guys awards for turning up, make up amazing categories, most beautiful smile, most glamorous diva, best actor. So we all turn up because let's face it, we're suckers. Anyway, they turn up when they probably shouldn't. And get this award. And at the same time, whatever brand you're sponsoring, face of the year. And what really disturbs me is that – nobody's making a funny joke. But they intercut it with everybody laughing, right? There's a laugh track. So it's a con. And the only people really being cheated are the audience there.

AC: That are buying into it?

SAK: Buying into this. It's completely false. There's not enough money spent on the humour, the entertainment. Of course, the songs and dances and everything that suits the sponsor is happening. They all try and create an alternate universe. If I need the money, I'll go. But if I can help it, I would stay a mile away.

AC: Kevin Bacon, the American actor, got a prosthetic disguise. He got this nose and these teeth to see what it felt like to be anonymous again. So he goes to the Grove, which is that lovely shopping mall in LA. And he said it really sucked because nobody recognised him. How invested are you in the fame?
SAK: I'd love to say I'm not interested in fame. I like money and I like privilege. But I think sometimes in India, if you're privileged, it just gives you human rights. It's something we're used to. I'd love to say, it's not important. If I were an Ambani, could I not have privilege that way? It's not particularly exciting giving selfies at the airport. I could do without that. Is that what fame is?

AC: Yeah.
SAK: No, then please take it all away. If nobody ever recognised me ever, ever, I'd be the happiest guy in the world. But, I can buy a first class ticket and get pranam service at the airport. Things like this, I want. I want to go on holiday and most of these things money can buy.

AC: Right, exactly.
SAK: I don't want fame at all. But I want to get paid as an actor. And I like acting a lot. But if I could act, and respect on set is nice also. I don't want to be just one mazdoor actor – idhar khade raho, line bolo. You give a mind-blowing shot, that cut, hato (Stand here, say your line. You give a mind-blowing shot, cut, now move).

AC: You don't like the airport look in the papers?
SAK: I hate having to dress up. Can you imagine having to dress up for the airport? And people should understand that.

AC: Listen, your wife sets a high bar.
SAK: That's okay. I'm sure she enjoys it at times. And it's quite normal, she's a star. And she's lovely. But—

AC: Not for you?
SAK: No, I'm saying, there are all these traps. You've got to dress a certain way for this. People commented. Honestly, I just want to act. There are many things I want which are . . . . But I don't like not being free. If I

want to do it, great. Glamour is another complicated thing. There are so many amazing people here. So it really has become a little bit hollow in that sense. Because all the focus has gone on to social media. And nobody's interested in talking to you anymore.

AC: Absolutely, I can't tell you. It's very scary. I've been to parties where literally people are just posing.
SAK: They don't want to talk. And you're like, the photo should be a reflection of the cool party. But there is no cool party.

4 October 2017

27

'Enrich Your Soul Through Your Job': Irrfan Khan

Anupama Chopra: You know, Irrfan, I read somewhere that after Sharmila Tagore saw *The Namesake*, she sent you a message saying, 'Thank your parents for giving birth to you.'
Irrfan Khan: I swear, sometimes, I've got the kind of praise or acknowledgement from people, which is so moving. It's like somebody has, you know, just poured their heart out.

AC: So, Irrfan, what are the choices that have made you the man you are today?
IK: Just to avoid getting bored with oneself . . . [I had] to keep my profession, because I had no other way to keep myself engaged. No other way. I had choices when I was a teenager, you know. I could have indulged in a few things, and it could have . . . kept me engaged. But somehow, my naive mind kept telling me that you need to find *your* space where you can engage yourself. Because I'm terrified with myself. I have a lot of anger, a lot of anxiety. And I could never fit into the system, any kind of system.

AC: But are there any favourite failures?
IK: Oh, yes. There are favourite failures. I won't call it a failure, but a kind of traumatic experience. When I was seven years old, I was passionate about flying kites, and we were not well-to-do. Although I belonged to a feudal family, my father didn't take dues from anyone, so we were still living in a rental house and our terraces didn't have protection. And in the evening, I was trying to catch a thread hanging from an electric wire. And I fell down. I broke my wrist and elbow. And it took at least two years for me to recover, because my father was not there. He was a hunter, so he was out. Nobody knew what to do. So, it stayed like that.

AC: It's still bent?

IK: It is still bent but I am okay with it. Kids are spontaneous and they don't understand what cruelty is. And they indulge in making fun of each other. The whole school used to make fun of me. So, I started getting into my shell. I was a very shy guy. And suddenly, I lost all confidence and everything, you know. I was just living in my dreams at the time. I lost so much of my strength that I used to keep lying in bed all the time. I used to play this game where I would check where my hand would fall. Now this side, and then that side. So, this traumatic experience made me notice that whatever I am, people are not perceiving me like that. People don't know what lies inside me. So, there was a kind of organic need for me to come out ... and do something so that people realise what I am.

AC: But, Irrfan, how does a child who grows up very far away from anything to do with cinema find the courage to pursue acting and go to drama school? And then I read that you were so insecure about the way you looked that you would sleep with a pin on your nose. How do you then get past all of that and say, 'I am going to make this work?'

IK: I pumped myself with inspiration. Sure, this is the kind of thing which I was suffering from when I came to this city. In Delhi, there was an atmosphere where I could watch international and European cinema. I was introduced to this kind of cinema, and that was my source of inspiration. I have learnt a lot from those movies. When I came to the city, I was almost like in a middle of a mandi. Nobody talks about cinema, nobody discusses it. My struggle was to just keep my inspiration going. The first thing I bought with my income was a VCR and I was looking for films. And that time I realised that this is not my real drive – otherwise, the inspiration would have been there even without watching films. So, that time I realised that this is a cultivated interest of mine. *I* have cultivated it and so I have to keep it going. I needed to watch good cinema so that my inspiration was pumped up.

AC: Irrfan, you are perhaps the only actor in the world who has worked with both Ang Lee and Anees Bazmee. There is no other person on the planet who has managed that. You have made it look natural and easy at both ends of the spectrum. What does that take?

IK: Because I am still struggling to see myself as an accomplished actor who is playing with the craft. I am still struggling. The thing is a lot of my time is given to Hindi cinema. I am still working on my craft. I am not as easy as Mark Ruffalo. So that keeps me going.

AC: When you were talking about Hindi cinema, you said that we can live without nuance here. You said what we need more is attitude. So even if you give a superficial performance, it can still work. Because we are not aiming for nuance. But what does it take to give that superficial performance? Does it require a high level of skill? What do you do to create that attitude performance as opposed to what you do in the West?

IK: That is just there. You don't need to work on it [the character]. The only work you do is that you don't work too much. That you don't put your own sensibility onto it and make it a liability.

AC: So you purposely dumb yourself down?

IK: Don't research on that character, find its background or see nuances of its behaviour. This is there to give goosebumps to people. Don't bring in all those shades, don't work too much over it. Just flow with it. Have a good time when you are doing Anees Bazmee's movie! You have to relate to that humour, enjoy on the sets and have fun.

AC: And that's it?

IK: That's it. There is no single formula that works when you are working on a character. You will keep discovering new ways of doing it. You have to discover that each and every character needs a different kind of approach to reach him. I was doing a movie with one of my favourite directors, Anup Singh. When he narrated the story, I just realised that I cannot work on this character. Because his narrative is musical. He sees music in everything. Even in your behaviour he sees music, rhythm. An earlier film, *Qissa*, I was not ready to do because it was too dark a subject. I said, 'Anup, I don't want to fu*k myself, you know. I can't live in that complicated state of mind for two to three months.' For the next film which I did with him recently in Rajasthan, I didn't work on the character at all. I just went on the sets without preparation. I used to have great time at night, partying, you know. I used to go to the sets, see the atmosphere and act spontaneously. That gave me a lot of freedom. That gave me a lot of courage to just dive in and see what happens. I loved that experience.

AC: Irrfan, one thing really fascinated me the last time. Remember we'd had a conversation and you had said that Bhatt Saheb had sometimes, during directing, told you, 'Irrfan, please act terribly!'

IK: Yeah, spoon-feeding.

AC: So, how does an actor of your calibre purposely do bad acting when instructed?

IK: He didn't mean I act terribly. He meant I don't personalise it. For the audience, you know, like in Hindi cinema, an actor serves as a magician. Because there is no language in camera work here. It is just covering the frame. There is no form of cinematic language; the lines are all flat. So only an actor can do some form of magic to it. He meant, 'Don't personalise it so much. Just say the lines with flourish.'

AC: Is that hard for you to do or can you do that easily?

IK: At that time, I was doing two kinds of series which were equally popular. *Banegi Apni Baat* and *Chandrakanta*. Now *Chandrakanta* was completely about line-baazi (dialogue delivery) and no character research. It was all about how to convincingly say your lines. And *Banegi Apni Baat* was very realistic. So somehow, my background and my choices helped me do this.

AC: You can juggle between the two?

IK: But the stylish version, you know, nobody bought it in cinemas. Although [this kind of character] was popular in series . . . in cinema, nobody was ready to give me that kind of opportunity.

AC: The stylish version of Irrfan...

IK: The stylish version of Irrfan! I am thankful to them, you know. Otherwise, I would have got sucked into it miserably and lost my path.

AC: A couple of weeks ago, I was talking to Arjun Kapoor and we were trying to address the issue of an actor as a celebrity versus an actor as an artist. And I was saying to him that, 'Now actors are not just acting. You are doing award shows, endorsements, panel discussions, television serials. Does that distract you in any way from being an actor?' And he said, 'Look, in our ecosystem, we are actually entertainers. And this is all part of being that.' Do you see yourself as an entertainer?

IK: I see myself as an entertainer. But as far as art is concerned, whatever responsibilities you have just mentioned, art doesn't fit in any of those. Art only comes when you start making things personal and when you start reflecting on those things. Life around you, whatever you are absorbing as a human being, you are then communicating that observation, your own point of view about society and human beings, through those stories. If that is not happening, then art is not happening. You are just an entertainer, an actor, a celebrity, whatever you want to call it. But art only happens when you start reflecting, when you start personalising things.

AC: So you can compartmentalise in your head that here I am an entertainer and here I am an artist?
IK: Yes, you have to. Otherwise, you will confuse the story, and you will confuse the other people as well. You will confuse the audiences also. Whenever I am doing a film which is just about one-liners, I have to deliver one-liners and enjoy it. You shouldn't be sceptical about it. Just have fun, you know. You start playing that game and if it suits you, please continue playing it. Whatever works for you.

AC: Irrfan, you had also talked in interviews about the star system in Hindi cinema. And you said even the most interesting directors will at some point say: 'In the next film, let me get a star.' Is the star system frustrating for you as an actor or have you just made your peace with it?
IK: This made me feel helpless at one point of time. But there were so many things which could make you helpless and frustrated. That's again a challenge – how to stay positive and be interesting enough so that you can enjoy yourself. You don't let it affect you that much. But it happens. Because you are not bringing in that kind of money. The other thing is that if you are doing something which is not from the copy book, or if you bring in some new element to your craft which doesn't conform to the norms, there is a tendency of the establishment to feel threatened. Because they can't use that. They think, 'What is this new thing? Can I use it? If I can't use it, what is he doing?'

AC: While you were creating your own space, did you ever have a dark night of the soul where you just felt like you can't struggle against this anymore?
IK: There were times. Because of the way I was reacting to those circumstances. Mostly I have done movies with first-time directors. I have seen them change – the first film would be successful, and then in the next film, I wasn't important at all. And subconsciously, you start banking on this team because you have both done something new. Now I know not to depend [on directors]. I learnt my lesson. It would be unfair on my part to start expecting that the director leads their journey according to me. One film they do with you, and then it is, 'It was great working

with you.' And that's it! That was frustrating when I was doing TV. I used to feel claustrophobic, jealous and insecure. Because my juniors were getting breaks, they were doing commercial cinema. And I was struggling to just get one-minute parts in movies. I used to hear that Subhash Ghai watched *Safar*. He was talking to a director, 'Who is this guy?' So, that director came and told me. I used to wait and say to myself, 'Now any day, Subhash Ghai might give me a call.' But I never got that break in cinema until the time was right.

AC: I remember one discussion we had about the hundred crore clubs. Everybody used to say, 'My film earned hundred crores, mine did so and so…' And you were just coming off *Jurassic World*. So you said, 'Well, mine did about twenty-thousand crores.' I just love that you are functioning on another plane completely. But I remember you saying that it's not cool for actors to be discussing money.

IK: I don't have a kind of benchmark that if my film did so and so business, I am worth that much as an actor. That's too boring for me. What a scale to judge yourself, man! You are taking away all the mystery of storytelling. It's not a product which indicates your worth based on your sales. It's an experience. Sometimes, some stories are not made to make that kind of money. They are personal stories. On the other hand, there were films like *Baahubali*, where they would have imagined that it would do a business of forty crores on a Monday. Figures are just by-products, but a story is a living thing . . . it interacts with you because it's a creation. And I can give you many examples of how a story has come and nudged me, and created an atmosphere for me or challenged me. During *Paan Singh Tomar*, I got hurt so many times. For no rhyme or reason. I would just be walking, and there was a misstep and suddenly my back would go. Or I am playing cricket and suddenly a ball hits my eye. I tore my ligament in another incident. So many incidents with that film!

AC: And that's the film you won a national award for?
IK: And that's the film which exactly showed what happened to Paan Singh Tomar in his life. He was a national champion. And his name was not there at all when we started researching about him. It was absent. No record. Nobody knew him. Exactly the same thing happened with the film. It was made, and everybody was loving it before its release, but it was not getting released. We got so frustrated after eight to nine months. If anybody asked me what's happening with *Paan Singh*, I would say,

'I forgot *Paan Singh*, don't talk to me about it. It's gone, erased.' And then, suddenly the film came out without any publicity. And it must have gotten an opening of some eighty to ninety lakh rupees on the first day, and then it spread like fire. Suddenly the film stood on its own merit. So see the correlation between his life and the film, and how it interacts.

AC: What's the worst advice you see being dispensed in Bollywood?
IK: It all generates from a strange kind of insecurity to fall into a kind of formula. People who haven't reached there, they also have a kind of a say on how things work and what gives you success. And this premature way of understanding things is a kind of folly. That without having any real experience, you have devised a formula, and that if you follow this formula, it will definitely work. One must interact with oneself and see one's potential and what is unique about them. And evolve as an actor, I think. Falling into a formula is something which can reduce one's uniqueness and possibility of success.

AC: We always think of you as this very intense, serious actor. But I remember reading this interview Rohan Joshi from AIB did after they shot that amazingly funny video with you. The club song. And he said that they were all so nervous about meeting you, but he said you were very chill. So what are you like when you're not working?
IK: When I'm not working? I'm scattered, actually. I try and find a space for myself wherever I am. I tell myself that I will sit in this spot and rest and have my coffee or tea, and I'll read. But all those spaces remain as they are. I roam around the entire house. When I'm reading a script, it is in one room and I am reciting lines in another, and then I forget the line and then I'm like, 'Oh fu*k, where is the script?' I'm not an organised man. When you see actors doing wonderful roles or when you see people changing themselves completely and getting into it, that cannot happen spontaneously. You have to work on yourself. And diligently work on yourself.

AC: Which you do…
IK: I do, I do. Because characters excite me. I have abused myself and my body a lot. Now I've slowed down, but I'm a very reckless man. I used to carry a lot of anger, which I have controlled and dealt with. So the whole being is your tool. It becomes a kind of a responsibility to take care of yourself.

AC: Take care of your soul, also…

IK: That's what it is. To enrich your soul through your job. It has to have communication both ways. Otherwise, you're doing injustice to your job. You're killing a possibility.

AC: So lovely, so instructive. I am going to remember your words. 'Your job has to enrich your soul.'

8 May 2017

28

Twenty Years of Kareena Kapoor Khan

Anupama Chopra: It's your twentieth year in the movies. We want to take you through five milestone roles. I want to start with Poo.

(A clip from *Kabhi Khushi Kabhie Gham...* plays)

Kareena Kapoor Khan: I can't even look at myself. That time was so different. I was, what, twenty. We were shooting in 2000, 2001.

AC: It released in 2001.
KKK: That person was very different. I don't know if I could be Poo again. But, it is truly iconic. I don't think you've seen a mainstream actor do this kind of role or dialogues.

AC: She gave me hours of joy. I still go back and watch it for her. Karan said that Poo was him. What was his brief to you?
KKK: He was acting every beat out. This character's energy is a bit like Karan. Flamboyant, lovable, all heart. He knew this character the best. I was just following him. It's been one character where a director actually performed each shot. The only director who has shown me that.

AC: This character is over the top. It's a very fine line. How did you guys know how not to cross that?
KKK: Poo was, like you said, slightly annoying. But the way I played it, she just was very lovable, her innocence. Half the world believed that this is me, it was so real.

AC: Did people really think this is you?
KKK: Of course. It took me till *Jab We Met* for people to know there's also another person in there. Because of her flamboyance, the lingo, it was quite millennial for its time.

AC: They are still quoting, 'Good looks, good looks, good looks.' Karan said that you and him were the only people who liked her before the film released.

KKK: Everyone was like, *yeah, you know, she's ditzy, this is the entertainment in the film.* But when the trial happened and people saw the film, they were like, 'Oh my God, we've never seen something like this.' And Poo was just fabulous. You could have actually hated her, but nobody did. Everyone just ended up wanting to be like her. Karan always like, 'Trust me, everyone's going to love it.' I was like petrified. Other actresses were doing all the emotional scenes. Comedy, I feel, has now started getting its due. Earlier, it was like, why would a heroine of the film be doing this kind of comedy? But once the film released and they started reviewing it, it became like this cult figure. And still is. I can't walk the streets of London without people addressing me as Poo. I don't want my son to be like, *oh my God, why are they calling you Poo?*

AC: Let's go to Dolly, *Omkara*, 2006.

(Dolly's death scene from *Omkara* plays)

KKK: Unbelievable scene.

AC: It makes my hair stand. This is so out of your comfort zone. How did you become Dolly?
KKK: *Othello* is a great story. When Vishal called me, I was always doing commercial films.

AC: Very urban, very glamour.
KKK: Exactly. And then when Vishal actually had the conviction to call me, his belief made me believe I can do this.

AC: You said yes immediately?
KKK: Of course. Desdemona is the only female character that Shakespeare wrote so well. I saw *Maqbool*, always wanted to work with Vishal. And the cast. But it didn't hit me till I was on set. I adapt really well. I am a chameleon. I've always wanted to act. When you put me in that setting, I become that person.

AC: In this scene, when you realise this is over, what was his brief?
KKK: All these shots were actually one take. One or two, maybe for sound. We were all really prepared. I had become Dolly. This was one of the last scenes we shot. I miss playing Dolly.

AC: Really?

KKK: Yeah. Her story ended really fast. There was so much more she wanted out of life, out of her love. It's still in me, lingering. When I'm done with the film, I can't be that character again. But, Dolly is still very much a part of me. I miss being that character.

AC: What do you remember? It was one of the first contemporary movies to go out into UP and those kinds of terrains.

KKK: And Saif playing a negative character, Langda Tyagi. There was Vivek, there was Bipasha. The cast was attempting this genre for the first time. There were so many of us coming out of our comfort zones, and that energy just worked.

AC: Where was it shot?

KKK: We put up a set in Wai, outside Mumbai, to shoot the village. We were there for like forty to forty-five days. And Lucknow. Everybody was so secure with their parts, really confident. For the first time you had six characters playing strong parts in a story.

AC: Everybody was so good.

KKK: We were all so excited to work with Vishal Bhardwaj. And loving *Maqbool*. The way he projects rural and UP, I think that's his...

AC: It's his forte.

KKK: He brings it to life. He brings even a character, I mean, an urban girl like me, he made me become that.

AC: Let's go to the role that everyone thinks is you, Geet, *Jab We Met*, 2007.

KKK: Another character that no one's—

AC: Forgotten.

KKK: —yeah, and everyone thinks that's me! Honestly, I don't think even Imtiaz knew what we were doing.

AC: The magic you were creating.

KKK: Imtiaz is a passionate filmmaker, really intense. We're both very different people. Imtiaz just really gets into the character. I want to rehearse, I want to know my lines. He'd want to constantly discuss. I was shooting for *Tashan* and giving *Jab We Met* some attitude. That, listen, I'm working with Yash Raj Films with Anil Kapoor, Akshay Kumar, Saif Ali Khan. I am playing the main part. I've become size zero. I'm going to wear a bikini and I'm going to kill it.

AC: So I'm doing you guys a favour.
KKK: Yeah, I'm going to be like *Kill Bill*. And I was very like, *I need to constantly train*. Ten days I'm shooting for *Jab We Met*, ten days for *Tashan*. Shahid actually said that I should hear the script of this film. And he kind of actually got this entire project together in a way. We went our separate ways but this movie came out of it.

AC: Isn't that amazing?
KKK: And that's the time I had to do *Tashan*. I met Saif.

AC: And this is the one that changed your career!
KKK: So I just feel that it was all like really karmically connected. And this was God's plan. It was literally like chess. This is Imtiaz and Shahid and my best film, I think, till date.

AC: Every woman in an Imtiaz film is compared to Geet.
KKK: Everyone wearing patiala salwars and t-shirts. Everyone started making Punjabi films.

AC: And these energetic, small town girl characters.
KKK: But this film just happened. No rehearsing or prepping. Imtiaz would tell me, take it a notch down or up.

AC: Were those discussions you guys had? Because again, this is a very energetic character.
KKK: Yeah. Imtiaz is very involved, like a one-man show. He gets into every little thing. The music was amazing. Shahid was very involved in the music. This small film has become a benchmark for love stories today.

AC: You've said this is one of the hardest roles you've done.
KKK: This girl was constantly babbling. I don't know what she was on. You have to constantly keep up that energy in every scene.

AC: In the first half.

KKK: And then, her entire life changes. A lot of my life took a turn as well during the making of this film. And it came pretty organically, shooting, performing. But my hope was always on *Tashan*. And when *Tashan* bombed I was shattered. Depressed for almost six months.

AC: And you never imagined that she was going to be another iconic character for you.

KKK: I knew that the film and the music and everything would be amazing. But I didn't know that Geet would be etched in stone. This film was a team effort. Imtiaz, Shahid and me will always be karmically connected.

AC: Okay. Mahi Arora in *Heroine*, 2012.

KKK: I'm glad it's in the top five characters you've selected. I feel this performance didn't get its due.

AC: And you were really naked?

KKK: I gave it my all. The audience also at that time was not ready.

AC: Yeah, her desperation is…

KKK: It's uncomfortable. And the film was out there, bizarre. That's the kind of films that Madhur has always made. And I believed in the world. I think people don't want to see a few hidden truths in the films. But I was just so happy, and proud. I enjoyed the experience. We had so much fun.

AC: But was it hard?

KKK: Of course. I would come back home disturbed. I have a child at home. Even though I'm the kind of actor that can leave when the film or shoot is done. I can leave. I gave it one thousand per cent. I'm happy that it's a part of my repertoire. And it is definitely part of my top five. I went down to the deepest, darkest areas that I would be scared of. And Madhur is a brilliant director. He can make you feel uncomfortable as an actress. And he did it beautifully well in all his films, whether it was Kangana or Priyanka. Tap a side of them which you would never see. He has this ability because he's a very nice guy. He makes you touch the bottom pit of your heart. I'm happy that I went down there.

AC: Are you good with coping with failure?

KKK: In this industry, if you're not, you're not going to last two decades. You need to wear the oxygen mask, sinking jacket and wear that suit and just brave the storm. It's like war. You have to make yourself like that. I wasn't like that, but over twenty years, I'm immune to it. Sometimes I get unnerved because millennials now are used to instant success, instant gratification. Friday the film is released, 20-crore-rupee numbers. Saturday it's like, bam, bam.

AC: Also because of social media.

KKK: Yeah, of course. They have to last twenty to thiry years. If this is instant the gratification, maybe the audience's taste is also changing faster.

AC: They'll find a new flavour very quickly.

KKK: Everyone just has to brace and always prepare.

AC: And the last one. A film I really loved. *Udta Punjab*, Preet.

KKK: It was just a brave film. When I was offered the film, Alia and Shahid's track was the track of the film. My character Preet was a parallel track. I felt it was the wheels of the film. It took the story ahead – getting down to the drug bust. They had all the empathy and sympathy. When I read the script, I knew this was Shahid and Alia's film. But I still wanted to be part of this world. Even if I wasn't the central character. Their love story had all the meat, the screaming, all the lines, emotion, wrath. But there was something about Preet. I wanted to be a part of this movie that was saying so much. Seeing me in this setup would be very different. I think we're here because of my choices. An actor is defined by the choices and decisions they make. I made some good choices. The part might not be huge but is impactful. When you're choosing the script in your living room, that's the toughest part. That's where you're the actor. Being on set and performing – it comes. The hardest part is deciding whether to be a part of the film or not. That defines you. And I think that's what's defined me. To have that ability – to do *Udta Punjab*, *Ki and Ka*, to work with Irrfan.

AC: For *Angrezi Medium*.

KKK: For *Angrezi Medium*. Radhika is a father-daughter story. Homi spoke to me and said its a small part but kick-ass. 'You as a cop, never seen before.' Important in the second half, to the twist of the film. And he was like, 'I don't know if you'll do it.' I said, 'Why not? Why are you afraid that a mainstream actor would not want to?' I'm at the stage where I would want to do different parts. So again I think that . . . . That's a brave decision. It will have a payoff. It's a great world, a great story. And a really cool part. Radhika is the central character. But that doesn't make me less as an actor. If I do my part well, people will say, 'She was really cool.' And most Hollywood actors do that. They all pick up parts. That's what defines me – being a little fearless. It's not like I just want to work opposite big stars. I have done that and will continue. But I'll also pick up parts that work in totality. That's the intention. Hope we have another twenty years of amazing parts.

AC: After all these years, what do you think is key to being a strong actor?
KKK: The key is to not be vain.

AC: Is that hard?
KKK: In today's age it is. I was like, I can't be dressed up when I'm talking to Anupama. Everyone's very caught up in our looks. We have to have that couture look. I feel we need to drop that guard. Just be more fearless. The younger generation have that. But to have twenty or thirty years . . . . People have seen me in every form. What else now? Pick up fearless parts, relevant films, keep reinventing. Keep it real . . . as much as possible.

AC: Did this lack of vanity take a while to come?
KKK: When you're young, you want to really look good. And wear a gown, look stunning at the red carpet. Now I'm just like . . . 'Listen just click me at the airport, in my chappals. I'm exhausted.'

AC: You're so over it.
KKK: You see me on screen – I look really good. I've just come back from a shoot. I can't have an airport look. I'm actually apologetic about it. But it's fine.

AC: And it's all about what is in that frame.
KKK: Yeah and it's nice for fans to see – 'She's also as real as any one of us.' I'm very happy.

AC: What can you tell us about *Laal Singh Chaddha* and *Takht*?
KKK: Well I think *Lal Singh* will be fantastic. I hope he doesn't kill me, but I think it's going to be Aamir's best work. And mine. I think he's a genius. The way they've adapted it is superb. There's a long way to go, but

I think people are going to be proud. And *Takht* is going to be fabulous and just opulent. And a brave movie. If someone had to make a film on the Mughal Empire, with this setting, star cast, in this age, it's Karan Johar. It's a difficult script, but he's ready for it. He's always done different films. *My Name Is Khan*, *KANK*, *Ae Dil*. He's constantly tried to evolve. I've never done this genre.

AC: He described it to me as the *K3G* of the Mughal era. So life goes a full circle!
KKK: Absolutely.

20 February 2020

29

The Inner World of Konkona Sen Sharma

Anupama Chopra: Konkona, it's lovely to have you on Now Bingeing. This is our signature show where we celebrate streaming, and you are a full-on streaming star.
Konkona Sen Sharma: Aren't we all nowadays?

AC: No, but Konkona, look at the work you've done, *Dolly Kitty Aur Woh Chamakte Sitare*, *Mumbai Diaries*, *Geeli Pucchi*. And now *The Mirror* with *Lust Stories 2*. The first guest we had on this show was Manoj Bajpayee.
KSS: I watched that! I adore Manoj. Finally Manoj and I have worked together.

AC: Ram Gopal Varma said, 'God made Manoj for OTT.' Is that also true for you? I feel your instinct is towards material which is complicated, thorny.
KSS: That's true. A few years back, it was all multiplex. Before that, studios. New things will also come. But right now, it is streaming. I'm okay with wherever the films come out. We're here to communicate some ideas. I personally love watching stuff on the big screen, but I don't think that my shows or series or anything needs to be watched only on the big screen. I really enjoy watching things on my own, or on a flight on my laptop. I find it a very intimate, individual, intense experience. I think something happens [mid-air], with the low pressure, emotions are heightened, taste buds a little dull, there's nothing else.

AC: That's so funny. Is the on-air experience even...?
KSS: I think it's something to do with the pressure.

AC: You've always said, 'I'm an accidental actor.' But that it was not some burning desire.
KSS: Yeah. I thought publishing, advertising, whatever any respectable BA honours person does.

AC: And then you become one of the finest actors we've ever had. Your second film wins you a national award, *Mr. and Mrs. Iyer*. You become a director and say, 'I'm terrified, everybody will figure out I don't have technical knowledge,' and then you make one of the finest films of the year.
KSS: You've always been so sweet about *Gunj*, I'm so happy.

AC: Is there some jadibooti (medicinal herb) Aparna fed you?
KSS: She never let me watch the mainstream Hindi and Bengali films of the 1980s and 1990s. A few slipped by – *Mr. India, Masoom*. I remember when *Bold and Beautiful, Santa Barbara*, was a big craze. I was not allowed to watch. The soaps I was not allowed to watch. *Ramayana* and *Mahabharata*, when they first came, I was not allowed to watch. She said, 'First you read the epics. Your first exposure should not be somebody else's imagination. It has to be first your own imagination.' Of course, I never read the full *Ramayana* yet. *Mahabharata* I have. But I think, because I wasn't . . . we were watching a lot of world cinema. Regional cinema. Even with books, I remember when you go through a phase as a child, I'm only reading Enid Blyton. One day she said, 'No, bas ho gaya hai (enough of this), you have to now move on from this.' What an obedient child I was!

AC: You did it?
KSS: I was like, 'Okay, yeah, okay, let's watch, you know, try something else, watch something else.' That may have helped to an extent in expanding the worldview, horizons, being open to different kinds of narratives and art forms.

AC: But that's still just a palette, right? Talent kidhar se aaya (Where did the talent come from)? Craft kahan se aayi (Where did the craft come from)?
KSS: You know, ye sab toh, I mean, pata nahi, ho gaya (I don't know about all this but it just happened, you know). Baar-baar hoga ki nahi (whether it will happen again and again), you don't know. In real life also, I feel like I have to be myself. I have to try and be as honest and as truthful in the situation. Maybe that has something to do with it? That I am also mostly not trying to please anybody else. I'm mostly just trying to see if I'm excited by an idea. What am I trying to communicate? I think whether it's films, books or any kind of artistic expression, it's really just, what it is to live – this weird human life that we're living. It doesn't always work, and

sometimes I think I'm communicating this, and something else is getting communicated, but maybe it lands nearby.

AC: So, you don't seek external validation in the way that most people in showbiz do?
KSS: I don't think I seek external validation. I think that very early on was wiped out. As a kid, I was a very bad student. And I became a very good student, but only after class nine. So, when you've been a terrible student, I think you don't seek external validation. And my upbringing, my mother always gave so much respect to me. I was always given a certain space and agency of my own. I always read a lot, had a very rich inner world. So, agar mil gaya toh mil gaya, agar nahi mila toh nahi mila (so, if I get it then I get it, if I don't then I don't).

AC: You're not hungry in the best way possible?
KSS: Hopefully, and let's see how long it lasts. Life itself. My personality also, I mean, it's not like I'm this or that.

AC: You're many things.
KSS: Yeah, it's changing, it's fluid, it's seeping out of this direction, leaking in that direction.

AC: You are also a 'nepo baby', right?
KSS: I'm a nepo baby of sorts.

AC: Your mom is a movie legend. And yet, no matter how shrill the conversation around nepo babies got, your name was never flung around.
KSS: Yeah, but I sit and feel guilty on my own a little bit, sometimes.

AC: Because that's just who you are.
KSS: That's just who I am but also maybe it didn't get called out because I was never part of the Bombay mainstream industry. Aparna Sen has done some Hindi films, but not too many. And as an actor she was a big commercial star but I never really did that in Bengali films myself or in Hindi. I feel like I'm a nepo baby in the best sense because, I have been around film sets since I was a kid. I've also watched my mom editing, dubbing, mixing, doing budgets, having pre-production meetings, it's a familiar world. But it's not like she had networks or connections like that

in Bombay as such. It's always lovely to be extended the respect that was accorded to her. I'm lucky.

AC: But it might also be because you're so talented. Talent speaks for itself, right?
KSS: Yeah, and it's very subjective. There are all kinds of talents and some people like this and some people like that, and it's nice to have a wide variety of things happening so that people can also pick and choose.

AC: Yeah. One of my favourite films is Zoya's *Luck by Chance*.
KSS: Mine too.

AC: That scene when you, as Sona, are saying to that producer that you should be given work because you have talent and he says, 'Lekin woh kise chahiye (But who wants that)?' I've never forgotten that.
KSS: What a script that was! What a film that is!

AC: Yeah, yeah, it was just fabulous. Do you feel that in 2023, talent is a major priority?
KSS: For whom?

AC: For producers, for the gatekeepers.
KSS: I don't think so. I think even more than talent, people who are putting in money want stars and I mean, why not? And many stars are very talented and perhaps some aren't as much, but I think that even for OTTs there's definitely a move towards stars.

AC: Really?
KSS: Yeah, 100 per cent.

AC: It is . . . a star system is setting in?
KSS: Yeah. There's a lot of pressure to take stars. As an actor also, and as a director also, there's a lot of pressure to cast big stars.

AC: Karan was saying, maybe stars are still a requirement but, 'You can't just be a star, you also have to have the talent.'
KSS: Yeah, maybe. Maybe, that is possibly true and that's the best combination isn't it?

AC: Absolutely yeah.
KSS: Best and rare.

AC: When you were younger, you said you were judgemental of your characters.
KSS: My characters, yeah.

AC: You said, 'If I didn't approve of their behaviour, I wouldn't have sympathy.' Did this change?
KSS: It's changed. I remember my mom pointing it out to me, because I was always like, 'Ugh! Why is she behaving like this? Why doesn't she have more dignity?' I had this slight attitude sometimes. My mother said, 'But, you know, this girl doesn't have any other weapons. She feels she has to behave a certain way,' and that really helped. I have to say thanks again to streaming, that one is getting interesting roles also. Good things have also happened, you know. Like, *Dolly Kitty*. Dolly is a strange character – a lying, cheating, stealing kind of a woman, not always a great mother. Fantastic, I love the way Alankrita portrays women. And even *Geeli Pucchi*. Also, format-wise, you can do a short film, documentary, docuseries, short miniseries, films, all of that. As far as I know, series don't need censorship.

AC: But tell me about this empathy with your characters. Does that show in your performance when you are judging your characters?
KSS: Probably, it will come through. The aim now is to try and connect. We have everything already within us. Like, all the emotions and all the feelings, and at different points in the day or in our life, different elements of ourselves come out. And when you get a character, you do the Venn diagram and find the overlap. Sometimes it's useful to find a real person as an approximation. 'Ah! This one is like my cousin,' or something. The other thing is – I've actually caught myself doing this – I start behaving like my character in real life.

AC: Really?
KSS: Yeah. So, for example, if I'm largely an angry person, I've also in real life become slightly – things which may not have bothered me, I've let it bother me. If in character I have to confess something, in real life also I'm like, I can't almost help it. It's a very risky business.

AC: I was just gonna say!
KSS: Playing with your life!

AC: Doesn't this get really tricky?

KSS: It can. It's a good thing that I caught myself doing it. Then you're like, 'Are you sure? Is this worth it?' It's fun taking some risks and living a little on the edge.

AC: You're going through the day and then you stop and say to yourself, 'Am I being so and so or am I being myself?'

KSS: No, I realised this when I had to do a scene where I'm distraught and anguished. As I'm leading up to that scene, one or two days before, maybe it's somewhere on my mind, I found myself inviting the anguish in my life. I would normally take a moment and calm down. But I found myself – because I have to go do this, let me anyway do this beforehand a little, and then just cheat and transplant.

AC: Just prep me for that.

KSS: It's not like I planned it.

AC: That's so funny!

KSS: It's so interesting!

AC: And you're able to kind of, see yourself in third person and say, 'Konkona, you're doing this now.'

KSS: In the last few years, maybe to a certain extent. Also, nowadays with all that mindfulness and all the Insta nuggets you're getting all the time, 'identify the emotion.' It could be a factor of age, being more self-aware. Now, sometimes if I have a negative emotion, I am trying to train myself a little bit, 'Oh, I am feeling this.' It's a helpful thing.

AC: What about becoming a director, has that helped you to be a better actor?

KSS: I think to a certain extent it did; when you're acting, it's more insular. And as a director, you have a more macro view. I also realised that anybody's performance is such a collaboration of everybody. I became a little more sympathetic also to my directors, to delays and things like that.

AC: You, as an actor, have played such a variety of roles. In *A Monsoon Date*, you were a trans character. In *Geeli Pucchi*, a queer, Dalit woman.

There's so much polarised conversation about who gets to play who. What is your sense of this?

KSS: It's tough, we're just all of us figuring out and learning. It would be ideal if we could have a bank of trans actors. But I mean, it's not happened yet. It should and it will, I'm sure. Shohini Ghosh said, 'I will always choose skill over identity, just like I would for brain surgery.' So, that is also a factor. Of course, there should be actors from all communities, to portray these characters. But, one also has to apply the filter of skill. You can't just take somebody because they're from that community and they don't have the skill, it's not a documentary.

AC: Yeah, this is very complicated.

KSS: It's tricky terrain.

AC: There's so much conversation after *The Mirror* came out. 'How do we get Konkona to direct more often?'

KSS: You started it! That was so sweet, I loved it! 'Petition to get Konkona to direct more.'

AC: How can we do it?

KSS: My favourite thing is just jamming with people, you know, whether it's writing or world-building.

AC: The brainstorming.

KSS: With actors, cinematographer, production designer. So, if somebody else is just taking care of the nitty-gritties of life, maybe I could do more of that. But also, one has to be excited about an idea, let things percolate and maybe be allowed to fail.

AC: So, now there's too much expectation?

KSS: No, I don't know about others but I just feel, do baar toh ho gaya thik-thak, ab pata nahi third time kya hoga (that it has worked twice but I don't know what'll happen a third time).

AC: Low on confidence?

KSS: I actually like a little bit of self-doubt in people. Very overconfident toxic positivity, it's not something I can even really relate to. A little doubt is nice and you can learn.

AC: Is there a burden to being perceived as really smart?
KSS: My image in other people's minds is none of my business. I'm sometimes a little smart, sometimes a little stupid, I can be very funny, sometimes I'm a little duh. I don't think one really gets a sense of a full person from the roles they play. From my work, the only thing that's really me is *A Death in the Gunj*.

AC: What's next?
KSS: *Mumbai Diaries*, season two, coming out soon on Amazon. And I'm really excited to work with Abhishek Chaubey and Manoj and Nasir [Nasser] Sir in *Killer Soup*. . . . And my mum's film, *The Rapist*, at MAMI later this year – I'm excited about that.

AC: That film got under my skin.
KSS: You've seen it!

AC: It premiered at Busan.
KSS: I'm so glad.

AC: Very complicated film and I kept second-guessing my own feelings about what was happening.
KSS: Absolutely. When you're reading something about an issue like this, you're like, 'Oh, but this angle?' It's such an ambitious project, but at the script level, I remember thinking, 'Let's do this.'

AC: Just leaving you with the earlier petition, direct soon!
KSS: I'm so happy, thank you. Yes, I hope so.

AC: What type of a binger are you?
KSS: I don't watch as much as my friends, my peers. The way people are consuming, it's amazing. But once in while, there's a show which I will just, finish in two nights. I love *Tabbar*.

AC: Me too.
KSS: I really got into it. I just believed everything. I enjoyed *Trial by Fire* as well, though I didn't binge it.

AC: It was a tough one, yeah.
KSS: But they saved it for that last episode. I loved *Beef*. I was so happy, to see that kind of rage on screen. We rarely see women so angry. And

I also love playing characters who are angry, it's so taboo in real life to just lose your shit. *White Lotus* also, I enjoy that world. Second season, I really missed that hotel manager. I love watching stand-up.

AC: Who are the Indian comics you like?
KSS: Biswa of course, Zakir, Abhishek Upamanyu [Upmanyu], Bassi – there are many.

AC: Your preferred genre?
KSS: I'm genre agnostic. If something is well made, I don't care what the genre is. I'm a little scared of horror. The film may have finished, but me and my mind, we have made sequels.

AC: You had very scary moments in *Gunj*.
KSS: I want to make a small indie horror movie. Subtle horror.

AC: What are you watching right now and why?
KSS: I'm not on a series right now. I have to watch *Succession* and *The Bear*. I feel a little, 'Ugh,' when there's a lot of hype. *Game of Thrones*, I just couldn't. Fantasy is not my favourite genre. Also when everybody's watching it, it feels like...

AC: Let the hype go. What's a performance in a recent Indian show or film that's made you jealous?
KSS: I love Tabu, Vidya, Shefali . . . . I can relate to a lot, I guess.

AC: All-time favourite film?
KSS: One of my all-time favourites is *Day for Night*. Truffaut's. It's a film about making films. *Jules et Jim*, *Day for Night*, I love voice-overs like that, really fast . . . . It's like, when you hear an article or podcast, you're like, 'Hurry up!' because so many thoughts are coming in.

AC: You've said mainstream Hindi cinema was never your thing.
KSS: But there are a few! *Main Hoon Na*, *Om Shanti Om*. I really liked *Darlings*. *Mard Ko Dard* [*Nahi Hota*], *Ishqiya*.

AC: If you had to do a mainstream Hindi film, which director would you choose?
KSS: Sriram Raghavan. I'd love to work with him.

AC: And if somebody didn't know you, what's the first film you would recommend?
KSS: *A Death in the Gunj.*

AC: What's a recent character you've played or created that stayed with you?
KSS: *Geeli Pucchi*'s Bharti Mandal. I had a chance to kind of unleash my inner man. Being feminine is something that is learnt. In real life, one is often quite neutral. I am. Neeraj and I would talk about it. But a different man came out of me. It's not like it was planned, but there was that person inside who I've never even given the permission to come out.

AC: It was such a fantastic performance.
KSS: Thanks to Neeraj and Sameer Saxena, the writer, and Aditi and everyone.

AC: Okay, and if a book has been made into a film, book first?
KSS: Nothing like that. And there are rare exceptions. *Clockwork Orange* is at par. A couple of films have come close. It depends. I always go by the reviews, of films, books. Also from certain friends and colleagues that I trust. I want to recommend *Tomorrow and Tomorrow and Tomorrow*, what a fantastic book! They're probably making it a movie already.

AC: Favourite superhero?
KSS: *Across the Spider-Verse*! What have they done! My son is watching a lot of superheroes.

AC: And is he inducting you into the fold?
KSS: He tries. He sometimes tries to quiz me on *Avengers*. I love being deliberately obtuse, to just show my disdain. Some of them are obviously good, but a lot of them, I try to tell him that they're just making these again and again to make money.

AC: Is there a superpower you want to have?
KSS: I'd like to be invisible. You can observe.

AC: What are some other shows you've loved?
KSS: I binged on *The Diplomat*. *Bad Sisters* was super fun. It's about these five sisters – one of them is married to a prick and right at the

top, all the sisters are trying to kill him and they're botching it up. *Severance* – I love.

AC: Very unnerving!
KSS: The sense of claustrophobia, so relevant.

AC: We're going to the last segment, 'Imagine This'. Inspired by your film, *Yun Hota To Kya Hota*. These are basically imaginary scenarios. So, would Aisha and Sid have lived happily ever after?
KSS: No, I doubt it very much. They would have had a few good years maybe.

AC: What would be an alternative profession for Sona from *Luck by Chance*?
KSS She's very resourceful and jugadu (innovative), she would have made it in films. She would have killed it at streaming, I think.

AC: Where would Shutu be if he was still alive?
KSS: Maybe sitting and writing a novel in like Finland.

AC: What is Bharti Mandal doing right now?
KSS: The stats are so sad, but she she's trying to live her best life and she's helping others too.

AC: I feel like she could have taken over that factory.
KSS: Oh yeah, like this (snaps fingers).

AC: Woh toh baaye haath ka khel hai (It was easy). Complete gender equality on a set, what would that set look like?
KSS: It's so sad – it might look very much the same. Because, sometimes, from the outside it looks equal, but women are doing everything in high heels, with the baby at the back. So, on the outside, it looks the same, but maybe they would be a little more relaxed and have less to deal with.

11 August 2023

30

'Every Day Is a New Costume': Mohanlal

Anupama Chopra: Sir, such a pleasure to have you. Congratulations on the stupendous response to the trailer of the *Drishyam* sequel. I cannot wait to see if George Kutty gets away with the perfect crime. I'm sure you're not going to tell us anything.
Mohanlal: Even I don't know. He's unpredictable.

AC: True. The brilliance of the first film was that incredible screenplay. But you left us wondering about George Kutty. That last scene – you're asking for forgiveness but not with great emotion. Is George Kutty a good man?
Mohanlal: He is unpredictable. Even I don't know George Kutty still. After all these years, after the shift. His state of mind. What are his emotions? His intelligence? He can be a big criminal, he can be a good family man. He is scheming so many things I don't know. *Drishyam* changed how the world looked at Malayalam cinema. Part two is a big challenge – the script more than George Kutty. Jeethu has done a wonderful job. Even for *Drishyam 1*, he spent around six or seven years. *Drishyam 2* also. This film is full of emotions and family drama, I cannot say it's a thriller, you have to decide after watching.

AC: Do you judge him as a human being at all?
Mohanlal: For him, nothing is bad. He'll go to any level to protect his family.

AC: The first film was seven years ago. Did you slip into character easily?
Mohanlal: For me, when you say, 'Start, camera, action', you are in. The actor knows about the surroundings, his house, his car. I can read the scene and I know how to perform. George Kutty is close to my heart. It's not just me but my co-actors Meena and the children too – they know each and every corner of the house. They know what happened in this house six years back. So the acclimatisation was perfect.

AC: The sequel was announced during the lockdown. Did you always imagine it would end up on a streaming service?
Mohanlal: We were trying to make a movie which can bring people to the theatre. We were not prepared to do *Drishyam 2* at this time. On a sudden call, Jeethu said, 'Okay, we'll try.' People started writing about *Drishyam 2*. And later, Jeethu told me the storyline. And it was brilliant, an intelligent film. But theatres were still a question mark. People want to watch this film, so we got an opportunity like this.

AC: Was it tough to make that decision?
Mohanlal: No. For our production company, we did a big film called *Kunjali Marakkar*. We are holding that. All over the world we have to release. For *Drishyam 2*, luckily we got this platform. It's all God's blessing.

AC: You've done 345 films on IMDb. It's 365 now. Your forty-third year, five national awards. You said, 'It's an unknown energy helping me.' But that's not a satisfying answer.
Mohanlal: You tell me . . . . Because it's a mystery for me. I don't want to 'reveal' it, it is happening . . . . That's the best answer I can give. I don't know. It's a practice. We do rehearsals. We do a lot of things. Then your colleagues will join. It's a big congress happening. So if you ask, 'How do you act?' – I don't know.

AC: Is there ever a moment or a day when it just feels like a job when it's not exciting?
Mohanlal: When I feel this is like a job, I'll stop acting. For me, every day is a new day. New costume, new dialogues, unrealistic things, fighting, singing. It's a beautiful revelation. When you start thinking, 'Why do I want to do this job?' I will stop acting. I promise.

AC: What's really amazing is that you're a brilliant actor, but also a massive star. All the box office milestones of Malayalam cinema have been your films. When you decide on a script, how much are you thinking about the box office?
Mohanlal: I never do that. That's the brilliance of the producer and the director. Of course, it's my production also, but with a good script, we cannot say, 'Oh, this is going to collect 200 crores.' I believe in happenings.

AC: So, how do you choose your scripts?
Mohanlal: I believe in my directors and the script. Nobody can say, 'This is going to be a big hit.' We don't know the recipe. You get a peep when reading a script. Sometimes things click. Now producers, directors – so many people hear the story. I am not the deciding factor. But I'll say things that help it go better. Like *Lucifer* – when you read it, you feel, 'My God.' Then you feel, 'Oh, this is going to be a nice character.' If you perform well, shoot it well . . . . If it's not conducted properly, people won't watch. Each film has a pace. You have to be careful with everything. The film should have a soul. You have to communicate. After watching, you have to carry something back – a character, a scene...

AC: I really enjoyed Lucifer. Tell me about *Empuran*, the sequel.
Mohanlal: We cannot commit to anything because we don't know how it is going to be. We planned to do it in 2021. So, if everything goes well, it can happen in 2022 beginning. The storyline is ready. They have to write.

AC: What is happening with your directorial debut, *Barroz*?
Mohanlal: Same thing, Covid. *Barroz* was supposed to start by January. Most of the actors are from Spain, Portugal, the US, Ghana. So, they have to come again. Our action director is from Thailand. We are trying to start by mid-April.

AC: Are you nervous about directing?
Mohanlal: I never thought of directing. It happened when Jijo narrated this story. I asked, 'Who is going to do this?' It's beautiful, like a fairytale. It's about a genie, treasure and a girl. The child in me said, 'Do it.' Forty years back, I walked into his room. He selected me as an actor. Then he said, 'With all my blessings, do this.' It's a 3D film. They did *My Dear Kuttichathan*. I thought, 'Why do a simple film? I'll do a complicated one.' Barroz is a four-hundred-year-old ghost. So I thought, okay, I can live for 400 years.

AC: The level of fame, does it put responsibility on you in terms of the scripts you do?
Mohanlal: I am a performer. My social commitment is to do what I get perfectly. I do theatre, magic, dancing and I sing. My passion is to do things which nobody can do.

AC: I was watching *Iruvar* recently. Your performance is brilliant. When it released, it didn't work. But today, it's a classic. Tell me about your relationship with Mani Ratnam.

Mohanlal: Mani Ratnam saw the second film I did in Malayalam. His second film *Unaroo*, he called me to do. People said it's the story of MGR, Karunanidhi and Jayalalithaa. After the film, I asked, 'Why did you call me to do this?' He said he doesn't know. It was a big thing for me to do that role. And it was one of the best films. But the censor problem happened. Ministry changed. But it's one of my favourite movies. After that, Mani Sir called me for some other movies but at that time, I was confused. I have great respect for Mani Sir. And of course, Aishwarya Rai too, it was her first film. Craft-wise, if you watch the film again you can see how they've done it perfectly.

AC: There's been such a sort of renaissance in Malayalam cinema. How do you view it? And who are the directors you want to work with?

Mohanlal: Let it happen. It is more than the director, the script and of course, the executives as well. You do whatever the film needs.

10 February 2021

31

Vikrant Massey Spills the Tea

Sneha Menon Desai: Welcome, Vikrant. Do you cycle around?
Vikrant Massey: In and around Yari Road–Versova. Parking is such an issue nowadays. And thodi exercise bhi ho jati hai (it doubles up as exercise too). I love physical activity.

SMD: I have landed up literally under your building. You are a Bombay boy – didn't move to the city to become an actor. Do you live in the same building that you grew up in?
VM: I was born and raised in the adjacent building.

SMD: Let's go there.
VM: I was almost raised here because I used to live here. All my friends used to live here. Deewaar taapke yahan aa jaya karte thhe (So, we used to come here by climbing the wall). That's my school.

SMD: Oh, your school is right here! So, one more deewaar (wall) and you were in class.
VM: We used to play here. Cricket all day. Let's begin at the beginning. I would love to take you where I was born.

SMD: Do you live with your parents here?
VM: No. My parents are just ten minutes away. I am on my own.

SMD: What's this house like? What's the vibe?
VM: A lot of mess. It's a small 1BHK.

SMD: You are a messy guy or you are a busy guy?
VM: I am a Massey guy.

SMD: Right.
VM: There is clutter in this house at this point in time, because I have just come back from an outdoor shoot. Still haven't completely unpacked, it's been ten days.

SMD: Living out of a suitcase.
VM: But I love that. White linen, organised room service – wish I had something like that here. My parents keep jumping in and out, my father walks in this park every evening. After that he comes home for his cup of tea.

SMD: You literally have your old house, your current house, your school and the park.
VM: The park where I used to play a lot. Itna nazdeek hoga ye nahi socha tha (You didn't think it would be this close by).

SMD: Yeah, it's a beautiful park.
VM: They have also installed those community workout machines and everything.

SMD: Are your building friends still your friends or have you become that Bollywood guy?
VM: Nahi, aisa nahi hai (No, it's not like that). I still do retain my relationship with them. But honestly, we don't catch up as often as we used to. That's the house I was born and raised in. Woh jahan pe bada dish antenna laga hua hai (Where that big dish antenna is installed)? That's on rent right now.

SMD: Oh, okay.
VM: Woh maine rent pe chadha diya woh ghar (So, I have rented out that house). Yeah. Thodi tarakki ho rahi hai zindagi mein (Life is getting a little better). This is exactly where I was born and raised, in this building. Bombay mein itna bada ground (such a big ground in Bombay)…

SMD: I was just going to say!
VM: It has some six or seven cricket pitches.

SMD: You had a great childhood.
VM: I was so fortunate.

SMD: You are the right candidate for a childhood tour. My poor son is not going to have this.

VM: Life back in the 1990s was incredibly different. We used to play here. And I still have a lot of other friends around. So, this is the building. You can see a lot of it is furbished, a lot of it has changed right now. Let's enter.

SMD: Do you walk the streets around here? Or are you slightly more conscious of how you are looking?

VM: Not at all. In fact, what you see now is the polished me. You will see me in shorts and chappal, hair completely dishevelled.

SMD: But you know we live in the times of the paparazzi?

VM: Not for me.

SMD: Well, you entered on a cycle. So, I believe you.

VM: A lot hasn't changed for me. You can see that little store there. Uske baaju mein shaam ko panipuri wala aata hai. Uske bagal mein humara gola wala khada hota hai (Next to that, the panipuri guy comes in the evening. Our shaved ice guy stands next to him.) Aaj bhi woh jo gola wala wahan pe khada hota hai, mujhe aaj bhi usko udhari deni hai meri, school ki (even today, the gola guy who stands there, I owe him money, from school days).

SMD: Are you serious?

VM: Bolta hai, 'Arre bhaiyya, aap abhi film star bann gaye hain, toh aapse kya lenge paisa? (He says, 'You have become a film star now, what money will I take from you now)?'

SMD: Have the neighbourhood aunties' attitude changed towards you? Were you a naughty kid?

VM: I was very naughty, but I was also very loved. Matlab, shaam ko hum khelte thhe, toh main rehta tha four maale pe yahan pe (I mean, we used to play in the evening, so, I used to stay on the fourth floor). So, every minute used to be so crucial for us. Toh one maale pe jitni bhi auntiyan rehti thi, unki shaam ki duty thi, fridge mein shaam ko char-panch baje hi humare liye, you know, badi one litre ki bottle mein Rooh Afza banake rakh deti thi, ya Rasna banake rakh deti thi (So, all the aunties on the first floor, it was their duty in the evenings, so some of them, at around four or five in the evening, would keep a one-litre bottle of Rooh Afza or Rasna in their fridge for us).

SMD: Sweet.
VM: Jab itne-itne thhe hum (When we were small), this place used to look so big.

SMD: What was a six?
VM: So, we used to bat there. And yahan pe 6/4 hua karta tha, over here (it used to be six/four here). Plastic ki kursi lagake we used to play, box cricket hota tha literally (So, we used to play cricket by putting a plastic chair, it was literally like box cricket).

SMD: Was there anything filmy about your upbringing in any way?
VM: Not at all. The only filmy thing was Renuka Shahane being our neighbour.

SMD: Ohho! So, when did the acting bug bite?
VM: I always wanted to be an actor. But mujhe aisa lagta tha ki hum middle-class log hain, pehle padhai-likhai apni puri karenge (But I used to think that we are middle-class people, we will finish our studies first). But then television happened very early. At sixteen. And then...

SMD: And good, big shows.
VM: The big ones started trickling in after like, two or three years of work. I did small bits here and there. I did a show for Doordarshan. In front of the chroma key green main rakshas se baat kar raha hoon (I am talking to a demon) as huge as this tree right here.

SMD: If you can be convincing like that, you can do anything. Did you confide in anyone – friends, family that you want to be an actor?
VM: When I started dancing in school, a lot of my teachers pushed me already in that direction. I used to be out of the class all throughout the day.

SMD: Enthu wala (The enthusiastic one).
VM: Totally. I was average or above average in school. I would also be outside the class most of the times because I used to play a lot of cricket. Jab PTAs hote thhe aur PTAs ke alawa jab shikayat ke time parents ko bulaya

jaata hai, uss waqt kehte thhe ki yaar ye kuch issi field mein karna chahiye bachcha (when there were PTAs and apart from PTA, when parents are called at the time of complaints, they used to say that this child should do something in this field).

SMD: Also, good looks were on your side. So, you would have been popular...
VM: I was actually not at all popular. I will tell you why. I was unpopular for all the wrong reasons. Because gora tha main bohot matlab (I was very fair, I mean).

SMD: But India mein (in India), that's not a bad thing.
VM: But the other guy friends would be like, 'Aye chikne, aye chikne (Aye whitey, aye whitey).' I had a lot of pimples on my face, and my nose was like, really long.

SMD: What about the girls?
VM: Haan matlab (yeah, I mean), on and off.

SMD: Achha!
VM: But my school never had good-looking girls, yaar.

SMD: They could be watching, and they're not going to be happy.
VM: I want them to listen!

SMD: Was the Bollywood struggle a big part of your journey?
VM: Yes, my struggle made me the person that I am, growing up. But I think sab apne-apne sphere mein struggle karte hain (everyone struggles in their own sphere).

SMD: But what was your struggle?
VM: Auditioning and everything happened much later. Very basic, regular, identifiable, lower-middle-class struggles, nuclear family. Do ladke hain, maa-baap hain (Us two boys and our mum and dad). Father is a salaried man. Pehle ke dus-pandrah din mein paise saare udd jaate hain acting toh bohot baad me aayi (In the first ten to fifteen days, all your money flies away, acting came much later). I was working in a coffee shop for eight to nine months. And then, Shiamak happened during my tenth standard break. Struggle sabke apne-apne hote hain (Everyone has their own struggles).

SMD: It's relative also.

VM: It's relative. Comparatively, I had the privilege of having my family here. I did not have to leave my city and come back. When I hear stories from other people who have come from places like Punjab or Delhi, woh apni kothiyan chhodke aaye hain (they have left their huts). Away from family and everything. I knew that I had a place to come back to. All I need to do is just be up, eat and go out and do my stuff.

SMD: You chose to star in smaller parts, in bigger roles. *Lootera, Dil Dhadakne Do, Half Girlfriend,* you really proved yourself. Today, we are talking about a film opposite Deepika Padukone. Was that a conscious route or did you just know not know better?

VM: I really don't know.

SMD: Because in retrospect, it's cool to say, like, 'Wow, this guy really worked his way up.'

VM: But that was also the idea. Today, in retrospect, when I look back I think, 'Okay, I was a professional dancer.' The Hindi film industry, even today, centres around song and dance. Sometimes, I think I should have done that. But, when I'm all by myself, I'm very happy with the calls I've made in life. *Maqbool* changed the way I started consuming entertainment. And . . . Irrfan Khan has played a very important role in my life.

SMD: You wanted to be an actor after you watched that film?

VM: After I watched that film. When my parents lived in Janki Kutir – I was not even born then – my mother always stood in the balcony and saw this really lanky guy jo jhola leke aata hai wahan pe, ghanton-ghanton baithta hai aur shaam ko chala jaata hai (who brings a tote bag and sits there for hours and leaves in the evening), who eventually turns out to be Irrfan Khan.

SMD: What?!

VM: Maybe in his mid-thirties or forties, jo maine dekha, jo thairaav unme tha, jo ek acceptance unke chehre pe hume dikhti thi (the way I saw him, the way he was determined, the acceptance that we used to see on his face) which sort of drew us closer to him. I always wanted someone to feel for me the way I felt for Irrfan. I feel like I haven't even started doing things that I want to do. I'm just thirty-two.

SMD: But what changes when you sign a so-called big film in Bollywood? Do more people try to sign you up?

VM: Yeah. You have no idea the number of calls and scripts coming in my inbox. Toh haan perception hai (So, yeah, it's a perception). But agar aap mujhse puche toh (But, if you ask me), I don't think anything has changed from the way I see it. And no, I'm not trying to be modest. I really don't want to think about what is going to happen or focus on what people are seeing me as. What's more important is that I continue, stick to my basics and make sure that people are happy with the performances they've seen.

SMD: But how are you keeping out the clutter and just focusing on the craft?
VM: I don't know.

SMD: It's new, right?
VM: It's fairly new but not entirely new. The magnitude of it is new.

SMD: What can you tell us about the schedule?
VM: It's been good. It's been far more focused. I have more responsibility. The only thing that I am focused on right now is to not think about the peripherals. Agar apna kaam achha rahega toh phir uska result bhi milega (If our work is good then we'll get the results as well). My family keeps me sane. My lifestyle hasn't changed. Shaam ko, you'll find me playing carrom in the adjacent building with my friends. Toh wahan pe hum carrom khelenge, 10–10.30 p.m. baje tak ki permission rehti hai. Then I come back. Zindagi mein ye nahi karna hai. Karna kya hai woh sabko pata hai (This is what not to do in life. Everyone knows what to do), ups and downs are a part of this thing.

SMD: You learn.
VM: You learn.

SMD: You also talked about how actors are judged by social media presence.
VM: Everybody is asking me this question. Kuch galat kaha maine (Did I say something wrong)? Ek second haan. Rekha Aunty!

SMD: I fully agree with what you said, which is why I want to talk about it.

VM: No, see what I actually meant was, social media today is very important. For a lot of people it's a form of making money as well. But it's a very thin line. 'This person is extremely talented, but we cannot hire because they don't have Instagram following.' Now, that is ridiculous.

SMD: And you're an actor at the end of the day.
VM: It's also because I have seen the other side. Audition space is actually like an examination space. I still test today. I prefer it. You've seen what I offer as an actor in front of the camera. I really want my producers and writers to be absolutely sure.

SMD: But what's different today?
VM: Bas ye hai ki abhi wait nahi karna padta hai. Ab wahan pe jao toh woh ready rehte hain (You don't have to wait. Now, when you go there, they are ready).

SMD: Alag alag looks don't need to be carried in your bag, perhaps?
VM: Woh bag mein jaata hai samaan (One carries things in the bag).

SMD: So, people are clearly watching your social media. There is a certain girl in your life that you've kept very . . .
VM: She's out there on social media. We've been together for nearly four years now and it's good.

SMD: Does fame make it harder to go places together?
VM: Not at all.

SMD: You make it sound too easy.
VM: But why is it tough? Stepping out for dinner with the person you've been with.

SMD: How have you not got papped?
VM: Because I don't call the paps. That's the only difference. Hum dono aaj bhi shaam ko general store jaate hain, D Mart jaate hain, ration bharte hain (We both still go to the general store in the evenings, to DMart, fill up the ration).

SMD: Selfies?
VM: Nahi, woh hai (No, that's there). There are people who come over.

SMD: And you're okay with that?
VM: That validation is what we work for, you know.

SMD: The last time we met, ek manager tha (there was one manager) which you had finally succumbed to. Aaj kaafi saare hain (Today, there are many).
VM: Yeah, but I think a lot of my peace of mind is also because of them. I have some really great minds helping me.

SMD: Strategising brand 'Vikrant Massey'.
VM: It's new territory for me. If I have really skilled people around, a lot of my time is saved. A lot of other things are also saved. What has changed tangibly is that I am happier today as a person. Scripts are coming my way and there are more people who are wanting to know me.

21 May 2019

32

'I'll Graduate Life with Honours': Sushmita Sen
With Ram Madhvani

Sneha Menon Desai: In my ten-year-career as a film journalist, I have always maintained that there are literally just two people that can enter a room and command it: Shah Rukh Khan and Sushmita Sen.

Sushmita Sen: That's a huge compliment. Shah Rukh does that.

SMD: And so do you. What is the secret sauce? Does it ever get exhausting?

SS: That's a beautiful question. I became famous because I wanted people, not awards. And when God gave me that in such abundance, I have looked at it every single moment. Does it get tiring? Yes, but that thought kicks: 'This is what you've always wanted. I'm forty-eight years old and I've been famous longer than I have not been.'

SMD: I was going through the ORMAX report of the most-watched OTT series in 2023. She is literally the only actor that has two shows up in the top ten, a cumulative watch time of 35 million people. And that also makes you the most watched Indian female actor in 2023.

SS: I never thought of it like that.

SMD: Break that down for me.

SS: 2023 was a very cathartic year. *Aarya* came like a manifestation. I waited and kept saying no because I was waiting for The One. I walked in to KBC, met Mr Ram Madhvani. I had manifested this human being, this director, his vision and *Aarya*. It was a 'yes' in five minutes. As an actor in my second innings, I wanted to do different things. I've always known ki main duniya ki sabse kamaal actress nahi hoon, chalega. But main duniya ki sabse hardworking actress honi chahiye. (It's ok if I'm not the best actress in the world, but I should be the most hardworking actress in the world.) So where I don't have talent, I'll put in the work. So, with that thought, when *Taali* came, everyone around me said, 'Don't do it. There'll be public opinion, the transgender community.' But it's the one thing I had again manifested, I'm a very inclusive human being. Gauri Sawant wanted me to do it. And then my audiences accepted *Taali*.

SMD: 35 million on last count.

SS: Thank you for the specific count. But that's what breaking it down is. And then I had victory with my health in 2023. The Sherni (lioness) and the Shakti (power) we speak of when we speak of *Aarya*, I experienced that in real life. I think it just gave me a whole new lease to life.

SMD: But the truth is, we are sitting on the eve of the release of part two of *Aarya*, season three only because in 2010, you did a film called *No Problem* and you then realised that you, in fact, had a problem with the kind of roles that you were getting and decided on a ten-year hiatus. Was that audacious?

SS: My mum would always tell me, 'Beta, you get in life what you have the courage to ask for.' I went myself; I met all the heads myself and I said, 'I'm Sushmita Sen, I've been in the industry a long time, don't have too much work to show for it, but I would like to be a part of OTT. I want an author-backed show, a character and I want to headline the show.' So, that was not audacious, that was asking for jo mera haq hai (what I deserve). And I believe that everything that I don't have in talent, I have in hard work. Everything worked itself out and I've been very blessed, I have had an audience that has believed in me. They've said, 'No, she didn't get her due.' They stood up for me and honestly, it is because of this audience that I walked away eight years ago. I said, 'It's not the fault of the industry, it is my fault because I'm accepting it. I'm saying no. And this could be the end of a career or could be the beginning of another one.' Thanks to my audience, it became the beginning of another one.

SMD: Yeah. Being a mother myself, it hit hard when you said, 'My children were very proud of the person that I was but not so much of the work that I was doing.' And Renée is in the audience as well today. Did their validation shape your decisions?

SS: No, I think how they impacted my life the most is, as mothers, hum apne bachchon ko humesha bolte hain, 'Ye sahi hai, ye galat hai (we always tell our children, this is right, this is wrong), don't settle for less in life.' Your children look at you, ki aapne jo sikhaya hai woh samajh gaye, magar ab aap kya karte ho (whatever you taught them, they understood. But now, what do you do)? My children became a driving force for me to show them what I've always been talking about. That was scary, because I wasn't just coming to learn. I had to unlearn first. And then come back to learning a new way. I have been scared of theatre. Live audience nahi chahiye (I don't want a live audience). You know, 'Cut, take, one take, okay?' Chalega (it's fine). But I'm like a sponge. I absorb energy. So, a person like me, I have to be very careful of the energy that I take in and give out. So sorry, you were asking me?

Audience: Theatre!

SMD: Yes, theatre!

SS: See, ha, there you are. I was scared of theatre because of this awareness. Ab mujhe milte hain Ram Madhvani (Now I meet Ram Madhvani). Aur woh mujhse kya kehte hain (And what does he say to me)? 'Kuch mat kijiye (don't do anything). Three cameras are going to follow you. You don't have to look at the camera. Seven-page ka scene hai, ek saath shoot karna hai (It's a seven-page scene, you have to shoot it all at once).' 'Matlab? Six log aa rahe hain, Six log ja rahe hain, phir wahan se ek gaadi aayegi. (I mean, how? Six people are coming here, six people are going. Then a car will come.) Poonam is the housemaid. 'And she will come and serve coffee.' 'Ye real time mein kaise hoga (How will it be done in real time?)' 'Woh aap hum pe chhod dijiye (Leave that to us).' Every take of *Aarya* is between roughly twenty-six to forty-five minutes long. And that is why she comes across as so real, because everything is just around her. She is not performing. Nobody is performing. Everyone is just in the moment. But what it does is theatrical. Ab woh darr mit gaya hai (The fear I used to have is now gone), thanks to him. Renée is about to take part in her first play ever. Life comes full circle.

SMD: Not many of us can boast of becoming a student in their forties. I had the chance to speak to your acting coach Atul Mongia.

SS: Oh, you did?

Atul Mongia (on video): Hi Sushmita. I really admire this universal love that you carry in your heart and it oozes out of your entire aura. And the other thing that I really love about you is that how you are not just a student – a good student in a workshop or at work – but of life. You love learning, growing. And every single day I feel that you wake up with that zest. I am so fortunate that I got to work with you. And it may seem like I was the giver, but I think I have received as much if not more.

SS: I love you.

SMD: How lovely! I want to talk about being students of life. What does it take after doing this for this many years to say, 'I want to learn'?

SS: When I first started as an actor, I didn't want to be an actor. Bhatt Saab said, 'Ek film kar lo, *Dastak* ke baad (Do one film, after *Dastak*), leave.' But aisa hota nahi hai (This doesn't happen). Time, money is invested in you and there is the business side. And then there is the art. I was never interested in the art, unfortunately. Had I been, I would have learnt so much. This time, I chose it. So, I wake up every morning knowing that this is what I want. It's no longer a by-default process. And I have no set of people that I have, 'Mujhe sirf inke-inke-inke saath kaam karna hai (I want to work only with them).' I have had at least five or six first-time directors. Incredibly talented. I want to work with people who bring out the best. You are living it together. And I don't want to waste my life. So, I wake up every morning knowing I am doing what I love. Today I did not get the job I really wanted. Maybe tomorrow, day after. But come it will. That feeling is a celebration and also, if you have come near death twice, you look at life differently. So, you make it count and say, 'I have no regrets.'

SMD: I saw this video of your father collect your honorary doctorate.

SS: Very proud moment.

SMD: But it actually takes me back to a story. When you were crowned Miss Universe, your dad was crushed that you didn't finish your degree. You told him, 'Baba, don't give up on me just yet.'

SS: 'I'll graduate life with honours.'

SMD: How's Baba feeling now?

SS: Very proud. He cried. That day I had a viral fever and a bad throat. And I called Baba, he's in Kolkata, and said, 'Daddy, will you please go receive this for me?' 'What? Do I have to give a speech? Do I have to go up on stage?' Because my father is a very simple man who gets flummoxed when there are too many people and attention. He's a rock-solid human being. My brother told me that he came out and he just kept crying – I've seen him do that twice – once when I won Miss Universe, not because it's a pageant, but because I wore India and that for him as a patriot, a defence person, was everything. And then, to see his daughter be 'educated enough' to get a doctorate, even if honorary, he spoke to me afterwards and he was very emotional.

SMD: It's all written.

SS: Beautifully executed by God.

SMD: You said, 'One of the best things about turning forty is that it teaches you how to give a damn elegantly – but give a damn you must.' What do you give a damn about now?

SS: I'm a loyalist. When I call you family, you are my family. I don't have this sense of khoon (blood) and rishta (relation) but I don't make family easily. But when I do, I protect mine and I am preserved. Like *Aarya*. Aarya has three kids and I have many. The whole world that returns love belongs to me, in that sense. I give a damn about my beliefs very strongly, but I don't scream and shout. I think when you know the truth, you don't fight for it. Only you're not sure, then you fight. I love my voice – I mean the ability to express myself. I will never be silent if I need to speak. I don't give a damn about settling down. I love and respect the institution of marriage. I do very much. And I've had the blessing of knowing some incredible people, including my director and my producer, one of the most beautiful couples I know. But I'm a big believer in companionship, dosti (friendship). And freedom. So, I give a damn about freedom. And I give a damn about my work. My children. Anything to do with their lives, I give a damn about and they know that. One says, 'I'm too old, I can handle this.' And the other one is saying, 'I'm studying abroad, I, in any case, handle things on my own.' So, I'm suddenly jobless. Now suddenly I'm on a set and I'm just like, 'Yeah, yeah take your time.'

SMD: You've been a single mother for so much of your life and suddenly, an empty nest syndrome, what does that do to your personality?

SS: How old is your baby now?

SMD: Six.

SS: Wait for it, it's coming!

SMD: Are you discovering new sides to yourself, more space for work, for love?

SS: Oh, thank God, I never had to turn and tell them, 'Because of you, I did not do this.' I did what I needed to do, they did what they needed to do. (To Renée) Why are you smiling? I want to know, what is it? (To SMD) What were we talking about?

SMD: Has it helped you sort of see new facets to your personality?

SS: I do have more room, yes. But my personality, I was always in touch with, I never compromised on. I do discuss some big decisions with my children, but most of the time, they're like, 'You've thought this through? Then do it.' Every action has consequences. So, if you say, 'I will take this action and I'm ready for the consequence,' go for it. But if you take an action and say, 'Aisa reaction kyun hai (Why is this reaction like this)?' Toh gadbad ho jayegi (then it will be a problem). Alisa at age fourteen has done a PhD in that, she's telling us about everything deep and profound. I chose to make a life the way I have lived it and built it. I used to joke that, 'Kal ko chali gayi toh (if I die tomorrow), I have no regrets.' Ab maine woh joke karna band kar diya hai (Now I have stopped joking about it).

I'm lucky to have a foundation so strong, my mum, dad, brother, my daughters, God.

SMD: And some incredible collaborators. Can we bring on stage your partner in crime and the man behind the resurgence of Sushmita Sen, the creator of *Aarya*? Welcome. I actually want to take you back to that first meeting. It took you five minutes to convince her?

(Ram Madhvani arrives on the stage and hugs Sushmita Sen)

Ram Madhvani: First of all, this lady is intimidating.

(Audience laughs and agrees)

SMD: What went down that day?

RM: You're always nervous as a director, 'I don't know whether she'll say yes.' And, she says yes. And then I walk out to the lift after she's left. And I tell Amita, 'Do din ke baad pakka (definitely after two days), she's going to say no.' Be prepared, because rejection is the game. And then I realised with Sushmita that when she says something directly, she means it.

SMD: Good, bad or ugly.

RM: Good, bad or ugly. She's direct. Over the last four years we've been working together, I've begun to hugely respect that.

SS: And the next thing we know, Amita is like, 'Hi, Sush. I'm landing at 9 a.m. tomorrow morning.' She's the Lakshmi. She sets foot and everything is go.

RM: I'm very happy that she said yes. I don't have the power to greenlight anything. She does. I'm so happy that she manifested.

SS: I also have been manifesting a love story that he has to direct, with me in it.

SMD: You heard it here first!

SS: He is such a sensitive director.

RM: Thank you.

SS: He needs to delve deep into romance.

SMD: You refer to yourself as an eight-quadrant director. What is the trick?

RM: After I made *Neerja*, Sooraj Barjatya came and said, 'Ram-ji, Namaste. Maine aap ki picture do baar dekhi. Dusri baar maine apni family ke saath dekhi. Bohot kam log family ke liye pictue banaate hai. (I saw your film twice. The second time I saw it with my family. Very few people make pictures for family.)' And this affected me. I come from a joint family. TVs are not in bedrooms, they are in living rooms. Dadaji (grandfather), nephews, Mausi (aunty), everybody is walking in and out. The value system should reach out to the families. So, more than 30 million people, I want to reach out to 800 million.

SMD: He says he is in the business of feelings. Why is that so important for a director?

RM: I did a course in Indian aesthetics at Bombay University. And then I went to New York. I have a teacher-friend called Malia Scotch Marmo, who teaches screenwriting at Columbia University. So, I spoke to her and tried to see how I could balance an Indian and a Western way of telling. Because otherwise, you get culturally colonised.

SS: Well put.

RM: Cultural colonisation means you follow the three-act structure. And before you know it, all stories are the same. So, I said, 'I'm going to learn about the Rasa theory.' There are two systems over here. The Western system is going to give you, let's say, bones. But the Eastern system is giving you all the feeling. And I'm interested in tragedy. *Aarya* is a tragedy.

SS: Hum log sab subah ye practice karke aate hain set pe (We all practise this in the morning on set). '*Aarya* is? A tragedy.'

RM: We laugh a lot off camera. But when we're shooting . . . . I think we have lost the tragic hero. Dilip Kumar, Meena Kumari, now we have Sushmita Sen as *Aarya*. Season 3.2 tells you the price that she has to pay. And that's my value system. If you're going to do bad shit you're going to—

SS: Pay for it!

SMD: What really amazes me about OTT is the feedback. Do you get the opportunity to make something of that feedback?

RM: My pet peeve is when somebody tells me, 'Dekho, aap audience ke hisaab se dekho (Look at it from the audience's perspective).' Toh main kaun hoon bhai (Then who am I)? You've already put yourself on a pedestal. Sometimes I get deeply upset.

SS: I would like to respond to this. Very important. Everybody else can be objective. Everybody. But if you are the one creating it . . . yes, we are the audience.

RM: Sushmita Sen is the audience. Then why am I not the audience?

SS: I watch everything like an audience, even my own work.

SMD: Can you do that?

SS: I'm very detached.

RM: Why can't I do that?

SS: We have eight episodes of *Taali*, six remain. That's how objective. It's not an attachment to what you have put in. It's an attachment to the final thing.

SMD: But are you listening to feedback?

RM: I like the word detached attachment. Humbly arrogant.

SS: Agree to disagree.

RM: I also come from advertising. I value what people are going to say. And at the end of Season 1, they said, 'It's a little slow.' So first episode of Season 2 was thirty minutes. Hotstar said, 'What's wrong with you? Make it forty.' I said, 'But logon ne bola fast pace karo (People said make it fast paced).' They said, 'No, Aarya is also slow, it's got emotions.' We came to a balance. Then in Season 2 they said, 'Aarya's becoming weak. Audience wants Aarya to be badass.' So, I said, 'Achha, aisa hai (Is that so)?' Now we made her badass in 3.1; now they're saying, 'Arre, she's becoming too badass. Can you make her more emotional?'

SS: Kisne bola? Meko toh kisine nahi bola. (Who told you that? No one told me that.)

SMD: Ram Madhvani doesn't say 'action'. Instead, you say?

SS: You have to experience a Ram Madhvani film's hospitality on set. Huge round of applause for Amita Madhvani. We don't take rooms in a hotel. We block the whole palace. Aangan par tents, roz shaadi wala buffet. Saare actors, directors, sab milke wahan par apne din ki discussion karte hain because sab apni families se dur aaye hue hain. (A courtyard where tents are set up. Wedding buffet every day. All the actors, directors, all get together and discuss their day because everyone is away from their families.) You bond, feel like kings. Next morning, labour class, back to set. They have figured out how to get the best out of people in a creative way.

RM: Thank you. We say, 'We don't organise the shoot, we host the shoot.' I don't say action, I don't say cut, we were at a press-junket kind of thing and the people who were shooting would say, 'Silence!' Why would you say that? As soon as you even say the word 'action', it changes the molecules in your body. So, I'm normally giving a sign. One of our directors, Dravid, put it into practice, 'Go when your heart says.'

SS: We as actors know, 'Go when your heart says' means, 'Ek, do, chalo' (one, two, let's go).

RM: But it allows you to relax and breathe. I'm not going to say, 'Roll camera', 'Silence', 'Action', 'Cut'.

SMD: And no chaos on set?

SS: Oh, none. Nobody is allowed to speak in high volume. Aaram se baat karo (Talk peacefully).

RM: Achha, light toh hai nahi (There is no light).

SS: *Aarya* mein aapne dekha hai? Hum actors, street lamp ho ya ghar mein ek chota sa bulb jal raha ho set pe, hum saare actors ghuske wahin pe scene karte hain, because we want natural raat ka feel (In *Aarya*, have you seen us actors, whether it's a street lamp or there is a small bulb in the house on the set, we all actors enter and shoot a scene there because we aren't given lights). So, we are all struggling for light. Whatever the crisis, we'll deal with it. What a team to work with. The only show in my life – film, anything – in which I have not had a single member of the managerial team on the set. It's been managed by the RMF family. This never happens.

RM: People work with the handcuffs of the industrial processes of filmmaking and we should stop that. I'm here to be in the service of my actor.

SS: He says that always, 'I'm here.' He's a director here, but when we are filming, he will always say, 'I am just a floor manager.' He will walk around behind the camera like a shadow. You won't even know he's there. He's so quiet.

RM: Yeah, I don't like being at the video assist.

SS: Yeah, he's never there.

RM: I'm with my DOPs, and this time we've had two female DOPs, Kavya and Priyanka. They are incredible. Most of my team is women, thank God.

SMD: And look at the magic that they can create. Proof of what you can achieve when the handcuffs are removed.

SS: Well said.

RM: If your quest is truth and reality, you need to have the freedom to allow that. I'm here to capture that energy. Actors are actually wild animals.

SMD: In the nicest possible way. Sherni (lioness), yes.

SS: Can we discuss this later?

RM: At least I didn't say actors are cattle. Then you have to basically cajole and coax, without them knowing you're meant to cage them.

SMD: You're letting out all your secrets!

SS: Oh, but we know when we're caged. Can you imagine this banter and making a series through it all?

RM: But I'll tell you one thing. She's very courageous. When I give her the opportunity to jump off, she jumps and she doesn't even know that there's going to be a safety net.

SS: I know I do. You wait for him to say, 'Jump!' because that's when you know something will come. Because this is not a rehearsed system. You're not allowed to read the lines of your scene. And hawk ki tarah ten log dekhte rehte hain, set pe, ki, 'Ye do actors kyun baat kar rahe hain? Alag karo.' (And there, ten people are watching you like hawks on set, like, 'Why are these two actors talking? Separate them.') You can't even tell each other, 'Tu aise mat bolna, aise bolna (Don't say it like this, say it like this)', you can't do anything.

RM: I don't do rehearsals because in life there's no take two. You create the environment for the actor to give that.

SS: This is the system in which you are stuck.

SMD: You've now been spoilt.

SS: Yeah. No, we are stuck. Because if he says, 'Jump' – you know that you don't know what to do, except jump. And then the magic happens.

RM: She just lands.

SS: I land because of knowing that.
RM: She's not scared. Some actors would hold back. There's one scene which – spoiler alert – which is going to come up in 3.2.

SMD: Close your ears.

RM: There is one scene where I said, 'I have to give Sushmita Sen a drunk scene. Now jump.' And she's landed, you have to see that scene.

SS: Aditi, why is he allowed to say all this and my briefing says I can't talk about it?

RM: Okay, this is going to get cut.

SS: No, it was nice, I am also looking forward to seeing that scene.

SMD: And before I open it up to the audience, I want to ask the two of you about your mental and physical health.

SS: You go first.

RM: Okay, so I think over the last ten years, Amita and I have decided that we would take different kinds of holidays. So, you need a holiday with your friends, very indulgent. One of my friends, Bunty, is over here . . . I call them my public, with the family it's a different kind of holiday. But the health holiday means you go for a detox, so, I normally go to some Ayurvedic centre, because I can't lead a disciplined life.

SS: I also don't know.

RM: So you need to have a health holiday. I do have a meditation teacher, and my Ayurvedic doctor, Dr Shailendra Chaubey, he comes, for half an hour to forty minutes every day. My team says, 'You should meditate for two hours. Half an hour is not helping your impatience, Ram!'

SMD: We insist!

SS: I train. I listen to music. I have the most amazing playlist. I travel. And I detox from people.

SMD: Wow.

SS: You can't always be running away from 'this energy doesn't work for me'. So I detox from people, usually in Europe, away. But I have discovered a couple of places in India where I am going to just be the third wheel.

SMD: Can Sushmita Sen walk the streets and be allowed to?

SS: Nobody has to disallow. I will walk the streets! I make more friends when I walk the streets. Any envy that there might be, it's when you're in your car. The minute you step out of it, it's gone.

RM: But obligations of stardom and fame, for her those are not obligations. Because we've seen people who treat it as a duty. For her, when she walks into a room, it's like: energy shifted; Sushmita Sen has walked into the room.

SMD: That's true.

RM: Whether it's the chef or the person waiting on your table – I've seen her interact with these people – there is no obligation of fame.

SMD: She wears it so lightly.

SS: No, I wear it as a job.

SMD: What do you guys do?

SS: You guys want to listen to everything we have to say, then you also have to share. What do you do? (In response to audience) Doctor. Student. CA? Phone number! Being an actor is my job; it's funny, being famous is also my job, a side effect of being an actor. That's the beauty. Once you are aware.

RM: They can co-exist or they are not separate.

From the floor: Q&A

Audience member: This is about *Aarya*, but I have been a fan since the 1990s. I remember watching the movie *Zor*. How do you divest out of a role that you're doing? How do you not get emotionally attached?

SS: Aarya exhausts you so much on the set itself; it is easy to leave her behind. *Chingaari*, a film I'd done many years ago – I consider myself a strong woman, with a voice – that character and the way that I was spoken to and behaved with. Main bohot royi hoon uske baad, ki main maanne ko taiyyar nahi ki ye kisi ke saath hota hoga because meri rooh mein dard ho rahi hai. (I cried a lot after that, that I'm not ready to believe that it could happen to someone because my soul is hurting.) What I have to do is breathe, breathe, breathe, because that's the only way to come back to the present moment. It needs work sometimes, not always.

RM: Except the gun that she carries in her bag.

SS: It has real bullets in it! He always does this in every interview!

Audience member: I often wonder, how do you recognise which people are real with you or which people are just there with you to be attached with your fame?

RM: I am not a good reader of people, so I just take people at face value. And then maybe a year or five years later, I say, 'Oh man, what happened over here?!'

SS: Main ulti hoon (I'm the opposite). I am a Scorpio. I don't trust easily. And I think being a single woman, I protect myself. When I trust, it's hundred khoon maaf hain phir (everything is forgiven). Because I put my faith in you.

5 February 2024

Acknowledgements

I have to begin by thanking my husband Vidhu Vinod Chopra. *Film Companion* was his idea. After my Star World show *The Front Row* wrapped in 2014, I was pondering the next act and he suggested that we start a YouTube channel because reviews and conversations should not be appointment-based viewing; they should be available whenever the consumer needs them.

Our first video – my review of Salman Khan's *Kick* – was posted on 25 July 2014. Even though *Film Companion* never covered Vinod's work (conflict of interest), he was the spine of the project. As our team grew, many wonderful people became part of the journey. But there were a few pillars of the platform: Mohini Chaudhuri, who multi-tasked as editor, writer, ideator supreme; Baradwaj Rangan, who built *Film Companion South,* and Vishal K Menon, who carried forward the torch; Rahul Desai, critic extraordinaire, and Prathyush Parasuraman, writer extraordinaire; Tanvi Ajinkya, who helped set up Film Companion Studios (our boutique long-form production arm) and steered our first documentary *Modern Masters* on S.S. Rajamouli to the finish (it's streaming on Netflix); Suchin Mehrotra, who covered streaming with passion, and Sucharita Tyagi, who brought her singular style to reviews (her take on *Kabir Singh* got over a million views). And most of all, Sneha Menon Desai, a force-of-nature journalist-producer, who got behind all my nutty ideas and who never once suggested that texting routinely at 6 a.m. is perhaps taking our passion for film too far.

There are perhaps few offices which have the joy and camaraderie that *Film Companion* did, which is perhaps why our work endures. To all those who joined me on the journey, thank you.

Thanks to Chirag Thakkar, my publisher, and team Bloomsbury India, for thinking of this book. To Vaishnav Praveen, who shot the portrait for the cover of the book. Thanks to team A Suitable Agency for representing me.